ISLAM
AND THE
WEST

ISLAM
AND THE
WEST

A DISSONANT HARMONY OF CIVILISATIONS

CHRISTOPHER J. WALKER

SUTTON PUBLISHING

First published in the United Kingdom in 2005 by
Sutton Publishing Limited · Phoenix Mill
Thrupp · Stroud · Gloucestershire · GL5 2BU

British Library Cataloguing in Publication Data
A catalogue record for this book is available from the British Library.

ISBN 0-7509-4104-9

Typeset in 10/13pt New Baskerville.
Typesetting and origination by
Sutton Publishing Limited.
Printed and bound in England by
J.H. Haynes & Co. Ltd, Sparkford.

Contents

List of Illustrations

Preface

I am grateful to a number of people and institutions for help and inspiration in this task. Thanks are due to the late Dr Lofthouse of Worthing for teaching me some Hebrew while I was still a schoolboy, and leading me to an interest in other Semitic languages and cultures. More recently I owe thanks to David Taylor for answering many questions, and to John Waś for help with translations. Roger Lockyer has been unfailingly helpful. I owe Marius Kociejowski a special debt of gratitude. Judith Curthoys, archivist of Christ Church, Oxford, kindly answered my questions. Simon Curry has challenged ideas. The librarians of the British Library, the London Library, Dr Williams's Library, Harris-Manchester College (Oxford) and my local Hammersmith and Fulham Public Library are to be thanked too for help and for answering many queries. I cannot omit an expression of thanks to Christopher Feeney, Hilary Walford and Jane Entrican for their patience and forbearance. I am grateful too for sidelong help gained from catalogues of London's book dealers and auction houses, where one may find descriptions that illuminate details of history, landscape, reason or religion. The final responsibility for the contents of this book is mine alone.

❖❖❖

I have avoided diacritical marks on Semitic names, and have preferred the spelling 'Koran' to 'Qur'an'. Likewise, as regards dates, I have kept BC and AD, preferring them to BCE and CE. It seems to me that extraneous complexities, however well intentioned, impede a narrative and obstruct ideas.

Introduction

In the eras of both Queen Elizabeth I and Queen Victoria, England established informal alliances with the Ottoman Empire. The two great monarchs favoured the Muslim empire above other, Christian, empires. Queen Victoria even threatened to abdicate unless her government took a firmer line in support of Turkey. Yet neither of them, separated by three hundred years, has ever been accused of betraying Christendom, or been regarded as a cultural traitor. What does this mean in terms of Islam and the West?

Other instances may lead us to question any fixed categories of East and West. Francis I of France, the Most Christian King, made an alliance with Islamic Turkey to guarantee independence against subjection to Emperor Charles V. Before the battle of Lepanto of 1571 – seen as a display of Christianity, turning the tide against Ottoman Islam – the pope invited the Persian shah to join in. Faith, it seems, could mutate from being the defining issue in war and diplomacy to being just one element among many.

In the current climate, it is probably not necessary to explain the origin or relevance of a book on Islam and the West. But, for the record, this work did not develop from the events of 11 September 2001; it found its origin in the decade which saw the destruction of the Babri Mosque in Ayodhya, east of Delhi, by militant Hindus, a defining event in the modern history of extreme religion. The Balkans, too, witnessed violence shadowed by the rhetoric of faith. Faith worldwide seemed, and still seems, to be going through one of its periodic crises, as it had in Europe during the Crusades, and at the time of the Reformation. So a study of relations between West and East seemed appropriate.

In part, this study is one of the manner in which two systems of belief, often seen as universal but with their own internal fractures, have lived and continue to live – and sometimes failed to live – side by side. Islam was not initially radically different from the Christianity which was its neighbour, and was far from appearing as its shadow-side, on the way to being castigated as paganism. It looked like a cousin of the Christianity of Syria and Mesopotamia. Its unitarian theology was reflected in the writings of some of the early Christian Church Fathers. Even in early modern times, when the advent of rational Christianity compelled a reassessment of Islam, it could be classed, by John Hales for instance, as a Christian heresy.[1] Neither Hugo Grotius, the founder of international law, nor John Locke, whose philosophy has shaped the modern world, considered Islam to be alien or 'other'. These thinkers championed Christianity as true and reasonable; yet both held that Islam constituted a valid way by which the Deity could be approached. Nevertheless, in the eleventh to thirteenth centuries, at the time of the Crusades, Western Christianity had erupted into an assertion of itself as something radically different and militant, and this attitude continued selectively until modern times – although there has always been a section of western humanity prepared and able to consider Islam in non-bellicose terms.

The crusading expeditions had been phenomena driven primarily from northern Europe; Eastern Christianity never developed the language of visions and prophecy with which Western Christianity upheld its right to assault Islam. Southern Europe was often keener on coexistence. Christianity and Islam mingled contentedly in the Sicilian court of the two Rogers and Emperor Frederick II; and in Spain, in the early years of the Reconquest, Islamic learning was held in honour by the Castilian kings, who avoided rhetoric.

It seemed right to end in 1914, on the grounds that the subsequent period has been well covered; the date represents the emergence of the contemporary world, whereas my concern has been to rediscover and I hope illuminate the background, the hinterland, to a perplexing and highly charged issue, capable today of catching the fire of international conflict.

CHAPTER ONE

Sophronius and Omar

Helena, the mother of the Emperor Constantine, first accorded Jerusalem a central place within Roman Christianity, by making a pilgrimage there probably in the year 326. According to the pious historians Socrates Scholasticus and Sozomen, she discovered the site of the Holy Sepulchre. At the time of her visit this sacred place was occupied by a temple built by the Emperor Hadrian and dedicated to Astarte. The devout lady pilgrim, granted the title of 'empress' by her imperial son, dutifully sought out other sites connected with the life of Jesus, and discovered a holy relic of deep and lasting significance, that of the True Cross. Her devotional travels inaugurated the powerful and lasting tradition of Christian pilgrimage – the process whereby inner spirituality is strengthened and enriched by an outward journey of aspiration, physical hardship, attainment, presence, recollection and meditation.[1]

Astarte was the local cult-name for Venus, and even in pagan times an aura of sacred suffering and renewal hovered in the darkened grotto. The rites of Syrian Adonis, the annual life-replenishing corn-god, were celebrated here in springtime. A link has been suggested between 'Adonis' and 'Adonai'; the womb which nurtured the fresh-limbed god of springtime became the tomb of the Son of Man. Perhaps we can also find here a continuity of female presence, with Astarte foreshadowing Mary Magdalene and the other women at the empty tomb, who in turn could be linked to the historical figure of Helena. The ambience was in contrast to the robustly male environment of the other great sacred place, the former Jewish Temple, manifestly masculine in its pagan Roman form as the Temple of Jupiter Capitolinus.

Christianity had evolved from being a faith of the oppressed into a triumphant imperial religion. From being a subversive doctrine challenging the divinity of the emperor and waiting expectantly for the end of the world, it was on the verge of granting legitimacy to imperial

1

rule. The faith was now bound up with temporal power; it was about to become a partner to the political order. The emperor came to be seen not only as the commander-in-chief, judge and legislator, but also the living symbol of the Christian empire, with a status as God's first servant. He became the object of a cult, which was enacted with reverential ceremonial. His person came to be held as sacred. Here was a great change.

There is a paradox in pilgrimage, especially in a journey to sacred sites undertaken by the emperor's mother. The Roman Empire took on the aspect of a universal empire; the earthly embodiment of the unbounded spiritual realm. Its universality was limited only by its proximity to another empire of equal power and magnificence, that of the Sasanid Persians. Rome implanted within the minds of the people of the Mediterranean seaboard, of Anatolia and of some of Europe, a notion of world citizenship. Here the idea of Christianity as a universal religion found fertile soil. A universal empire, where the universal gospel could be preached to every creature without distinction, was a harmonious pairing. God could proclaim his universality, his non-totemic lack of a specific locality, by his reflection in universal empire. Yet now Helena, at the moment that Christianity was affirming its universality, was by her pilgrimage subtly undermining the idea of universal empire and faith. Her devotion emphasised the individual localities of the origins of Christian faith. Undoubtedly a pilgrim's journey can refresh and renew faith. But pilgrimage may also lead to a privatisation of piety. The notion of the universality of Jesus may shade into his being a local sacred figure of Palestine. Pilgrimage can make the inner lamp of the soul shine more brightly; but it can also fetishise a land mass, and imbue a locality with a specific devotion which may diminish the aspects of faith that aspire to worldwide validity. Helena's own intention would have been sacred recollection, not local idolatry; but for lesser persons than herself, it was a short journey from the pilgrimage of the soul to a cultic reverence for relics of saints, the sacrality of remains, and other totemic detritus of regional superstition. Erasmus would later remind us that, by the sixteenth century, a merchant ship could be built from the fragments of wood said to be relics of the True Cross.[2]

Jerusalem, like other cities in Asia, passed in and out of the control of the later Roman, or Byzantine, Empire. When the Persian Sasanids, in one of their almost annual campaigns, stormed out of their capital Ctesiphon in the year 615, they conquered Anatolia and Syria – the whole of eastern Byzantium.[3] They seized the alleged relic of the True Cross, and carried it home in triumph. Palestine was wrecked, and thereafter Jerusalem never regained the opulence it had known during Constantine's reign. The Persian rage for conquest was said to have resembled that of 'infuriated beasts and irritated dragons'.[4] Two years later the same unappeased invaders hungrily eyed the great city of Constantinople from the Asiatic shore of the Bosporus. But the Emperor Heraclius gave them no quarter, and after campaigns lasting more than ten years drove them from his lands and regained possession of the 'True Cross'. In the struggle the empires of both Byzantium and Persia drew their inspiration from sword-driven faith. In 629 Heraclius finally earned the laurel wreath of victory. The war had been in part a typical war of imperial rivalry for territories and access; but it also drew some of its force from the urge to regain totems of faith. It showed aspects of holy war. The court poet saw it more in intellectual and metaphysical terms. Celebrating a triumph, George Pisidis wrote an ode to Heraclius: 'O capable intelligence and most acute nature! Fire of analysis energetically pursuing profundity!'[5] Heraclius' victory was so monumental that it found echo far away, with a report of the sacred struggle reaching Arabia, where it is mentioned in the Koran.[6]

Few victories have been more filled with irony. For the struggle of empires, the cataclysmic duel between Rome and Persia, the battles fought amid the turbulent rivers, harsh deserts, trackless plains and distant snowy mountains of Asia had exhausted both sides. Winning and losing their empires by the sword had left them prostrate. The future of Syria and Mesopotamia lay neither with east nor west, but with the south. In Edward Gibbon's words, 'The rival monarchies at the same instant became the prey of an enemy whom they had been so long accustomed to despise.'[7]

Islam had been born a few years before Heraclius' victory, in AD 622. On that date the dedicatedly monotheist prophet Muhammad undertook his flight (*hijra*) from Mecca to Medina. For a decade he built a state there, based on his prophetic messages. Following his death in 632 his mantle fell to his leading followers – although later it was to be contested in a bitter struggle between them and members of his family, which led to the division of Islam into two branches: Sunni, known as orthodox, and Shiite, from the Arabic word for 'partisan', since its followers were the partisans of Ali, Muhammad's son-in-law. The successor to the Prophet, and leader of the community of believers, was known as the caliph (*khalifa*).

Islam evolved in a milieu which was partly Christian, partly Jewish, partly pagan, but wholly Arab. The Christian influence came, in part, from the southern Syrian hills; here, desert Arabs, traversing great spaces, had been drawn to the play of light radiating from monkish cells. Distant flickering lamps were welcomed as points of illumination amid brooding night; they were visions of hope and longing, starry presences which lifted darkness from the soul.[8] The great pre-Islamic poet Imru' ul Qais, finely combining the sensual with the austere, proclaimed of his beloved that 'in the evening she brightens the darkness, as if she were the lamp of the cell of a monk devoted to God'.[9] We find a similar mixture of hedonism edged with Christian sanctity in the verses of al-A'sha, a contemporary of Muhammad: 'Many an early cup [glistening] like the eye of a cock have I drunk with trusty youths in its curtained chamber while the church-bells rang – pure wine like saffron and amber, poured in its glass and mixed, spreading a costly perfume in the house, as if the riders had [just] arrived with it from the sea of Darin.'[10] (Darin was a port near Bahrain, where musk from India was unloaded.)

The influence of the Christian kingdom of Abyssinia, Ethiopia today, was felt strongly in southern Arabia. At one time part of Arabia was subject to Abyssinia, an event which had occurred in response to the over-ambitious policies of a Jewish king who ruled south Arabia in the sixth century AD. There had been converts to Judaism, and more than one Arabian tribe had embraced Judaism. The Jewish faith, in its sceptical Sadducean form, where observance is minimal and faith is expressed in doing what is naturally good, was also present in Arabia. Its presence promoted the idea that, amidst different faiths vying with each other, an indistinct belief in One God was alone necessary, combined with an aspiration to do what was, on consideration, felt to be right. In the city of Mecca itself the mood was occasionally touched by the monotheistic currents which surrounded it. The rich families of that prosperous trading city remained devoted to pleasure and to polytheism – a polytheism which even here could develop into a kind of quasi-monotheism that has been called henotheism. (Monotheism indicates the idea of God alone, henotheism that of one supreme God among lesser deities, a less rigorous notion.[11])

In this ambience the new faith was proclaimed. What Islam uniquely brought was a universal message expressed within the Arab context; that is, it was a profound monotheistic message, using the imagery, social context and above all the rich and resonant language of the Arabs. Islam is not a specifically Arab religion; but its formulation and expression in Arabia gave the faith aspects which only the Arabs could have given it. Islam also unified them at a highly appropriate moment. Its success was due more to practicality than to religious enthusiasm (in the sense of extremism). Muhammad himself was too disciplined to be called a religious enthusiast.[12] If read carefully, the Koran reveals not a frenzy of enthusiasm and violence, but gratitude to God for his works and the Prophet's fondness for his native city of Mecca despite the materialism of its big merchant families.[13] The preaching of a new faith gave its propagators a powerful sense of zeal; but it was a zeal circumscribed by the founder's practicality.

The Koran should properly be known as the Qur'an; the word is cognate with the Syriac *qeryana*, 'reading', 'declaiming', and with the Aramaic *qeri*, 'to be read', a marginal indication of textual corruption found in the Hebrew bible. The language of the Koran is of central significance. Its power and beauty can soften the hearts of the most hard-bitten sceptics. As Peter Brown has written: 'For Muhammad's followers, this was no Syriac religious ode, a human composition offered by man to God. It was an echo of the voice of God himself, of a God who had never ceased, throughout the ages, to "call out" to mankind.'[14] The astonishing power of the language made it easy to believe that Arabic was spoken in paradise, and that any translation of the Koran, if not actually blasphemous, violated its essential spirit.

Muhammad had made no conquests beyond the Arabian peninsula. But in the immediate aftermath of his death the Arab horsemen, imbued with the mission to spread the Prophet's message, stormed out of the peninsula and within a comparatively short time were in control of vast tracts of land. Besides Asia they conquered westwards: Egypt, North Africa, ultimately Spain. The struggle was hard fought: Alexandria had to be conquered twice (in 641 and 645). But the story of the burning of the library of Alexandria is almost certainly a fake, since much of the library had already been destroyed – by Julius Caesar, by turbulent monks raised to wrath by theological niceties, and by an edict of the Emperor Theodosius dating from about AD 389. The story of the conflagration was first related by Abdullatif al-Baghdadi, who died in 1231, and it was copied by Grigor abul-Faraj, whose Arab history was translated in 1663 and became influential in the developing studies of the East.[15]

Just as the Persians and the Byzantines had fought tenaciously, so now the new invaders staked a claim to the land of west Asia, with the benefit of being more lightly armed. Their subsequent victory broke down the 'iron curtain' of antiquity, the Roman–Persian frontier, and united most of east Rome with Persia, fashioning a new realm which recreated the universality of the Roman Empire, but in a more easterly position.[16] The first caliph was an elderly, cautious man of integrity, Abu Bakr. His successor, Omar, saw Islam as a world phenomenon. (Some commentators have likened Omar's position in the faith to that of St Paul within Christianity.)

The campaign to capture Syria concluded with the battle of the Yarmuk in 636, when Arab forces under Khalid ibn al-Walid defeated Byzantine and mercenary forces led by the brother of Emperor Heraclius. Departing, the emperor memorably declared: 'Farewell, Syria, and what an excellent country this is for the enemy!'[17] The conquest of Syria had been made easier for the conquerors for two reasons. In the first place, Islam had the advantage of its simplicity. Christianity, to those who set their minds to work out its theology, had become very complex. The issue of the Trinity was the most perplexing: it was hard to see how one God could be Three, each of whom was fully God in his own right, while yet there were not three gods but One. (The view that the three persons of the Trinity were three differing aspects of the One God is heretical and Sabellian; the Athanasian view of the Trinity is that each of the three persons is fully God.) The puzzles concerning the nature of Christ were equally complex. Serious divisions had arisen, especially in Syria, concerning the connection between his human and divine natures: whether they commingled or remained separate. If they did commingle, then Christ was of a different substance from mortals. If they were separate, which substance died on the Cross? Then might we be not saved? All these issues were of prime importance at the time. The Syrian Christians had reached their own conclusions, but these were opposed as heretical by Constantinople. Islam allowed them to have the beliefs they wished. Those still puzzled by Christian metaphysics were offered a simple and direct formula: 'There is no god but God, and Muhammad is his prophet.' The duties of being a Muslim were equally straightforward: belief in God and his prophet, prayer, almsgiving, fasting during Ramadan, and pilgrimage to Mecca at least once in the lifetime.[18]

In the second place Arabs and Arab kingdoms had had a presence in pre-Islamic Syria. The Nabataeans had enjoyed greatness in the first century AD, and from the sixth century the Ghassanids of the Hawran had acted as Christian auxiliary soldiers to Byzantium, despite their dissident views on the nature of Christ. These kingdoms and linguistic groups felt an affinity with the Arabs of Arabia, a point which was reinforced when the Islamic conquerors allowed the Ghassanids to practise their own beliefs freely. This liberty of belief stood in contrast to the faith forced on them by the heresy-hunters of Byzantium.

Not all of the initial Arab conquests of the extensive lands of Eastern Christianity were straightforward, or occurred in the manner of liberation from theological tyranny. Much of the warfare was violent, harsh and inhumane. In seventh-century Armenia a part of the Christian population which had taken refuge in its churches was burnt alive by forces commanded by Abd ur-Rahman.[19] But even here there was only occasional pressure to convert the people to Islam, and Armenians reached high office as Christians.[20] As a European Islamicist of the seventeenth century was to write of the Islamic conquests in general, 'I own that violence had some place here, but persuasion had more.'[21]

Jerusalem had already established a place within Islam, since Muhammad had initially instructed his followers to pray in its direction, in the years before it became obligatory for them to address their prayers towards Mecca. Jerusalem was also, possibly, the site of the Prophet's journey into heaven, according to a text in which the term 'the Further mosque' appears.[22] 'The Further mosque' is a translation of 'al-Aqsa mosque'; however, confusingly, this is not the site of the present-day Aqsa mosque, but that of the Dome of the Rock. (An added complication is that the term may have been intended as a reference to a place in heaven.) But early tradition, which always counts for much in religious matters, held that the sanctuary in Jerusalem – the Temple Mount, known to Muslims as al-Haram ash-Sharif, or the Noble Sanctuary – was, alongside Mecca and Medina, a most sacred place, appropriate for deeply devotional prayer.[23]

Christian chronicles and prophetic discourses of this time treat the coming of Islam and the Arabs for the most part as a matter of little contention. Theophanes, the Byzantine chronicler, did not see Islam as a radically new phenomenon. (Gibbon crisply comments, 'The Greeks, so loquacious in controversy, have not been anxious to celebrate the triumphs of their enemies.'[24]) Occasionally from a Christian source one finds a fierce polemic; but such things were exceptional. 'The Apocalypse of Pseudo-Methodius', a seventh-century Syriac document, treats the emergence of the new faith as a judgement on the wicked ways of the Christians, and a presage of the end of time.[25] When the Christian Syrian historian Dionysius of Tel-Mahre wrote about the Arab invasion some 180 years after the events, he gave a reasonably objective summary of Muslim beliefs, free from extreme language. He believed that God had nodded in assent while the Arab empire waxed in power.[26] A Syriac chronicle of AD 724 calls Muhammad the 'messenger of God' (*rasulo d-alloho*).[27] The patriarch of the Christians of the East, or Nestorians, writing during his patriarchate of AD 650–60 to the archbishop of Persia, said, 'The Arabs, to whom God at this time has given the empire of this world – behold, they are among you, as you know well, and yet they attack not the Christian faith, but, on the contrary, they favour our religion, do honour to our priests and the saints of the Lord, and confer benefits on churches and monasteries.'[28]

The Armenian history attributed to Sebeos – who may have been a bishop in eastern Armenia – also contains an unvarnished description of the coming of Islam. The narrative (perhaps dating from 660 or 661) sets out starkly, in its earlier sections, the unrelenting conflict between Rome and Persia which preceded Islam, a struggle described by a modern commentator as 'total war'. Sebeos, the chronicler, goes on to note the appearance among the 'sons of Ismael' of a man whose name was Mahmet, 'a merchant'. His presence had been manifested, the author declares, 'as if by God's command . . . as a preacher and the path of truth. He taught them [the Arabs] to recognise the God of Abraham. . . . Abandoning their vain cults they turned to the living God who had appeared to their father Abraham. So Mahmet legislated for them . . .' Sebeos held that the expansion of Islam had occurred in response to divine command; it constituted the accomplishment of God's will; though later, when the Arab caliphate had grown powerful and was fighting bitter battles against Christian Byzantium, he castigated it as wicked.[29]

In the West, the Venerable Bede noted the coming of the Saracens without rancour, despite the fact that their conquests had been halted in the south of France. The battle of Poitiers, and the Arab presence on the world stage, made no great impact on his consciousness. Bede was more interested in the Biblical genealogy of the Saracens, and their descent from Hagar and Ishmael.[30]

Two years after the battle of the Yarmuk, the Arab armies were encamped at Jabiya near the Jawlan (or Golan) Heights, which was the former capital city of the Christian Ghassanid Arabs. From this base they captured Jerusalem and thus completed the occupation of Syria. Their commander was Abu Obaidah. Different traditions have survived concerning the circumstances of the city's capitulation. What is known is that the caliph, Omar, came to Jerusalem in order to play a defining part in the settlement which followed its Islamic conquest. In one of the traditions Abu Obaidah summoned Omar to Jabiya to discuss the future of Jerusalem, since the population of that city, led by the elderly and saintly patriarch Sophronius, refused to capitulate without the presence of the highest Muslim dignitary. In another version, Omar came to the Muslim headquarters of his own free will, and after a short campaign, the terms of Islamic Jerusalem were agreed.[31]

Both the caliph and his general approached Jerusalem. To the patriarch the Muslims' appearance seems to have called forth a mood of deep gloom: Omar's arrival indicated 'the abomination of desolation spoken of by Daniel the prophet, standing in the holy place'.[32] How are we to take the elderly patriarch's utterance? The city's capitulation was a loss, a cause of great sorrow to an old man; maybe it seemed like the end of, if not the world, at least his world. Perhaps Sophronius saw domination by Arabs, despite their monotheism, as little different from the occupations which had followed the victories of the pagan Sasanid Persians; he might have recalled the ferocious and unqualified demand of the Persian emperor Chosroes (Khusrau) II: 'I shall not spare you until you renounce the Crucified One, whom you call God, and worship the sun.'[33]

But the commonest currency of opinion is that Sophronius was disturbed – affronted even – by the casual clothing worn by the conquering Muslims. Their style was too much at ease. The historian Theophanes describes Omar approaching clad in 'filthy garments of camel-hair';[34] another writer has him wearing a coarse cotton shirt and a sheepskin jacket. Abu Obaidah is reported as approaching in a similar non-triumphalist manner. The casual garb, redolent of equality, was a matter of comment. The people of eastern empires were used to something smarter. Sophronius' tradition held that conquerors should be gorgeously robed. The Persians themselves had shown a correct imperial bearing: in 622 the Sasanid general Shahrvaraz (in Greek, Sarbaros) had, in defeat, handed over 'his golden shield, his sword, lance, gold belt set with precious stones, and boots'.[35]

The Muslims to whom Sophronius was signing away control of his city cared little for gold belts or precious stones. They were almost certainly making a point by wearing everyday clothes, shunning the splendour to which the patriarch, as a ritual perfomer of the greatest act of the greatest empire, was accustomed. To a Muslim, the wearing of fine robes was an act of arrogance in the sight of God. It was almost as if there were a divine message of classlessness. This view could hardly be further from that of the Orthodox Christian liturgy, where religion was the mystical partner of empire. The celebrant officiated in the unique mystery whereby the people could partake of that greater realm of Christ of which the emperor's was a reflection, or a rehearsal. So the patriarch expected that those who came as representatives of another faith should appear wearing clothes fitting to an office similar to his own. Clothing to him was an indicator of religious and social position. Casual clothes were deemed incorrect, in a context where rich robes indicated proximity to God.

The Muslim ethos, though monotheist, was markedly different from that of Byzantium. In Sunni Islam there is no intermediary between God and man. Robed priests, and the sacrament of the eucharist, with its solemn internal processional drama, its ritual moves from penitence to absolution and adoration, are alien to it. The unitary God of Islam is compassionate, but distant. There is no question of incarnation, of spiritual intimacy, or of the freedom of access granted by the sacrament. The idea that there might be a Holy Family, or that Mary might be Mother of God, is unacceptable. Belief in the Trinity is almost indistinguishable from polytheism. To the philosophical problem of the otherness of God (the puzzle of reconciling the absoluteness of God with the possibility of his caring for humanity), Islam has maintained that God remains far off, virtually an abstract idea, intelligible only through faith, devotional practice, deeds and intellect. 'The rest is not our business.' There are no sacred mysteries. The humility of man before God was appropriate and important; but there is little personal closeness or intimacy. God could not suffer and die on a cross, nor was he such that he could ever share a meal with human beings. Nevertheless the Koran holds that Jesus – Isa – was a unique person, and a very great prophet sent by God; in some places he is declared to be the awaited one. But not the actual son; and certainly not sharing (as Athanasius demanded) the same metaphysical substance as God.

Following the city's capitulation, Omar agreed the terms for its citizens: that the city's Christian inhabitants would be granted security for their lives, property, churches and crucifixes, that the Jews were not to live among them, that churches were not to be used as living accommodation, and not dismantled or reduced in size. Christians thus retained their religious liberties. (Theophanes the historian speaks of 'a promise of immunity for the whole of Palestine'.[36]) In return they had to pay a poll tax (*jizya*), and to assist in defence against the armies of Byzantium.[37]

The time for prayer had arrived. Omar and Sophronius found themselves on the steps of the Church of the Holy Sepulchre. But Omar refused to pray. In Gibbon's words: '"Had I yielded," said Omar, "to your request, the Moslems of a future age would have infringed the treaty under colour of imitating my example."'[38] Omar would appear to be quietly pointing out that, in the context of a universal deity, true devotion can be shown by being cautious about zeal; that prayer can be at its most profound by delaying or refusing to pray. His unique and generous act of sacred diplomacy, a repudiation of local fetishism, did not prevent the subsequent violent abuse of faith.

Omar looked elsewhere for a place to pray, and observing that the sacred area of the Jewish Temple, unoccupied and ignored for 600 years was covered in filth – it seems to have served as the city's septic tank – demanded that the area be cleaned, and that it be made a place of prayer. The caliph himself assisted in the clean-up by shovelling up some of the septic material.[39]

Sophronius had taken Omar's at-ease dress as a sign of 'devilish pretence',[40] but there is no evidence that Omar was insincere. So far as is known, the details of the treaty were adhered to, and Christians in Jerusalem did not suffer unduly following the first encounter of substance between Christianity and Islam. The treaty was lenient for a conquered people, more a matter of reinforcing former privileges than of compelling a new and drastic way of life. It was a largely sensible, rational and non-triumphalist treaty; maybe it was hard on the Jews, but they had been supportive of the Persians, and Jews and Christians at this date had not yet achieved a modus vivendi. Over the next 500 years they were to find their way back to the holy city.

Jerusalem continued to be accessible to Christian pilgrims; the Gaulish bishop Arculf visited the holy places in 670 or thereabouts. On his return he was shipwrecked off the Hebrides. Here he recounted his experiences to Adamnus, Abbot of Iona. He described the Church of the Holy Sepulchre as being supported by 'twelve stone columns of marvellous size'. He also mentioned a rectangular 'house of prayer' which the Muslims had built on the reclaimed site of the Temple.[41] Arculf's spirit had been touched and elevated by his pilgrimage. Christian visitors were well treated under the new dispensation.

11

The lands of Islam still took on the nature and aspect of a universal realm; but despite the breaking-down of the former iron curtain between Persia and Rome, a new barrier descended within the faith at this time – not of iron, being more gauzy and permeable, but of deep and ineluctable significance. The fourth caliph, Muhammad's son-in-law Ali, had been challenged by the governor of Syria, Mu'awiyah, who was proclaimed caliph in 660. He was the very able leader of the Umayyad clan, which became the dynasty forever linked with opposition of the 'partisans of Ali', or Shia. On Mu'awiyah's death this opposition blew into a revolt, focused around Husain, the son of Ali and Fatima, and grandson of the Prophet Muhammad. He set out for Iraq to raise a revolt, claiming that the Prophet's family had a superior right to the caliphate. In 680 Umayyad forces confronted a small escort (of only about 200 followers) gathered around Husain. A desperate and tragic battle was fought at Kerbela, in which the overwhelming forces of the new caliph Yazid, which he had raised in the city of Kufa, attempted to encircle Husain, his family and followers,[42] and to parch them with a terrible thirst as the rival armies stood motionless. In the words of R.A. Nicholson, 'All the harrowing details invented by grief and passion can scarcely heighten the tragedy of the closing scene.'[43] Gibbon describes it thus:

The enemy advanced with reluctance, and one of their chiefs deserted, with thirty followers, to claim the partnership of inevitable death. In every close onset, or single combat, the despair of the Fatimites was invincible; but the surrounding multitudes galled them from a distance with a cloud of arrows, and the horses and men were successively slain: a truce was allowed on both sides for the hour of prayer; and the battle at length expired by the death of the last of the companions of Hosein. Alone, weary and wounded, he seated himself at the door of his tent. As he tasted a drop of water, he was pierced in the mouth with a dart; and his son and nephew, two beautiful youths, were killed in his arms. He lifted his hands to heaven – they were full of blood – and he uttered the funeral prayer for the living and the dead. In a transport of despair his sister issued from the tent, and adjured the general of the Cufians that he would not suffer Hosein to be murdered before his eyes: a tear trickled down his venerable beard; and the boldest of his soldiers fell back on every side as the dying hero threw himself among them. The remorseless Shamer, a name detested by the faithful, reproached their cowardice; and the grandson of Mohammed was slain with three-and-thirty strokes of lances and swords.[44]

In some respects the passion of Husain came to be as emblematic and as filled with inner sanctity as the passion of Christ is for Christians. Every year, on the tenth day of the Islamic month of Muharram, the Shia recall, with deeds of anguished devotion, the sacrifice of Husain at Kerbela, not far from the Euphrates.

Within the Islamic empire Christians continued to live in their native cities. The early caliphs of the Umayyad dynasty had no desire to convert them, since they were a source of handsome tribute; besides, the Damascus caliphs liked their city, and were too busy living a metropolitan life to resort to religious zealotry. The early Umayyad rulers took on some of the appearance of late-Roman emperors; a visitor to the Umayyad ruins at Ainjar (or Anjar) in Lebanon today, who is shown round by the Armenian guide (who hales from the nearby refugee camp, set up near the site in the years before the Second World War), may wonder: are these elegant ruins of the east or the west? Do they not have more in common with Rome or Ravenna than Baghdad or Iran? R.A. Nicholson summed up the best of the Umayyad rulers as 'strong and singularly capable rulers, bad Muslims and good men of the world, seldom cruel, plain livers if not high thinkers'.[45] One of the leading Christians of Umayyad Syria was St John of Damascus, the last of the Church Fathers. He had been a friend of the caliph Yazid in his youth and, following his father and grandfather, he became a servant in the household of the Umayyad caliphs; his father was head of the revenue department. The family lived a freely Christian life at the Islamic court. The son seemed destined for the same high civil service position as his father, but he received the calling to monkhood, and left the civilised pleasures of the city to take vows at the monastery of St Saba, in Palestine.[46]

At this wildly desolate monastery in the Judaean hills, together with his spiritual brother Cosmas of Maiuma (a town close to modern Gaza), he wrote hymns, and tracts against the iconoclasts, who were then in the ascendant in Byzantium. His arguments in favour of icons were imbued with the spirit of Christian Neoplatonism. St John of Damascus understood the world itself as an icon of God's thought; and if the Deity could have an icon, why should not man, his creature, do likewise? As regards Islam, he was no polemicist, but was concerned rather to refute its 'errors'. To John, Islam was a Christian heresy. He acknowledged that both Christians and Muslims worshipped the same one God. He criticised Islam for not accepting the divinity and crucifixion of Jesus; as a result he could not accept either the prophecy of Muhammad, or its corollaries, the notions that the prophet of Islam was the 'seal' of the prophets – that his revelation was the last and fullest revelation – and that the Koran was literally divine. Perhaps the most important points about St John of Damascus were the courtesy and scholarly manner in which he conducted his disputes with Islam and the ordinariness of his Christian devotional life under that faith. Occasionally his monkish superiors would make him return to Damascus, where he would be sent to hawk baskets in the city streets for the good of his soul.

The Umayyads were overthrown in 750, to be followed by Abbasid rule from Baghdad. Tolerance and accessibility continued for Christian pilgrims journeying to Jerusalem. Within the caliphate weaknesses appeared after about 840, when the rulers ceased to be concerned with government and farmed out power and administration to slaves.

The shift of the caliphate to Baghdad had a significant effect on the worldwide spread of Christianity. The Eastern Christians, or Nestorians, had been held in great esteem by early Islam, partly because of the legend that Muhammad had developed his sense of spiritual mission through the agency of a Nestorian monk he had met on a journey, and partly because they were the educated class in the east. With the establishment of the caliphate in the east, and with now-monotheist Islamic protection, Nestorian preachers were able to set out across Central Asia into China, in perhaps the greatest Christian missionary enterprise ever undertaken. Their presence among the Turkish tribes, and the respect that was felt towards them, is signified by the likely derivation of the word *çelebi*, a Turkish word, meaning 'gentleman', brought from Central Asia into Anatolia in Seljuk times. Almost certainly it is derived from the Arabic *salib*, meaning cross or crucifix, and had originally been applied to the Nestorian missionaries and clergy proselytising in Central Asia. The unequivocal evidence for the vast enterprise of Nestorian Christian mission work undertaken from Islamic lands is the tablet of Si-ngan-fu, a town in Shensi province. On this stone there is an inscription in Chinese and Syriac, which records the excellent qualities of the Christian religion and its widespread propagation in the Middle Kingdom. The date on the column is 1092 of the Seleucid era: that is, AD 781.[47]

If Islam had broken down the barrier between east Rome and Persia, and allowed Christian missionaries to carry their scriptures into China, it had (so it has been claimed) erected a tough barrier in Europe. The theory, set forth by Henri Pirenne in 1925 and elaborated in 1937, is that 'without Islam, the Frankish Empire would probably never have existed, and Charlemagne, without Muhammad, would be inconceivable'.[48] The new Islamic order in the Mediterranean and southern Europe broke down the north–south social unity within Europe, blocking off northern Europe and forcing it into itself, from which it emerged in the person of Charlemagne and in the condition of medieval feudalism. The theory is alluring, and will be debated for decades.

It is hard to deny the likely truth of its basic outlines. Nevertheless, the northern-European kingdom was not hermetically sealed. Its isolation was less than total. Coins of the Abbasid caliphs have been discovered in Orkney, and Saxon coins, probably Danegeld, dug up in the Middle East. Offa, king of Mercia in the eighth century, adopted the gold dinar of Baghdad as his currency. A fine example of this coin exists in an Edinburgh museum, with the inscription in Arabic 'God is most great' surrounding the name 'OFFA'.[49]

Although Charlemagne's empire lasted for not much more than 100 years, that time was imbued with a quality of grandeur and magnificence which haunted Europe for a millennium, and which found a moment of splendour around 790–800, when the Frankish (that is, Germanic) emperor Charlemagne (correctly 'Charles the Great') sent ambassadors, one of whom was Isaac the Jew, to the court of caliph Harun al-Rashid in Baghdad. The caliph reciprocated with gifts: an elephant – the only one he possessed, named Abu 'l Abbas, which would find its way into northern-European manuscript illuminations – as well as ivory, incense and a water-clock (or *klepsydra*). In return Charles sent white and green robes to the caliph, and a pack of his best hounds. The spirit was akin to that later displayed by Henry VIII and Francis I at the Field of the Cloth of Gold: a generous and lavish show put on by rulers at the peak of their power, who understood the political impact of the gift of gorgeous artefacts. An establishment, part hostel and part hospital, of Charles the Great was founded in the centre of Jerusalem to attend to the needs of pilgrims.[50]

A legend grew up that Charles was sent the keys to the Holy Sepulchre, but this was almost certainly fictitious. What seems to have occurred is that the Patriarch of Jerusalem, in a gesture of politeness reflecting the warm diplomatic atmosphere created by the two sovereigns, sent to the Frankish emperor something that appeared to be the keys of the holy city, but which was really just a gift and a reminder: a kind of gilded tourist memento, roughly equivalent to a special edition of the imitation, resin-made artefacts that one finds in museum shops today. A similar item would have been sent by the patriarch to any distinguished sovereign or guest. A number of European commentators, seeking to justify the Crusades, have claimed that Charlemagne's actions, in receiving the keys and in building a hospital, amounted to establishing a European protectorate over Jerusalem; but one has to have a very vivid sense of European superiority to interpret the sending of such a present as the gift of a foreign political protectorate.

In the exchange there was, besides the pride and pleasure of showing off power, an element of great-power calculation. Charles was looking for allies beyond the Byzantine Empire, whose emperor had inherited the mantle of Rome; he was seeking to enhance his own imperial legitimacy by opening diplomatic relations with a great ruler one step further away. Harun al-Rashid was likewise glad of positive relations with the Franks, to counterbalance the dynastic claims of the Spanish Umayyads (scions of the Damascus caliphate, a single member of whom had survived the Abbasid revolution). Even at this date the part played by religion in the creation of alliances and hostilities among world powers could be placed second by powerful and charismatic rulers. The idea that geographically distinct communities sharing the same religion have been politically 'One', either in early Christianity or within Islam, is a piece of mystification, an attempt to make a case for unity when separation was more likely to be the reality. A ruler could make statecraft and religion travel in opposite directions. Except as an invoked prayer ritual, 'Christendom' was losing unity by the ninth century, as was the Islamic *umma*, or community. A central philosophical conflict of the Middle Ages was that of Realism versus Nominalism, one view accepting the objective reality of universal concepts such as 'church', 'nation', 'political party' or 'mankind', while the other denied such a reality in favour of the observation and description of particulars, affirming that there were only individual believers (or individual members) and that the overarching concepts were merely names. It is hard to deny that 'Christendom' and the *umma* were developing into Realist myths. They were little more than names, having only a tenuous external reality. There were no diplomatic instruments or objects of faith or society that indicated unity between the many differing and hard-to-reconcile strands within either of the universal monotheistic faiths. Each was appearing more as an articulation of the Nominalist position: just an aggregation of individual members. The supposed uniting factors may have found reality in the prayers of believers, but there was less evidence in the tangible quotidianity of lived life.

Bernard the Wise, a pilgrim monk, visited Egypt and Palestine in the ninth century, at the time of the Abbasid caliph, al-Mu'tazz (866–9), and stayed at Charlemagne's hostel: 'We were received in the hospital of the most glorious emperor Charles, where are lodged all those who go to this place for devotional reasons and speak the Roman tongue. Close to it is a church in honour of St Mary, which has a noble library through the care of the aforesaid emperor, with twelve dwelling-houses, fields, vineyards and a garden, in the valley of Jehoshaphat.'[51] He noted the continuing good relations between the adherents of the different religions: 'The Christians and the pagans [i.e. Muslims] have this kind of peace between them there that if I were going on a journey, and on the way the camel or ass which bore my poor luggage were to die, and I were to abandon all my goods there without any guardian, and go to the city for another pack animal, when I came back, I would find all my property uninjured: such is the peace there.' Bernard added that anyone travelling without a signed document was liable to be jailed until he gave an account of himself.[52] It was common sense never to travel without a passport.

Relations continued thus. In 869 the patriarch Theodosius of Jerusalem wrote: 'The Saracens show us great good will. They allow us to build our churches and to observe our own customs without hindrance.'[53]

There was an intellectual exception to the low-key, sacred interchange between Christian and Muslim. In one location the interaction of Christian with Muslim was not that of the penitent spirit harvesting the humble fruits of sanctity and cloistered devotion. This was Islamic Spain, where a culture of vitality and vibrancy had sprung up, and where as a result the sin-conscious, bowed-down life of the starved, contrite soul had been eclipsed by the colourful educated splendour of a multicultural civilisation. Here Jews, Christians and Muslims forgot their differences (and most of their sins) and embarked on a voyage through learning, literature and pleasure. The Cordovan Christian scholar Paul Alvarus was a bishop who opposed civilised early humanism, being more concerned with final judgement, the Antichrist, the Beast 666 and the Second

Coming, in the manner of Puritan Bible-literal end-timers both of the seventeenth century and of today. He became a prey to the uneasy thought-patterns that religion can create in the overdevotional cast of mind that excludes the broader elements of culture and civilisation. Writing in 854, in a mood of sorrow and censure, he said:

> The Christians love to read the poems and the romances of the Arabs; they study the Arab theologians and philosophers, not to refute them but to form a correct and elegant Arabic. Where is the layman who now reads the Latin commentaries on the holy scriptures, or who studies the gospels, prophets or apostles? Alas, all talented young Christians read and study with enthusiasm the Arab books; they gather immense libraries at great expense; they despise the Christian literature as unworthy of attention. They have forgotten their language. For every one who can write a letter in Latin to a friend, there are a thousand who can express themselves in Arabic with elegance, and write better poems in this language than the Arabs themselves.[54]

The same society found Samuel ibn Nagdela, who was Jewish, as vizier to the king of Granada in about the year 1050. Samuel, known as *haNagid* or the Prince, was (according to Cecil Roth) a 'generous and discriminating patron of letters' who had gained his position by virtue of his Arabic style.[55]

If the Islamic West was flourishing, in the east circumstances were changing. The times were witnessing the slow sunset of a tolerant order which had existed since the Muslim conquest of Jerusalem. Knowledge, which had developed powerfully in the years from 830, was harder to find in the Islamic East in the years following the mid-ninth century. Tolerance of the sciences gave way to persecution of these studies, since science and philosophy were suspected of leading to a 'loss of belief'.[56] This intolerance, combined with political weakness, gravely weakened the Baghdad caliphate, even though it kept its civilisation and some of its learning. The caliph started to employ ethnic Turks from the east as bodyguards. Al-Mutasim built the city of Samarra (outside Baghdad) for them. Soon they were powerful enough to hold their sovereign as prisoner.

The power of culture, language and poetry was always apparent in fashioning the raw elements of Islamic history as much as religious belief and militarily based political power. One example is that of the Samanids, a dynasty founded in the ninth century AD in Central Asia. There is a linguistic paradox here. In the Iberian peninsula Arabic eased out Latin and early Spanish and became the language of culture and refinement, of love and sociability. But in Central Asia the Samanids, who appointed ethnic Turks as provincial governors, people renowned for their Islamic orthodoxy and devotion to the Arabic language, found that Persian became the dominant language. Individuals like Mahmud of Ghazna (in Afghanistan), a successor to the Samanids, were captivated by Persian literature. Mahmud, who also holds an unenviable reputation as a great looter of Hindu temples, invited all the poets of Persia to his court, and patronised the great Firdawsi, author of the *Shahnama*, or 'Book of Kings', promising him (but not delivering) a gold piece for every verse. The poets of the tenth century spoke their verses in a language which came to be known as New Persian, and which was in essentials the language which developed into that of modern Iran, written in the streamlined, smartly abbreviated and elegantly sloping script that is in use today.[57]

Knowledge did not vanish from the Fertile Crescent, Central Asia or the Islamic Mediterranean. But in the east mysticism grew strong, weakening the desire to rule and control that the Arabs had initially inherited from the Romans and the Persians. The desire to rule diminished, just as centuries later British rule in India would grow untenable after the intellectual assault of liberal values upon imperialism. The faith in some quarters was seen as veiled. The Koran was looked on as a mystical allegory.

This sceptical and mystical temperament found expression in the quatrains ('Rubaiyyat') of Omar al-Khayyam:[58]

> There was a door to which I found no key
> There was a veil past which I could not see,
> Some little talk awhile of me and thee
> There seemed – and then no more of thee and me.

Among those in the forefront of resisting the embrace of scholarly hesitation were the Turkish palace guards. Both in Central Asia and in the Fertile Crescent, their martial competence was seen as their principal quality, which created a contrast to the new mood of the East, which was one of savouring and reflecting. The Turks took over the reins of power when the ruling imperial nation had lost interest in ruling and administration. At the same time the new militia guards followed the faith and rule of their sovereign–captives. The Central Asian newcomers proved able in their new role; but the intellectual excitement found at the courts of the ninth-century Abbasid caliphs had vanished.

In North Africa, Shii Islam took root in the tenth century. Soon much of the southern-Mediterranean littoral had adhered to a variety of Shiism. Egypt, an unlikely recruit for Shiism, created its own caliphate, named after Fatima, the daughter of the Prophet. A number of the representatives of this caliphate were tolerant men, who showed a spirit of benevolent indifference to their Christian subjects. They were educated people who encouraged the sciences and amassed great libraries. They observed the non-Muslim communities largely without fuss: the Muslim traveller al-Mukaddasi remarks, after a visit to Jerusalem in about AD 985, 'Everywhere the Christians and the Jews have the upper hand.'[59] But there was a violent and significant exception to this pattern. Just thirty years after the foundation of Cairo, a Fatimid caliph emerged who was to send a tremor of anxiety throughout the Christian world. Al-Hakim came to power as sixth Fatimid caliph in AD 996.[60] He was an extreme Shiite, and he may have driven himself half-mad by mystical exertions. The influence of hermetic, secret, Neoplatonic ideas lay heavily with him: the notions that some human beings were chosen to be, or might aspire to become, the elect, the privileged, the in-crowd, the clique – an idea which is always attractive to the human mind in its narcissistic mode. Every society has its private clubs and cliquishness. The Ladder of Perfection often has a hard heart of self-absorption, despising benefits to the wider community.

Al-Hakim declared himself a member of the most exclusive society of all. He was divine. His status was higher than that of 'divine emanation' accorded to other Fatimid caliphs. Although his views were offensive to Sunni Muslims, he placated them by concessions. But he was intolerant towards Christians and persecuted them until his death in 1021, reducing the Church of the Holy Sepulchre to ruins and destroying several other Jerusalem churches, probably in the year 1010.[61] He was said to have been particularly inflamed by what he perceived as the fraudulence of the Ceremony of Holy Fire, performed on Easter Eve. In a flash of residual rationality, he affirmed that the fire which illuminated the church for the Easter festivities, and which filled the souls of the devout with the light of faith at that pivotal sacred moment, did not (as the priests asserted) descend from heaven but originated in the spark of a deacon's flint.

Al-Hakim's whirlwind of destruction did not last, and within two years of his death calm returned. The Byzantine emperor funded the rebuilding of the Holy Sepulchre, and pilgrim trade revived. When the Persian pilgrim Nasir-i Khusrau visited Jerusalem in 1047, he described this central church of Christianity in all its magnificence: how it could hold 8,000 worshippers amidst decoration of coloured marble and adornment of fine sculpture. Walls were covered in Byzantine brocade worked in gold thread and depicting saints and martyrs. Here too were pictures of Jesus, portraying him riding on an ass. The prophets were shown in paintings varnished with oil of red juniper and covered by a thin layer of protective glass.[62] It was clear that the Holy Sepulchre, and Christianity in the Holy Land, had staged a brilliant and rapid turnaround.

Nasir-i Khusrau also describes a building which would have been Charles the Great's hospital: 'Great numbers of people are here served with draughts and lotions; for there are physicians who receive a fixed stipend to attend at this place for the sick.'[63] The Persian traveller also noted that 'From all the countries of the Greeks, and also from other lands, the Christians and the Jews come up to Jerusalem in great numbers, in order to visit the church and the synagogue that is there.' Jerusalem was a city of multifaith pilgrimage under the Fatimids. This point is also reflected in the annual Jerusalem fair which was held each September, in which commerce acted as a deterrent to fanaticism and extremism.[64] The Jerusalem fair unified the people of the Mediterranean and created bonds of human brotherhood. The spirit of the fair made sure that no one cared who was Jew, Christian or Muslim. All that mattered was whether you could buy or sell. Here, within an Islamic society, was a pioneering example of the commercial rationalism which, seven centuries later, Voltaire was to hold up as an example of a defence against murderous religious hate. In business, Voltaire quipped, the only infidel was the bankrupt.

Throughout Palestine and Syria the power of the Fatimids was waning, and Jerusalem was captured by the Seljuk Turks. The Seljuks had moved slowly westward in the previous hundred years, eventually defeating the Byzantines at the great battle of Manzikert in 1071, a defeat which left the eastern frontier of the Byzantine Empire exposed and undefended. The

Seljuks were a tribal configuration who believed above all in handing out power to members of their own family, a system which endured in western Asia for a century. In 1070 a Seljuk Turkish general, Atsiz, had wrested Jerusalem from the Fatimids.[65]

Rule by the Seljuks in Palestine lacked the broadness of Fatimid and Arab culture and sentiment. Libraries meant nothing to them. However there was no major or dramatic change for Christian pilgrims or for the native Christian peoples. Things continued largely as before. The impulse for the Crusades, the catastrophe which was to befall the region, came – like the invading armies – from Europe itself. The multitude of deaths which were to suffuse the lands of the eastern Mediterranean in blood were, in the context of the region itself, effects without causes. As the early centuries of Islamic Jerusalem draw to an end, the image that the city presents is of a rougher, divided place of sanctity, disputed between Shiite Fatimid and Sunni Turk, but still largely a peaceful, multifaith city, where the twin activities of pilgrimage and commerce could be carried on with little hindrance.

CHAPTER TWO

The Asperity of Religious War

In July 1099 the crusaders, 'sobbing for excess of joy'[1] amid scenes resembling those depicted on a medieval Doom, captured Jerusalem from the Muslims and proclaimed Godfrey de Bouillon their leader. Relations between Christians and Muslims, which appeared to have reached a tentative equilibrium in the preceding decades, were drowned in blood. Thus began two centuries of domination of the Holy Land by western Europeans, known as 'Franks', although only a minority of them bore any connection with Charles the Great's Germanic people.

The red flood-tide which coursed through the streets of the holy city took with it the severed heads and limbs of the thousands of victims, and in the area of the Temple (or Haram) the horses of the knights slithered in a shallow lake of blood. The victors reeked of decaying guts, and the air was filled with the pungent odour of burning flesh, for a community of Jews who had crammed themselves into their synagogue were incinerated. In control amidst the terror, the crusaders, 'dripping with blood from head to foot',[2] experienced a sense of release and satisfaction. 'Who could find time to recount in detail the joys of those who massacred and the sorrows of those who were massacred?' declared Raoul of Caen.[3] The pent-up rush of heavenly aspirations and inner frenzies, driven by the religious intoxication which had led them to the holy city, had now received catharsis. In the bloodletting – for the killings were done on principle, not for strategy or self-defence – they had become like votaries of a cult of death, whose fetish was human blood. After the slaughter, there was devotion in the Church of the Holy Sepulchre and the chant of their thanksgiving rang out loudly. But the sacred offering did not purge the desire to kill. They came again. Albert of Aix wrote of a further massacre, three days after the initial bout, which focused especially on women and their infants. Christian qualities such as compassion or benevolence were absent as the streets filled with the torn and mangled limbs of children. 'The Christians had delivered their souls to the passion for carnage,' mused Albert, in a glimmer of regret.[4] Zeal of faith meant that death was paramount. July 1099 saw its consummation in Jerusalem.

David Hume described the Crusades as 'the most signal and most durable monument of human folly that has yet appeared in any age or nation'.[5] To Gibbon they were episodes of 'holy madness', manifestations of 'savage fanaticism', whose participants were 'alike destitute of humanity and reason'. How, he wondered, could six succeeding generations have 'rushed headlong down the precipice that was open before them'? The knights, he noted, 'neglected to live, but were prepared to die, in the service of Christ'.[6] The distant graves of the crusaders, in the deserts of Anatolia and amid the rocks of Palestine, were 'voluntary and inevitable'. The eighteenth-century Scottish historian and minister of the Presbyterian kirk William Robertson called the ventures 'a singular monument of human folly'.[7] The learned German theologian and church historian Johann Lorenz von Mosheim struggled to comprehend them. Their origin, he ventured, 'is to be derived in the corrupt notions of religion, which prevailed in these barbarian times'. 'The truth of the matter seems to be this: that the Roman pontiffs and the European princes were engaged in these crusades by a principle of superstition only; but when in process of time, they learned by experience that these holy wars contributed much to increase their opulence and to extend their authority, by sacrificing their wealthy and powerful rivals, then new motives were presented to encourage these sacred expeditions into Palestine, and ambition and avarice seconded and enforced the dictates of fanaticism and superstition.'[8] A number of nineteenth-century authors – Charles Mills, and Besant and Palmer – concurred.[9] Set alongside the wisdom and civilised moderation of Omar's initial Islamic settlement of Jerusalem, the crusaders' actions seem to define barbarity with focused ferocity, adding in a streak of narrow narcissistic vengefulness. Here was the raging darkness of a Europe unwarmed by the south since the coming of Islam: Charlemagne's northern empire, but without his political genius, hurling iron shafts of ignorance against a sun-filled civilisation of the south.

But the contrary view has long been voiced, and words and phrases like 'obligation', 'veneration', 'chivalry', 'piety' and 'the duty of the West' have been an essential part of the discourse of the Crusades.

Shakespeare, at the beginning of *Henry IV Part I*, used the image of crusading as a symbol of the holy resolution of English civil strife:

> Therefore friends
> As far as to the sepulchre of Christ, –
> Whose soldier now, under whose blessed cross
> We are impressed and engag'd to fight, –
> Forthwith a power of English shall we levy,
> Whose arms were moulded in their mother's womb
> To chase these pagans in those holy fields
> Over whose acres walk'd those blessed feet
> Which fourteen hundred years ago were nail'd
> For our advantage on the bitter cross.[10]

This is the more popular and traditional view of the Crusades: that they were an expression and an exaltation of noble and selfless knightly virtues exercised in the recapture from barbarism and from the clutches of the destroying Muslim of the Holy Land where the Prince of Peace once trod. Islam in this context became virtually interchangeable with paganism, and destroying the destroyer was seen as unquestionably virtuous. By a process of sympathetic magic, and in retreat from the universal aspect of the Christian faith, the holiness of the land transferred itself directly into holy deeds. Even though thereby Palestine became akin to an idol, and Christianity veered towards the status of a tribal cult, crusading in the eastern Mediterranean came to appear to have within it an element of intrinsic good: goodness-in-itself. This robust view was held in the 1930s by René Grousset, who believed that the Crusades possessed an 'epic' quality, with deeds of valour performed by Christian 'heroes and saints'.[11] The great names of the European aristocracy were often listed in awe as the banners of great families fluttered, even though this process brought the faith close to ancestor-worship, and the reverse of the coin of chivalry and nobility was the murder of an infidel.

The traditional view is hard to sustain today, partly because interest has diminished in great family names, and partly because the ideological offspring of the crusading enterprise, European colonialism, is as dead as its sacred predecessor. Both crusaders and colonialists sought control of, and felt above, remote and distant territory. To the crusaders it was 'Outremer', the (unnamed) place across the sea, Overseasville, whose very namelessness indicated that it belonged more to a world of ordering about and internal control imagery than to any sort of inter-state reality. Jerusalem, Tripoli, Antioch and Edessa were all yoked together under the one vague name. Now that aristocrats are no longer deferred to and the trumpets of colonial command have ceased to sound, the views of Hume, Gibbon, Robertson and Mosheim seem more congenial; they are harsher and bleaker, but devoid of vanity and superiority, and so ultimately more universal in outlook, and more attuned to that elusive quality, the brotherhood of humanity. However it is only right to add that, in modern leaders' recent troubled confusion of Afghanistan with Iraq (a confrontational mentality which sometimes extends to Iran), the idea of warfare in a nameless Overseasville has taken on a new lease of life, embodying the notion of an alien 'them', 'out there', a formless shadowy Eastern other, where half-realised identities merge into one another, and where enemies are created and kaleidoscopically attacked for the deeds of others, and all resemble the shadow-self of some carefully preserved, wholesome, noble and knightly Western ideal.

Why did the pilgrim armies make their way to the eastern Mediterranean for close on 300 years, and occupy parts of the Holy Land for much of that time? Explanations such as the longing of the Christians for Palestine or the saving of the land from 'pagans' are inadequate for understanding the warfare undertaken in the name of the Prince of Peace. So are presumptions – such as that voiced by Dr Johnson in a discussion of the above passage from *Henry IV Part I* – that Islam entailed inevitable hostility with the Christian world since it was a faith built on war; to him Muslims were 'obliged by their own principles to make war upon Christians'. This was a viewpoint shared by Francis Bacon: in an argument that has foreshadowed later justifications of 'preventative war', he argued that Western Christian fear was a sufficient ground for invasive war, since it was 'a fundamental law of the Turkish empire that they may, without any other provocation, make war upon Christendom for the propagation of their law'.[12] Both writers seem to have ignored the diversity of interpretation and of political power within Islam, as well as the pacts and treaties between Islamic and European powers. Muhammad himself never sought warfare outside the Arabian peninsula. Indeed, in his youth he traded with Christian cities and had received a very significant moment of spiritual enlightenment in the cell of the Nestorian monk known in Christian literature as Sergius and in Muslim texts as Bahira. So one can rightly doubt any assertion about the permanent hostility between Islam and Christianity.

The centuries before the Crusades had shown that Christians could cooperate with Muslims, either as Eastern Christian neighbours, or as Western Christian pilgrims. Treaties with countries outside the Islamic community existed from its earliest years; we have only to recall the relations between Harun al-Rashid and Charles the Great. The Byzantine emperor Alexius I was making treaties with the Sultan of Rum (based at Konya, or Iconium) a decade before the Crusades. The proposition that Islam is permanently unstable, owing to the concept of *jihad* or holy war (a word which initially meant not much more than 'hard striving'[13]), is disproved by observing what happened in practice. Relations between Christian and Muslim powers could be as stable and neighbourly (or the reverse) as relations between any powers. In most theoretical studies, there was a separation of the Islamic world into two divisions, the *dar ul-harb* (house or domain of war: the countries which had not been conquered by Islam) and the *dar ul-Islam* (house of Islam), indicating that war was the necessary and permanent condition for un-Islamised countries. But in practice this distinction did not occur, and peaceful relations could be and were established between Islamic and non-Islamic states, especially between the caliphate and the Byzantine Empire. The reception of the Greek ambassadors in Baghdad was an occasion for magnificence at which no expense was spared.[14] Moreover Islamic jurists had propounded the concept of a *dar ul-sulh* (house of peace), indicating that peace could in principle be established between states whether Islamised or not. This concept was not developed by Islamic lawyers, but it remained an option.[15]

A new element, or a group of elements, entered the situation in the eleventh century; or perhaps some inner dynamic found fulfilment at that time. The outcome was the militarisation of Christianity against Islam, destroying relations between the two faiths.

Muslim society in Palestine had changed little from the days of amity and hospitality except in one way: its own internal divisions. Fatimid rule was crumbling before the assault of the Seljuk Turks, who since 1055 had taken control of the severely weakened caliphate in Baghdad. The Seljuk Turkish family confederation had scored a famous victory over Byzantium in 1071 at Manzikert – 'the dreadful day', as it was known to Byzantine historians. In that year a Seljuk appointee became governor of Jerusalem and conditions became marginally rougher (but not impossible) for pilgrims. It needs to be stressed that, in the words of Claude Cahen, the great specialist on medieval Islam, the coming of the Seljuk Empire 'brought no fundamental change to the lot of autochthonous Christians or to the treatment of foreign pilgrims'.[16] In other words, according to Cahen there was no justification, in the circumstances of the Holy Land itself, for the Crusades. In 1089 the (Shiite) Fatimids reversed some (Sunni) Turkish gains by recapturing the coast towns of Palestine, and by the time of the arrival of the crusaders the governor of Jerusalem was a Fatimid.[17] The quarrel between Seljuk and Fatimid, with its edge of religious contention, seriously weakened the capacity of the local people to withstand invasion.

Within Europe a number of elements changed the prevalent attitude from peaceful pilgrimage to violent conquest of the Holy Land. The first was the coming of the Normans. This people, originally from Scandinavia, had within two generations remodelled itself as a dominant force within the society of Europe. They were assertive, dictatorial, controlling and militant, though sometimes content to act as mercenaries. They liked social hierarchies. If they could not be dominant they were content with submission; with a tendency towards warfare, they seem not to have rated equality highly. Their position paralleled in a rough approximation that of the Goths within later-Roman society in Europe, and that of the Turkish guards within Arab palaces. But they were greater agents of change, perhaps as a result of their instincts for violence and hierarchy. They made their militant cause popular by gaining, where necessary, the blessing of the pope, but were unafraid of excommunication. They used the papacy as they saw fit, and the papacy made use of them. When William the Conqueror invaded England in 1066, his army was led by a knight holding a papal banner emblazoned with a red cross; the invasion of England thus took on the appearance of a crusade before the Crusades. In dating the capture of Jerusalem ('the event preferable to all events'), Foulcher of Chartres makes a point of indicating that it occurred twelve years after the death of William, King of England.[18]

The Normans were active in Italy too; under Robert Guiscard ('Robert the Resourceful') they seized Bari and Apulia and, in the course of a war lasting from 1060 to 1090, Sicily. The greater part of this territory was seized from Byzantium, while the rest was taken partly from either the Lombards or the Muslims. In the struggle against the Sicilian Arabs the Normans were inspired by a banner blessed by the pope,[19] even though in 1053 Robert had actually seized the pope (Leo IX) in battle. A codependency was developing between the papacy and the Normans.

Both parties sought to attack or subvert Byzantium. The Normans' ambition was to do serious damage to Constantinople and even to supplant the Byzantine emperor. In 1081 they seized the island of Corfu and went on to attack the mainland. Dyrrachium (Durrës today, in Albania) was briefly occupied.[20] Only quarrels within the Norman army about pay permitted the Byzantines to make a successful counterattack. In May 1084, in the course of his policy of supporting Pope Gregory VII against Henry IV, the excommunicated Holy Roman Emperor, Robert permitted Rome to be sacked for three days in a whirlwind of violence. Many treasures from antiquity were destroyed, and the population, maddened by the brutality, was driven to revolt.[21]

But once the Normans were established in Sicily, they appeared to lose some of the Manichaean, confrontational drive – the tribal impulse to permanent revolution. Instead they drew richly on the culture which surrounded them, part of which was Arab and Islamic. Roger I and Roger II of Sicily abandoned the barbarian war-culture of the north and allowed themselves to be warmed by the south. They immersed their courts in Arab and Byzantine learning and philosophy, and created a multicultural society. They showed the fertility of a northern Europe reconnected to the south which did not seek to dominate its neighbour. In a memorable and magnificent way, the Normans went native in Sicily, and as they relaxed their control, the science and art of the region flowed into the court; and future generations benefited from it. Roger II's geographer, al-Idrisi, was a man of real knowledge who understood that the earth was round and wrote a famed geographical study entitled 'The Delight of Those who Seek to Wander Through the Regions of the World'. The chapel that that monarch built, the Cappella Palatina in Palermo, is among the most beautiful palace-chapels in the world. It combines an austere Norman-French structure with the darkly glittering mosaics of Byzantium, decorated with vivacious Islamic lettering and ornament, the whole surmounted by breathtaking Arab-style stalactite roofing. The Palatine Chapel shows the great achievement of an eclectic culture that had abandoned aspirations towards domination and demonisation.[22]

But if art and philosophy grew rapidly in the sun-baked regions of southern Europe, the north was still pervaded by religious gloom and guilt. Although guilt had lain lightly with the early Christianised populations of Europe, its significance had grown throughout the Middle Ages. Private confession became more common, whereby the bishop or priest might interrogate a malefactor and impose his own punitive standards on an individual, driving some sinners to believe that their wrongdoing had left them almost beyond absolution. (The practice of the early church had been for confession to be voluntary and open.) The discipline of the medieval church amounted to a sacred legislation; and this was enforced by means of lawbooks, or penitentials. Fasts and prayers were set to atone for real or imagined wrongdoing. Punishments were heavy: a sentence of as much as three hundred years' penance might be imposed. Sinners could expiate their wickedness by means of indulgences, or clerical fines. An alternative manner of expunging sins was to submit to savage flagellation. By a 'fantastic arithmetic', a year of penance was taxed at 3,000 lashes.[23]

A sense of sin ran deep. Whether there was at this time more actual wrongdoing is disputable, but the medieval soul felt darkened to the pit of death. So when the pope offered a plenary indulgence – forgiveness of all sins – to all who would enlist under the banner of the crusade, his offer was broadly accepted. Here was a way by which the people, weighed down by hag-ridden consciences, might escape the burden. They could evade detailed interrogation of their lives by the bishops and priests (who may have undertaken their tasks with vicarious enjoyment, since the worldly delights of the common people were less accessible to them, and the enjoyment of a sinful story knows no limits of detail). Participation in the crusade would cleanse the conscience; it was a new path of salvation (*novum salutis genus*) for full and complete satisfaction. In this way the Crusades were connected to the penitentiary system.[24] The remission also held good for future sins that might lie glittering along the path to Jerusalem. The violence and criminality which took place on the way to the Holy Land grew naturally from the papal free-gift, add-on absolution.

Pilgrimages had been shading into crusades throughout the eleventh century. Robert I, Duke of Normandy, the father of William the Conqueror, had travelled to Jerusalem in 1035. An event in his pilgrimage provides a striking early example of the antagonistic rhetoric which grew to characterise the Crusades. As the Norman duke lay sick on a litter, carried by local Muslims, he proclaimed, 'Tell my people that you have seen me borne to Paradise by devils!' – an utterance which mixes self-righteousness, ingratitude and demonisation in proportions recognisable today.[25] Fulk the Black, Count of Anjou, tormented by guilt for violating the sanctity of a church and other nameless sins, made two pilgrimages to Palestine and planned a third. He dressed himself in a rough penitential garment and begged the people to scourge him through the streets of Jerusalem. While he was praying at the Holy Sepulchre, the stone was said to have become miraculously soft to his teeth, and in a detail worthy of Salvador Dali he bit off a portion and took it home in triumph.[26] In 1074 a pilgrimage of 7,000 people, headed by the Archbishop of Mainz, travelled to Palestine and reached the Holy Sepulchre largely in peace, despite a skirmish with Bedouin Arabs. Peaceful pilgrimage was still occurring just two decades before the pope issued his call to holy war.

The papacy, revived and confident, sensed that campaigns in Palestine could enhance its power and prestige. The moment was right for Rome's self-advancement for two reasons. In the first place, for decades the papacy had been locked in bitter conflict with the western emperor, principally on the issue of investing bishops, and needed a grand gesture to enhance its authority. Secondly, despite the frequent calls for patching up their differences, the Eastern and Western churches had, by this date, gone their separate ways. The dispute over *filioque* (whether the Holy Ghost proceeds from the Son as well as from the Father) was little more than a pretext. In a fine passage, Gibbon expresses it thus:

In every age the Greeks were proud of their superiority in profane and religious knowledge: they had first received the light of Christianity; they had pronounced the decrees of the seven general councils; they alone possessed the language of scripture and philosophy: nor should the barbarians, immersed in the darkness of the west, presume to argue on the high and mysterious questions of theological science. Those barbarians despised in their turn the restless and subtle levity of the Orientals, the authors of every heresy, and blessed their own simplicity, which was content to hold the tradition of the apostolic church.[27]

The Western Church was now more self-aware. Rome no longer respected the antiquity of Antioch, Alexandria or Constantinople, but asserted its dominance. The pontiff would work to end ecclesiastical diversity, leading to the submission of the ancient self-ruling sees to his authority. The papacy was after the Greek Church. Similarly, its interest in encouraging the *Reconquista* in Spain was less to attack the Andalusian Muslims than to bring the Spanish Church under its control. The pope had gained high moral ground by excommunicating Philip I, King of France, for his marital arrangements and his personal disposition of pleasant idleness, which left him uninterested in devout struggle. Emperor Henry IV, who was driven to mortified penance at Canossa in

1077, had a turbulent and non-devotional temperament, which left him unmoved by zeal.[28]

In practical terms it made sense to send unemployed young men overseas. The medieval feudal system was reaching a moment of crisis, with the division at death of land creating impossibilities of inheritance, since no position was allotted to younger sons of land-owning families. Their only option was to remain disconsolately at home making trouble. The chance of sending off the excess population to fight in wars across the seas was a welcome solution, although it was expensive.

The extension of guilt among the populations of Europe, the power of preaching, the rise of Norman power, the reforms and ambitions of the papacy and the incapacity of feudalism to cope beyond a certain stage: these appear to be the elements which converged in the creation of the Crusades. In the Iberian peninsula the *Reconquista* was carried out with fanfare and propaganda, despite the involvement of the papacy.[29] The victorious Castilian kings initially respected the conquered Islamic civilisation. Further north, the *chansons de geste,* which recounted feats of knightly bravery, were by contrast mindlessly proclaiming the virtue of crushing the infidel and (in the case of the *Chanson de Roland*) distorting the facts of Christian–Muslim relations in order to produce a fictionalised tale of the light, goodness and bravery of 'us' Christians against the dark, sinister and alluring wickedness of 'those' Muslims.

The relation of the *Chanson de Roland* to historical truth is significant. The origin of that knightly poetic fiction which was so pervasive in the high Middle Ages lay in an incident which had occurred in August 778. In that month the Frankish army, commanded by Charles the Great and in uneasy alliance with the Moorish governor of Barcelona, Suleyman ibn al-Arabi (whom he may have suspected of treachery), was ambushed and slaughtered by a detachment of Basques while crossing the Pyrenees at the Pass of Roncesvalles.

From this incident of Europeans killing Europeans, with apparently no more than a vague hint of treachery by the Muslim forces, a complex mythology was concocted and given poetic merit, in which Charles's enemies became not European Basques but Muslim infidels (with some of whom, in reality, he had been in alliance). The historical record shows us an ordinary event of ambush, plunder and murder. The mythologised version developed into an angelic–demonic confrontation, in which the adversaries were not an army and an irregular detachment of small-time, plunder-hungry opportunists but representatives of ultimate, eternal values, facing each other as representatives of truth and error, God's world and Satan's, the good West and the evil empire; us and them. The purest goodness (Western Christianity) appeared facing seething evil ('Mahound' and his 'paynims'), despite the real-life alliance between Charles and Suleyman.

One does not have to be a thoroughgoing Freudian to see that, in the *Chanson de Roland* and similar depictions of the wickedness of Islam, there is an element of projection: the Europeans projecting their own 'bad' sides, especially their weight of guilt, on to the unrepressed, unpuritanical and less guilt-ridden Muslims. The historian of Islam W. Montgomery Watt has pointed out that 'the distorted image of Islam is to be regarded as a projection of the shadow-side of European man.'[30] According to a Kleinian interpretation, the issue can be seen thus: that the concocted myth represents a vivid example of what is known as the 'splitting' of experience into two opposing categories, which is the manner in which the dawning consciousness of an infant copes with baffling experience. Events become divided up as either extremely good (us) or extremely bad (them), with no intervening grey area. This manner of comprehending experience remains an option for the human mind to return to at any time, even after it has progressed to more mature stages, when a realisation has developed that an individual is not the centre of the entire universe, and that experience is not simplistic and utterly light or dark but is characterised by shades of grey. Returning to the primitive state – 'We are all good and they are all bad' – is (like any regression) comforting in bewildering times, when issues seem intractable and life too complex. Gibbon himself held the Crusades to be 'holy madness', so it is only proper to explore that madness with concepts of our own time.

The acclamation of the thousands present in November 1095 at Pope Urban's sermon at Clermont was (for the literate) *Deus vult!,* and for those who remained with their local tongues, *Deus lo volt* or *Diex el volt:* God wills it. Here was a theological change. No longer were the people humbly asking for the will of God to be made clear; they were unqualifiedly declaring they knew what it was. There was an element of man projecting his own ideas into the will of God at Clermont. It was a case of what psychoanalysts call transference, in this case between man and God. *Deus vult* could be seen as an act of Freudian transference: humanity projecting its own intentions into the mind of God. Control is frequently at issue in such a crossing of boundaries. In this light, *Deus vult*, which at Clermont was not the passive acceptance of fate ('it was God's will') but rather the active principle of engagement, could be seen as man's attempt to control God – or, as the secular might put it, humanity's intention to have its will performed implicitly. 'God wills it' can be understood to mean 'I will it, and desire to have it done in order to crush my own sense of guilt.'

A frenzy of religious enthusiasm (in the sense of 'intoxication') followed, most of all in France and Germany. Arms were consecrated, vows renewed, land sold and horses procured. Signs and portents were seen; stars fell to earth foreshadowing the fall of the Islamic rulers; flames were seen at night, foretelling the destruction by fire of Muslim strongholds; clouds of a deep red hue hovered over the east, dyed in the blood of the infidel; a sword-shaped comet, signifying the sword of the Lord, appeared in the south; and people were said to see in the sky an army and the towers of a city.[31] The religious enthusiasm was not universal. In England William Rufus, displaying a sceptical wisdom and acting for once in collaboration with his archbishop of Canterbury, Anselm, forbade his clergy and people from taking part in the zealotry.[32]

Peter the Hermit gave voice to the yearnings of the people; in Gibbon's phrase, he was a man who 'excelled in the popular madness of the times'.[33] He had been born in about 1050 of a noble family in northern France. An unremarkable man of small stature, he possessed complete self-confidence and was capable of oratory which transfigured those who heard him and which answered their deep yearnings. In the words of the Byzantine historian Anna Comnena, 'It was as if he had inspired every heart with some divine oracle.'[34] His unswerving message was for the recovery of Palestine by Christendom. He had visited Palestine in 1093, an event which led to his hearing voices. At the Holy Sepulchre he heard the words 'Arise, Peter', an instruction which he naturally took to be divine.[35] On his return to Europe, he visited the pope. The meeting was fortuitous: Pope Urban recognised the potential of the movement that Peter could inspire, and authorised him to preach a crusade throughout Europe.

His simple message provided a way in which the people, confused by the unclarity of the world in which they lived, could make sense by returning life to a back-to-basics, perhaps never experienced, simplicity. He came to be revered as a saint; the smallest threadbare patch of his foul-smelling clothing became desired as a holy relic. His campaign received a boost with the call of Alexius, the Byzantine emperor, for mercenaries to strengthen his position against the Turks.[36] The Byzantine Empire no longer possessed the confident manned frontiers achieved under Basil II seventy years earlier. The battle of Manzikert had left it cruelly exposed. Nevertheless the emperor did not seek an army but rather a troop of mercenaries; and he had no intention of reconquering Jerusalem. The presence in the crusader army of Bohemund, the arch-foe of Byzantium who had attacked the imperial forces at Dyrrachium, created alarm. East and West held radically differing ideas of the venture: the European rulers sought territory and land, and the people's beliefs were edged with the apocalyptic notions of divine judgment and final fire, the imminence of the last days in which sinful souls would be redeemed through the capture of sacred land. Byzantium had in mind a less coloured notion, in which defence was paramount and warfare might begin where diplomacy had ended.[37]

So feverish and so instilled with religious keenness were the populations of northern Europe that the people set off for the Holy Land as soon as the frosts cracked in 1096. Walter the Penniless led one group, Peter the Hermit another. Everywhere they went they spread disturbance and massacre. The Jews suffered shockingly; periods of Christian religious excitement were extremely bad for Jews. The Jewish communities along the Rhine were mercilessly slaughtered. In Cologne and Mainz every Jew was killed, and even the Christian populations fled the sacred army. The attitude of the crusaders to Jews contrasts strongly with that of the sceptic William Rufus, the 'scoffing' and sexually dissident English king who was unimpressed by zeal and the general tenor of violent sanctimoniousness manifested on the Continent. Rufus's attitude to religion in general, and to Jews in particular, was devoid of extremism; on one occasion he declared that if his Jewish subjects were to win an open argument with the Christians, he would become one of them.[38] The clergy were scandalised.

Travelling east, Peter the Hermit's band slaughtered the Hungarians of Semlin (modern Zemun, outside Belgrade), who had complained about their violence and thuggishness. A further band followed, directed by a priest named Volkmar, and headed alternately by a she-goat and by a goose, each of which was said to be filled with the Holy Ghost.[39] Here the crusade provided an outlet for totemic and animistic yearnings, which had been dammed up and suppressed with the coming of Christianity. The Crusades seem to have reawakened aspects of the dormant pre-Christian religions of Europe. Jesus's command to his follower, 'Put up again thy sword, for all they that take the sword shall perish with the sword,' was too elevated for the violent aspirations of the times, and the crusaders turned to other religions. A spiritual regression away from universality to past cults was symbolic of the regression of the individuals, which was expressed in their division of experience into stark categories of light and dark. It was as though they had abandoned seeking to stand as pilgrims in the tomb of Adonai but would rather carve their way into the womb which annually bore Adonis. Their behaviour, too, showed a regression to an early, controlling childhood: the driven, demanding self-righteousness bore the hallmarks of a child who still believes it is the measure of all things. Paralleling the totemisation of animals was the totemisation of land, where one piece of land was sacred, divine and marvellous, and the rest – even their own homes – irrelevant and superfluous. They found safety in embracing fetishistic magic. This was part of the package of the crusade, which led to its popularity.

Sins were most eagerly indulged, for all sins were to be washed away by the recovery of the Holy Land. Every day could be enjoyed guiltlessly. Life for the crusaders presented aspects of a permanent Saturnalia. Their enjoyment of a life of licence was only curtailed by the onset of satiety and fatigue. Holy forgiveness would inevitably be theirs, so they could revel in theft, murder, rape and pillage while the opportunity was available.[40]

These disordered bands, known as the People's Crusade, never reached Palestine. They quarrelled among themselves and attacked their Byzantine hosts, despite the cautious welcome of the emperor Alexius. The surprise and dismay of the Byzantines at their appearance is summed up in his daughter Anna's crisp observation: 'Endless hordes of Kelts'.[41] The violence towards fellow-Christians destroyed any vestiges of 'Christendom'. Peter the Hermit blamed their faithlessness, but not his own leadership.

Following the collapse of the People's Crusade, a 'crusade of the princes' started out for the Holy Land. Led by Godfrey de Bouillon, Raymond of Toulouse and Bishop Adhemar of Puy, they arrived in Constantinople in April 1097. The event was also watched with eager ambition by the Venetian and Genoese merchants, on the look-out for financial gain. Although initially the merchants aided the crusaders, transporting men and supplies to the crusader-states, subsequent events showed that religious zealotry does not sit comfortably with the principle of gain, and may be undermined by it. The merchant republics discovered that they could make a profit by trading with the Muslims too.

In a similar manner the great September fair of Jerusalem, so flourishing before the crusaders appeared and destroyed the multifaith balance of the Holy Land, had taken the venom out of religious differences and created a community of buyers and sellers where faith was not an issue. Commerce could limit violent bigotry.[42]

Bohemund, the ambitious and crafty Norman detested by Alexius, achieved colonial success when he seized the principality of Antioch, a fertile and agreeable province, well away from the disputed Holy Land. Only thirteen years earlier this city had been a Byzantine possession. Now it became armed and turreted northern-European-style territory. His example led Godfrey's brother Baldwin to grab Edessa, similarly temperate, green and at an even more comfortable distance from the holy heartland.

Besides Edessa, Antioch and Jerusalem, Tripoli (today in Lebanon) became a crusader fiefdom too, in 1109. One detail makes the siege of Tripoli memorable. An educated Egyptian of the family of Ibn Ammar had amassed a fine collection of about 100,000 manuscripts here, which were housed in a learned institution which was part-college and part-library. It had been part of the ethos of the Fatimids to create large libraries and encourage learning. A crusader priest found himself surrounded by this monument to knowledge but was unable to read any of its contents (whose subjects anyway were held to be sinful and satanic). So he decreed that the library should be destroyed. He called for the assistance of the soldiery, who burnt the entire collection.[43]

The Muslim counterattack was not long in coming. In 1144 the county of Edessa was lost to Zengi of Mosul. Northern Europe was plunged once more into turbulence and writhed with zealous antagonism as though a sword had entered its vitals. But within reconquered Edessa the spirit of warlike religion was less in evidence. Here the air was gentler and the recapture was a moment for generosity and tolerance. A Syrian chronicler noted that 'When Zengi was in Edessa [in 1145], he greeted all the Christians with joy, kissed the gospel, saluted the metropolitan and asked after his health. He said they had come to supply what they lacked. He visited our Syrian churches, examined their beauty, ordered two great bells to be given them and hung on them, as was the custom in the time of the Franks.'[44]

The Europeans saw the loss of Edessa only as failure, and kings, rather than princes, joined to create the forces known as the Second Crusade, a coalition powerful in theory, but devoid of success. The crusaders' policy was certainly strange at this time. Previously they had entered into an alliance with the vizier of Damascus (who was himself alarmed by the growth of the power of Zengi's son Nureddin in northern Syria and sought Christian allies). But this useful strategic link was severed in 1147 for local short-term gains.[45] The crusaders exchanged alliance for assault. The result was a rout.

The skirmishes continued; the Muslim powers were united by Saladin in 1171 and the crusader kingdom of Jerusalem was lost in 1187. When Saladin entered the holy city he treated its entire defeated Frankish population with toleration and magnanimity, even though he would have recalled the manner in which the crusaders had entered Jerusalem in 1099. Europe again reeled in guilt and shock, and the Third Crusade, led by the energetic and resourceful Richard Coeur-de-Lion, followed.

Attitudes had developed as the crusader kingdoms entered their second century. Two or three generations had grown up in the Asiatic kingdoms which modelled themselves on the feudal realms of northern Europe. What were the people like who were, so to speak, Asiatic-born Europeans? They were known as Pullani, and some of the chroniclers expressed strong opinions about them. Jacques de Vitry, later a cardinal, said that the Pullani were 'brought up in luxury, soft and effeminate, more used to baths than to battles, addicted to unclean and riotous living, clad like women in soft robes and ornamented even as the polished corners of the temple . . . they make treaties with the Saracens, and are glad to be at peace with Christ's enemies. . . . They indeed pass their days in all good living, but in a moment they shall go down to the depths of hell.'[46]

The assumptions in this passage are telling. Permanent warfare was being proclaimed; there could be no rest or treaties. Nor was there any room for religions or ideologies other than the crusaders'. Even the normal dress of the region, designed to allow cooling air to flow freely, was a transgression; only the severe mailed tunic was permitted. Taking a bath was also an indication of consorting with Satan. A tendency to bathing was part of the evidence used by monkish chroniclers to demonstrate that the Hohenstaufen emperor Frederick II was the Antichrist. The liking for stylish oriental houses with courtyards and fountains was also seen as corrupt. Anything remotely civilised was condemned as wicked. Deviation from traditional narrow Northern values led to hell. Here, it seems, was a turn of mind recognisable as incipiently totalitarian, which derived from the mentality which the crusading endeavour had fostered.

Chivalry came to the fore with the Third Crusade, in which the lion-hearted king's love of fighting and of male company were equally pronounced. (He is perhaps the only bridegroom in the Western Christian tradition whose wedding party was peopled exclusively by male guests.) But the Third Crusade was likewise ineffective, except for the creation by the crusaders of the kingdom of Acre, a fiefdom memorably described by Gibbon as having 'many sovereigns but no government'.[47] Richard's jousts with Saladin are remembered from this time; but there was a dark side too. On the surrender of Acre, the English monarch slaughtered its entire Muslim garrison in contravention of the agreed terms.[48]

Moreover, following the loss of the kingdom of Jerusalem, there developed in England a hostility towards Jews. This was partly due to financial reasons, since they were perceived as rich, although there were of course numbers of poor Jews and all were taxed at a higher rate than Christians. The religious enthusiasm of the time led, too, to the activation of the charge of 'deicide' – that the Jews had killed Christ, which meant that all Jews, including those currently alive, had had a hand in Christ's death. By the time of Edward I, this charge appeared alongside the formal system of 'chivalry' (of which Edward I was a key proponent), a style of feudal theatre that was high entertainment to those within the hierarchy, but dangerous to those outside it, since it excluded true chivalry, such as Saladin had shown to the Franks in Jerusalem. The public attitude, deriving from crusading failures and Plantagenet noble play, led to the exiling or murder in 1290 of England's Jews.[49]

The medical techniques of the Franks stood in sharp contrast to those practised by the local Arabs. Usama ibn Munqidh (1095–1188), a Syrian gentleman, recalls an event in his memoirs. Two Frankish patients appeared and were treated correctly by an Arab Christian doctor, with warmth, rest, clothing and herbal infusions. Then a Frankish doctor appeared. He ordered a knight to chop off the damaged leg of one patient, and the other, a woman, was made to have her head shaved, which was then incised with a deep cruciform wound into which salt was rubbed, with the intention of driving out the devil. Both patients thereupon died.[50] (The claim in a 1999 book on the Templars that Frankish medicine had a worthwhile and beneficial quality is hard to square with this incident.)

The Fourth Crusade, of 1204, was cunningly diverted by Venice to Constantinople, and the great capital of the Christian East was sacked and wrecked to make way for rule by Western knights. For the Greeks, the blow was felt more keenly than the city's subsequent capture by the Ottoman Turks in 1453. The papacy claimed that it was not involved in the assault on the Byzantine capital, although it acquiesced in its capture as soon as the city was taken, and the holy benefits of crusading accrued to its destroyers.[51] Innocent III described its sack as a 'miraculous event'.[52] Furthermore, the force that looted the great city had developed from the idea and the ambience of Christian crusading. Within the fabric of the Crusades, and shown by the initial Norman desire to supplant Byzantium, was a sense of grievance that the crusaders held against the eastern empire, partly because they despised its civilisation, partly because they were freebooters and partly because the Westerners resented the empire's belief that territory reclaimed in the course of the crusading enterprise ought to revert to its control.

Crusading was changing at this time. It still drew its strength from an inner conviction of self-righteousness and intolerance and from a desire not to coexist but to assume an aggressive pose and smite enemies. But the balance between sacred aspiration and self-interest was changing in favour of the latter. The meaning of crusading widened too. The term ceased to refer only to military actions in or near the Holy Land. The crusade against the Albigensians occurred at this time, in which land-hunger and greed were elements as important as the extirpation of heresy. The Knights Templar launched a series of crusades against the pagan Lithuanians, annual campaign–binges which continued even after the Lithuanians had adopted Christianity. The cachet of a crusade outgrew its original intention. The notion of 'a crusade' still held a sacred allure and a knightly popularity but at heart it represented an image-driven addiction to warfare, an opiate of masculinity, a steroid of narcissism. In Lithuania the knights resorted to 'illusionism': the practice of pretending that their antagonists were wicked Saracens, when all the time they knew they were unoffending native villagers, a number of whom were Christian.[53] In this way the knights' blood-lust was roused; they were spurred to 'heroic deeds' and spared the fate of seeing their own pointlessness. In its self-reference crusading had come to represent a Nietzschean assertion of asserting, a waving sword seeking only attention.

The sad episode of the Children's Crusade occurred in 1212, a terrible tale of aspiration, deception, greed and death.[54] It stimulated Europe to a further effort, known as the Fifth Crusade. Here the crusading army under King John of Brienne (who had been crowned at Acre in 1210) and the haughty, inflexible, half-mad Cardinal Pelagius succeeded in taking Damietta on the Nile delta after a long siege, before being undone by a tactical blunder, in which King John's army misjudged the rising waters of the Nile and was forced to withdraw in muddy chaos. Victory was handed to the Egyptians.[55] By contrast the Sixth Crusade was something like a masterpiece: an astute product of diplomacy and a successful campaign for the recovery of Jerusalem for the Latins, undertaken without an arrow being fired or a sword unsheathed. It had at its head the brilliant Hohenstaufen emperor, Frederick II, grandson of Roger II of Sicily, known as *stupor mundi*, the world's wonder. He had inherited the kingdom of Jerusalem by marrying the daughter of John of Brienne. His Christianity was as rich, diverse and cultured as his Sicilian court; it developed from the multicultural bases of the two Rogers and was a world away from tame acquiescence in the authoritarian demands of the pope and the western bishops. Here was a man whom monkish chroniclers might rail against – one who, besides bathing, believed in negotiation rather than the sword.[56]

Frederick II was a crusader against whom a crusade was launched. In his oriental court, he emulated his Norman forebear and liberally conversed with mathematicians, philosophers and astronomers – that is, Muslim Arabs and Jews – and others who disbelieved in the papal variety of truth. In an remarkable act of statecraft, he collected together about 20,000 Muslims from Sicily and transplanted them to a new settlement at Lucera, near Foggia. (Undoubtedly this act created much misery, but what distinguished Frederick from other medieval rulers was that the refugee population were granted lands, not exterminated or left to fend for themselves.) Here they lived freely, building their own mosques and carrying on their lives according to their own customs and laws. The system bore a striking resemblance to the Islamic notion of the *dhimmi*, the protected religious minority, a system which was later to become formalised in the Ottoman Empire as the *millet* system. In Frederick's case the Muslims of Lucera grew devoted to their emperor and provided his bodyguard. He also entrusted his treasury to their city. Both parties benefited from what turned out to be imaginative tolerance and trust. Years later, in 1266, following the defeat of the Hohenstaufens at the battle of Benevento, Frederick's daughter-in-law and her children took refuge in Islamic Lucera; their flight there indicates the pull of the Muslim city. The community was compelled to abandon Islam and embrace Christianity in 1300, when the Angevin Charles II crushed this southern Italian multicultural experiment.[57]

As Frederick sailed for his crusade, he was excommunicated by Pope Gregory IX. But on arrival in the Holy Land, he was able to achieve by negotiation everything that Richard I had failed to achieve by war. By a treaty of February 1229 he gained Nazareth, Bethlehem and Jerusalem, and a corridor joining Jerusalem to Acre. The treaty was to be in force for ten years. It was not a product of cynicism or greed – Frederick was not out for loot – but it represented a masterly way of solving the tensions that had developed between pope, emperor and the local players in the Holy Land. It was also a chance to create, for most parties, a good dispensation. He virtually compelled them to share power.

Frederick entered Jerusalem, his capital, and proclaimed his own coronation; since no churchman would place the crown upon his head, he did so himself in the Church of the Holy Sepulchre. (The Latin Patriarch declared the church profaned as a result.) He did not stay long in Palestine, but while he was there the legal code that he ratified granted equal civil and religious freedom for Christians and Muslims.[58] The Christians were permitted to pray at the Holy Sepulchre, and the Muslims at the Haram, or Temple Mount. In Gibbon's words, 'the clergy deplored this scandalous toleration'.[59] Some Muslim leaders disapproved of Frederick's actions too, although al-Kamil, the nephew of Saladin and a man of learning and intellectual curiosity, approved of the order of Frederick, something which was attuned to al-Kamil's own civilised and educated liking (to the exasperation of his own chroniclers) for the 'blond men'.[60] Churches were restored and monasteries replenished by the Latins, who offered no words of thanks to the unclerical Frederick. The fortunate state of affairs, beneficent to members of all religions, was only ended by an irruption of Khwarezmian Turks from Central Asia, fleeing the onslaught of the Mongols.

Frederick's triumph was one of non-bellicose negotiation. It was of rationality and almost of modernity, and free of the religious fervour of those who, like Louis IX, the sainted king of France, believed that the only dialogue possible with a 'blasphemer' – that is, one of a different faith – was to run a sword into his guts up to the hilt.[61] This deathly intention is a reminder that, apart from Frederick, toleration was alien to European Christianity in most cases until the dawn of the Enlightenment, in contrast to the established toleration within Islam, which reached a high point in eleventh-century Spain.

There followed a series of crusades (known collectively as the Seventh Crusade) undertaken by Louis IX in 1245–60, which again centred on Damietta. Among his opponents was the only woman Mamluk sultan, the resourceful Shajar al-Durr, she whom 'no woman rivalled in beauty, and no man in determination'. (This is from Pococke's translation of Bar Hebraeus: '*Nec inter mulieres formâ, nec inter viros animi constantiâ, par fuit.*'[62]) All the efforts of the pious king were a failure, despite the crusaders' alliance with the Mongols, which united two forces of destructiveness. In the Eighth Crusade (according to the traditional numbering) St Louis found himself in North Africa. Gibbon's summary has stood the test of time:

> A wild hope of baptising the king of Tunis tempted him to steer a course for the African coast; and the report of an immense treasure reconciled his troops to the delay of their voyage to the Holy Land. Instead of a proselyte, he found a siege; the French panted and died on the burning sands; St Louis expired in his tent; and no sooner had he died than his son and successor gave the signal of the retreat. 'It is thus,' says a lively writer [Voltaire], 'that a Christian king died near the ruins of Carthage, waging war against the sectaries of Mohammed, in a land to which Dido had introduced the deities of Syria.'[63]

By steering the crusading endeavour towards Tunis, the spirit of European holy war had moved into the realm of, if not madness, extreme weirdness. Disillusion grew apace. The crusaders were appearing like embarrassing half-mad relatives. On the eve of the fall of Acre in 1291 Pope Nicholas IV could arouse little enthusiasm for its salvation. The development of education in Europe was undermining zeal.[64] The growth of knowledge was giving back rational mental function to the people of Europe, with the Universities of Paris and Padua in the vanguard. The military success of Muslim leaders such as Baybars, who could be as brutal as the Europeans and as keen on slaughter (and as hostile to knowledge and advancement), also weakened zeal. In Europe the dawn of the Renaissance was glimmering on the horizon. But this was not before the crusaders had inflicted a final shattering blow upon the eastern Mediterranean.

By the mid-fourteenth century Peter (or Pierre) I of Cyprus, of the Frankish Lusignan family, was the sole monarch with a theoretical commitment to crusading. He believed in the accoutrements of crusading: the knightly deeds, the fetishes of the names and insignia of grand families, the imported, cold, northern European package of battlefield confrontation: confronting, perhaps, the dark side of the crusader's own personality, an act in which he slew by proxy his own demons. One of the movement's earnest propagandists was Pierre de Thomas, a man noted for his diligence, wisdom and piety. As papal legate to Cyprus, his ardour for the conversion to Rome of the Eastern Orthodox Cypriots had led him to beg the Frankish authorities of the island that he might torture the Orthodox of Cyprus into Catholicism; but the king, after surveying the numbers involved, rejected the idea.[65] Pierre was a dedicated advocate of holy war against Islam.

Peter's crusade assembled at Rhodes in August 1365: an armada of 165 ships. In October they set sail for Alexandria. On their arrival the Alexandrians believed them to be a great merchant fleet, and went out to greet them. Within two days the city was in the crusaders' hands, and their celebration was one of savage butchery. No one was spared: Christians and Jews were slaughtered with the same ferocity as the Muslims. Even the Latin Christians who had established a colony in the city were hacked to death. Horses, donkeys and camels carried the rich loot to the ships, and when they had performed their task, these unoffending animals were slaughtered too.[66] Crusading reached a terrible climax in the bloodbath of Alexandria; the frenzy of antagonistic religion so possessed the minds of the crusaders that nothing meant anything to them except killing. No laws or conventions, certainly not chivalry, the allegedly beneficent code created at the time of the Crusades, steered them from their devotion to sanctified death. In this assault, the splitting of the crusaders' world into the simplistic categories of light – acclaimed in their own righteousness – and of dark – projected on to those whom they were attacking – led to an exterminatory orgy of slaughter recognisable as psychotic. Here the militant spirit received its apotheosis. The destruction was total and the ruin and wreckage appear as a climactic craving for nothingness. They had passed through Christianity, into a vacant spiritual landscape of nullity, then back to a relaunch of society and superstition, where murder was the only reality. It is perhaps possible to discern in their actions the violently nihilistic spirit that some 600 years later was to animate the totalitarian regimes of the twentieth century and that, in its absolute Manichaean division between good and evil (typical of incipient paranoia), also has much in common with ideological perceptions found in the forced distinction between 'east' and 'west' in the twenty-first century, seen among the promoters of such ideas in a nihilistic and destructive yearning for 'creative violence' in order to crush what is in essence their own dark side, mentally projected on to the world outside.

❖❖❖

With Peter's expedition to Alexandria, the 'epic' of the Crusades to the Holy Land reached a conclusion. Palestine declined in significance as a focused object of fetishistic interest and the primacy of its military conquest diminished. The Holy Sepulchre began to revert to its status of the tomb of Adonai, rather than the womb, sought by the swords' points, which nurtured Adonis. But the rhetoric of crusading and the actions inspired by that rhetoric continued to be found for at least two centuries. The pope continued to bless expeditions against the infidel, to which the knights responded by displaying their rank and taking advantage of the conditions which attended a plenary papal indulgence.

The Ottoman Turks, rather than the Egyptian Mamluks, came to be perceived as the Muslim power which best occupied the position of enemy. There was good reason for this change, since by the mid-fourteenth century the Turks were threatening much of eastern Europe. Their tactics of rapid, daring assaults and their flexibility on the field of battle outclassed any European opposition.

Serbia's fate was sealed on the Field of Blackbirds, at Kosovo in August 1389. Its independent existence was ended by the Ottoman army, led by Sultan Murad I. Hungary sensed a threat to itself, and Sigismund, its king since 1387, sought assistance from the pope and the French.

The papal answer was positive, if not strategically helpful. Purposeful zeal was still the driving force. Despite the disasters, there appeared to be few doubts in Rome about crusading, nor was there a wider morality of death and suffering. The aim was simply the triumph of the Catholic Church, to be signalled by the expansion of its doctrine and authority.

Pope Boniface IX duly sent out a holy call to arms. The familiar plenary indulgence was offered to all who would hasten to Sigismund's aid. In 1396 a roll-call rallied the grand families throughout France and Germany.[67] There was also an English contingent of about 1,000 men, but its fate and even the name of its commander are uncertain. This was to be a real show, an array of magnificence. The knights entered into the spirit of it by declaring that 'if the sky should fall, they would uphold it on the points of their lances.'[68] Their confident claims reflected the splendour of their presences. If success could be measured in the grandiosity of names alone, this crusade would have extinguished all failures: the count of this, the lord of that, the grand master of this order. (Just to *be* the Count of Katzenellenbogen seemed enough for eternal glory.) Fighting the enemy appeared to be a lesser matter than feudal display and the mutual flattery of titles. The sacred licence offered by the indulgence, set within the context of the certainty (proclaimed ever since Urban II's call at Clermont) that the crusaders were perfoming God's Will and Purpose, meant that matters of military tactics such as order and discipline were subordinated to grandeur, pride and the bullish virtues of lordly warfare. Assured of their unquestioned rightness, they could feel free to indulge their way to the crusade. God was on their side even when they were inert through gluttony, drink, rape and vandalism. He would win their battle for them.

Sigismund sought subtle and defensive tactics. Nonsense, declared the massed nobility of Europe; we will charge and conquer the whole of Turkey, march into the empire of Persia, seize the kingdom of Syria and deliver the Holy Land from the hands of the infidels. Near Orsovo (east of Belgrade, today in Romania) they began atrocities towards the Christian Orthodox Serbs, who, following Serbia's subjection by the Ottoman Turks, were now classed as the enemy. The crusading army seized Vidin and Rahova, slaughtering civilians in a bid for honour and glory. Then they reached Nicopolis (the modern Nikopol, Bulgaria), an Ottoman possession situated at the confluence of the Danube and the Olt, virtually midway between Bucharest and Sofia and which had been carefully protected and provisioned by the Turks. It consisted of a fortified city built at the top of a precipitous plain sloping to the south. The crusaders believed that the siege would be effortless and continued to pass the time in scoffing, quaffing, gambling and enjoying a general debauch.[69] Meanwhile the Ottoman sultan was leading a lightning troop from his encampment near Constantinople. On its arrival, the Hungarians, knowing the manner of Ottoman warfare, counselled caution, but the Franks, sensing glory and eager to demonstrate their prowess, grew tired of the blockade and went in search of the enemy. They also slaughtered some Turkish prisoners who had fallen into their hands by taking a wrong turning. A French nobleman, the *sire* de Coucy, won a skirmish with Ottoman troops. Higher-born crusaders expressed anger that he should thus have robbed them of victory. The main body of the crusaders determined on a frontal attack. Sigismund begged them to rethink their tactics, to no avail.

In the assault on Nicopolis, the crusaders were initially successful; but the Turkish defence was stubborn and eventually drew them into a trap, as if teasing their yearning for glory. The Franks continued to refuse to coordinate strategy with the Hungarian king. They rushed up the steep hill, according to a chronicler, like lions; but when they saw the extent of the army waiting for them, they grew 'more fearful than hares',[70] and they tore back down again as fast as they could. The Ottoman army had re-formed, and they were faced by a forest of lances both before and after. The result was a rout, in which Sigismund was fortunate to escape with his life. The Sultan had been particularly outraged at the crusader slaughter of prisoners, and took extensive reprisals. The fate of the defeated was death or slavery, except for the few who were able to pay a large ransom. The injured who managed to limp home arrived in Paris on Christmas Day. When they told their story, they were imprisoned for spreading false rumours designed to weaken morale.

At Nicopolis the knights from western Europe rallied for the last time for allegedly sacred purposes. Thereafter there were no more vast expeditions to remote places. The notion of crusading still drew wild warlike spirits. Henry V, the 'hero' of Agincourt, hungered to launch a new crusade as he yearned to crush France, and the motifs of the one spread into the other. It was the militant strenuousness of his faith, drenched in the crusading ideal, which permitted him to commit the cruelties on the French that he did with such impassivity. However, whether from lack of success or loss of will, such public ethics were in decline.

A further failed crusade, at Varna in 1444, deserves a brief glance on account of an issue of international morality that it raises. In the years preceding, the king of Poland and Hungary, Ladislaus, had sworn a truce with the Ottoman sultan Murad II. Under its terms Murad withdrew his forces and Serbia regained its independence. But the papal legate Cardinal Julian (Giuliano Cesarini) declared that it was morally right to break an oath made with the Turks, and that it was a crime to honour sworn undertakings which were, in his opinion, evil in themselves. Swayed by his fanatic preaching, the European powers turned from peace and looked for war. The cardinal absolved the Christian forces in the name of the pope from their oath to the Turks. Murad II for his part scrupulously adhered to the Muslim side of the bargain. Ladislaus, urged on by the cardinal, gathered an army – Poles, Hungarians, Wallachians led by Prince Drakul, or Dracula – and marched through Bulgaria, where towns fell without resistance. Murad heard the news, crossed into Bulgaria and, after initial losses, cut down the Christian forces, killing Ladislaus and winning a decisive victory. (The inflammatory cardinal was reported missing, presumed dead, in the forest.) Following their pope-inspired treachery the Christian forces had received another entirely self-inflicted disaster. Christian dealings at Varna were among the persuasive elements in the Ottoman determination to renew the assault on Constantinople nine years later. The events at Varna were later to be finely (if anachronistically) dramatised by Marlowe in *Tamburlaine the Great*, Pt II, Act II, Scenes i–iii. Present-day Western commentators – professors and specialists – who declare they have detected within Islam a propensity for declaring oaths and pacts made with European forces null and void are less forthcoming about this early treaty with a major Islamic power, which was deliberately dishonoured and nullified by Christian forces in the name of the pope, and which thereby set a deadly precedent.[71]

Although the papacy continued to use the terminology of crusading, warfare between European and Islamic powers was becoming no different from other warfare; the 'holy' peg was becoming little more than a contrivance designed to kindle zealotry and to evoke the death-or-glory mentality required for creating local cannon-fodder or as a diversion from internal policy. This latter motive lay behind Henry VIII's sending assistance, dignified as a crusade, to the Spanish king against the Moroccan sultan in 1511, an event which was driven, not by malice or fanaticism, but by the English king's need for a diversionary grand gesture. Henry, the pragmatic Tudor, had no actual belief in the sacred purpose of crusading; as a sensible statesman he disbelieved his own propaganda. The expedition ended farcically in Cadiz when the English contingent, unused to the local wine, smashed the place up in a drunken riot. The inner dynamic of failure was similar to that at Nicopolis: crusading was warfare in a sacred cause, so *ipso facto* any drunken violence which accompanied it was permissible. It was holy vandalism. Ferdinand of Spain thought otherwise. He quickly shipped home the English who had wrecked his city and concluded a treaty with the Moroccan sultan.[72]

In response to the Crusades the Islamic forces launched a kind of countercrusade.[73] This had its focus in Egypt, whose Mamluk rulers developed a notion of the sanctity of the land of Syria and Palestine similar to that of the crusaders. Islamic pilgrimage to sites in greater Syria became a fashion in the late fourteenth century. The countercrusade was a largely cultural movement, a reassertion of the situation before the irruptions. The profile of the region was raised within the consciousness of Islam. The Mamluks had conquered Acre in 1291, they seized Cilician Armenia in 1375 and finally they focused on Lusignan Cyprus, which had sacked Alexandria in 1365; the Cypriot king Janus was compelled to become a Mamluk vassal in 1426. But the spirit of confrontation was waning on both sides. Fewer recruits could be found for crusades, and the reality of inter-state relations, as outlined by Machiavelli, broke through the thin artifice and outdated propaganda of holy, knightly strife. Both Francis I of France and Queen Elizabeth I had their own reasons for making diplomatic openings to the Ottoman Empire. Even the pope (Alexander VI – admittedly the father of Cesare and Lucrezia Borgia) allied himself with the Turks.[74] The Ottoman Empire, moving from great strength to defensive weakness in a comparatively short space of time, soon found itself seeking contrasting (and willing) partners from among the disputatious powers of Europe. European crusading, which fuelled its players with an addictive mixture of display and violence, was falling on its own sword.

Crusading had arrived virtually out of nowhere. It followed centuries of mainly good relations with Muslims in the matter of pilgrimage to sacred places. Gibbon gave it the title of the World's Debate. But the acts of crusading themselves were manifestations of a World Arrogance. This arrogance, which led to disaster, was first manifested in the assumption that mankind could know the will of God. *Deus vult* is, if carefully considered, blasphemous in the context of belief, since it indicates a knowledge of God's will. To unbelievers it is a grandiose expression symptomatic of the beginning of a loss of sense. In the context of the belief of the times, it stood in sharp contrast to the old attitude of pilgrim humility, questing and questioning, and of gratitude that God had allowed pilgrims grace to visit the shrines at all. In accepting that the people could know the will of God, the papacy had honed a powerful political weapon. As for the knights, they used the assumed knowledge of the will of God as a vehicle for projecting their titles and showiness. It became a motive in their ranking and in their clanking of weapons. In reality it was a preliminary move towards their defeat, first because the plenary indulgence led to a lowering of tactical sense and to all kinds of indiscipline – there was no need to obey laws, since all sins would be forgiven – and second because it made the crusaders overconfident that they had God on their side. The sense of certainty resulting from declaring 'God wills it' represented an attitude similar to that today which leads teenage warrior-members of cult-like organisations to believe that they will be protected by the Armour of the Lord if they go to war unarmed or even naked. It was a variety of deluded self-absorption and self-righteousness which we recognise as bordering on insanity: the madness of trying to reclaim by force some entirely lost innermost space of the past, rather than quietly uttering a pilgrim's humble prayer in a shadowed tomb. In the cases of Nicopolis and Varna, the results were catastrophic.

As the years passed, the effect was kindlier on individuals of a knightly cast of mind. The mellow derangement of Don Quixote is an accurate picture of the outcome, after a century or so, of the succession of acts of, at worst, arrogance and blasphemy and, at best, arthritic vanity on a basically kindly individual whose imaginary world has been shaped by attitudes of necessary confrontation and the need to have an enemy. No bolts of lightning, just a gentle sighing into idiocy; an alarum against a flock of sheep, furious swordsmanship against the revolving arms of a windmill. One sees this too in Lewis Carroll's White Knight, endlessly falling out of the saddle. When the violence of the Crusades left no more trace than the crumbling castles and whitening bones in the desert, when the antagonism had finally abated and great spaces of the east were silent again except for the to-and-fro of traders and pilgrims amid the wind and sand, the figures that would haunt our imaginations were less the bold knights of warfare and struggle than the wispy semi-distraught knights-errant of fiction.

CHAPTER THREE

Europe's Loss and Recovery
of Knowledge

Warfare and polemic were unavoidable between Christianity and Islam. The proximity of two religions, each of which claimed world validity, contained an inherent instability. There is nevertheless another way to see the relations between members of the faiths, an alternative script to that of infidels and crusading. This was the way of knowledge and intellect, of philosophy and reason, of mathematics and science, eventually of commerce and diplomacy. This fruitful interplay is less known, since it is at variance with the basic thrills found in claims of ultimate rightness, the clash of weapons, the flying of dynastic flags and the din of war. But the quiet way of knowledge was arguably of greater significance in the long term, less for Christian–Muslim relations (for a market can almost always be found for confrontation) than for the internal development of medieval Europe.

The thought of Plato and Aristotle permeated the medieval mind within both Christianity and Islam and gave it its most significant structures, so it is worth seeing (in the roughest outline, for libraries have been written on the topic) what notions the ancient philosophers held and how they were seen at this time. Gibbon gave a succinct summary when he contrasted 'the strong and subtle sense of Aristotle' with 'the devout contemplation and sublime fancy of Plato'. Plato's theory of forms – that all the particular things that we experience around us, such as horses, doors and people, are merely inadequate copies of the ultimate forms of horse, door, person – was his central metaphysical theory. For Plato the forms are the only perfect and the only real things: the things we encounter are merely imperfect illusions. This conceptual structure was rich and elevated but in terms of a theory of knowledge (how we can be sufficiently sure of what we know) incomplete and elusive, and it led to a tiered view of society that today we might call elitist. Plato's philosophy found little place for the idea of change. In his thought the notion of the soul as superior to the body and capable of being free from the body first emerged coherently; to Plato, the soul was in the body like whisky in a bottle. This view has some correspondence with the idea of the Pythagoreans: that the soul was an entity which could slip into a new body. (The transmigration of souls can be seen as akin to decanting whisky into a new bottle.) The notion also mirrored Persian Zoroastrian beliefs. It was not a typically Greek view; Homer had viewed the body as the self. The identity of the Homeric heroes lay in their pulsating physical presences. The soul was a poor, shadowy, gibbering thing, gutless in Hades. Plato reversed this idea, and gave pride of place to the immaterial.

By contrast Aristotle had a fiercer, more concentrated mind and with ruthless precision he exposed the incoherencies in the theory of forms, especially in his *Metaphysics*. He was the philosopher of the world as it is and was out of sympathy with the over-the-horizon mysticism of Plato. To him the natural world was the real world. Aristotle was more concerned with organising and classifying knowledge; his early work, the *Categories*, which outlined under ten headings what we can say of people and things, sets the tone. He liked the particulars of the here-and-now (in Greek, τοδε τι), which Plato had despised as common and vulgar. His basic element of reality was substance; things were substances, and God, the unmoved mover and first cause, was a substance too. Substance, either as the earthy reality which dislodged Plato's immaterial forms or as the centre around which change took place, was all-important. Aristotle invented logic, and his analytical and scientific outlook left him dissatisfied with the Platonic idea of soul, which he saw rather as blended into, and impossible to separate from, physical existence, just as (we might say today) an architectural object cannot be separated from light, space, position, materials and purpose, or as the sentiment of a poem cannot be set apart from the sound, rhythm and feel of the words. As animals had 'animal' or 'sensitive' souls (which made the difference between a dead lump of animal-matter and a living animal), so a human being had a rational soul which, acting as an expression of ever-changing human physical matter, provided the animatedness which created the complete human personality. The soul, to Aristotle, was 'the form of the body', that is, the summing-up of the manner in which the body behaves. Without it a human being was either a dead body or a waxwork-type entity with moving parts, a zombie of matter with physical form, but without rational or expressive form. ('Form' is used here in a quite different sense from that in 'Platonic form'.) Aristotle's view of the soul was radically different from the 'ghost in the machine', the 'backstage artiste', of Platonic theory.[1]

Despite his demystification of philosophy, Aristotle brought a vast and systematic complexity into the subject. The distinctions between matter and form, and between substance and essence, were helpful up to a point but they were ultimately perplexing, as were his accounts of active and passive intellects and of material, formal, efficient and final causes. His logic, though, was without doubt a masterpiece, as was his approach to science, and specifically biological science, which foreshadowed Darwin's method. By attempting to classify creatures by habitat, structure and habits, he made steps towards the complex taxonomy that is integral to modern biology. Darwin himself expressed 'unbounded admiration' for Aristotle, considering him 'one of the greatest, if not the greatest, observers that ever lived'.[2] Despite its founder's lively capacity for observation and its capacity to create early science (which was absent in Platonism), Aristotelianism as a system eventually came to be a fossilised relic, a 'dry and barbarous lucubration' in the words of Bishop Berkeley, and, like other dynamic systems which became ossified by the pedantry of their followers, it actually came to stand in the way of the development of science.

After Aristotle, Platonic theory made a resurgence culminating in the success of Neoplatonism in the third, fourth and fifth centuries AD; the principal thinkers were Plotinus and Proclus. Their philosophy posited a hierarchy of reality: The One, Soul and Mind, concepts which if intellectually elusive were sonorous and consoling. In Neoplatonic terminology, Soul (which is temporal, a living one) is the metaphysical offspring of Mind (or Intelligence, which is unsleeping), both of which find their ultimate locus in The One, 'the ultimate unity of all things'. Here was an interesting scholastic trinity. Somehow Neoplatonism gained a widespread, almost democratic adherence and was to some extent taken up by the Church. An early spirit of Neoplatonism pervades the Fourth Gospel. Philosophy metamorphosed into a kind of mystic poetry, laced with magic; it became less an enquiry about knowledge than, in a manner both austere and calming, a kind of aromatherapy for the mind, a hazy perfume of inner peace. The popularity of Neoplatonism, combined with the authority of Aristotle, led to a number of Neoplatonic texts being ascribed to Aristotle. In medieval Islam, a text known as 'The Theology of Aristotle' consisted of the last two books of a work by Plotinus. This was certainly odd, since the Neoplatonic view of the soul was quite different from Aristotle's; in Neoplatonism the soul's link with the body was more tenuous than Plato had held it to be. The theories that the Neoplatonists posited were emanationist, that is, that we are all emanations from some ultimately existent thing to which we will all return, and that some are brighter and others dimmer emanations from that One. The magical and unearthly paragraphs of Neoplatonism were comforting in disturbed times. In its etherial texts humanity found an easier peace than in the wintry words of Stoicism, the challenging rigour of the atomism of Democritus and Epicurus, or the sense of here-and-now observation of the natural world which was integral to Aristotle.[3]

The world of ideas received two hammer-blows in the 520s of our era, which can be seen as a decade of intellectual death. In the year 524 or 525 Boethius, the last European survivor of imperial Roman culture, was murdered in jail in Pavia by agents of the Gothic emperor Theodoric after enduring severe tortures. Boethius was a man of learning who had translated two lesser works of Aristotle but whose personal philosophy remained Platonic. In prison this last Roman had written *On the Consolation of Philosophy*, a work which was to shine like a sun-filled island amid the barren, featureless, grey sea which was the sum of Europe's intellectual achievement during the succeeding centuries. King Alfred translated it and Queen Elizabeth I is said to have produced an English version of it in twenty-four hours. With Boethius' death western Europe (apart from Ireland) entered a dark age which lasted for the best part of 500 years. The light of scholarship and knowledge was, if not extinguished, reduced to no more than a guttering dimness, sending out pale shadows, like the images which danced on the walls of Plato's cave. Although, some 250 years later, Charlemagne was to sponsor the advancement of learning, he himself remained illiterate and after the brilliance of his comet-like reign the shadows re-formed.[4]

About five years later, at the end of the decade which saw the murder of the last Roman, an equally serious blow against knowledge was enacted in Constantinople. In AD 529 the Emperor Justinian closed the schools of philosophy in the Academy of Athens, ending systematic thought by declaring that knowledge could not be taught by 'persons diseased with the insanity of the unholy Hellenes'. Seven distinguished pagan philosophers were driven into exile – 'the quintessential flower of our age' as the poet-historian Agathias put it.[5] They were the last links of what was known as the Golden Chain, an intellectual succession which reached back to Aristotle's Lyceum and Plato's Academy. One of the exiles, Simplicius, has been described as 'the most acute and judicious of the interpreters of Aristotle'. But Justinian's concept of mindless Christian faith had no place for them. Fatal new laws swayed menacingly above them like nooses and they were compelled to leave. They had fortunately heard that in Sasanid Persia there ruled a monarch who was both wise and just and who had created Plato's ideal Republic. So, faced with the prospect of death at the hands of Justinian's pious agents, these wise men set off for Persia, quitting their own empire's devout ignorance for the star of knowledge which shone in the east.[6]

They were welcomed by the Sasanid monarch, Khusrau (or Chosroes) I, Anushirwan ('the immortal-souled'), who they found indeed possessed knowledge of Plato and Aristotle and the spark of intellectual curiosity which elsewhere seemed dead. Together the monarch and the philosophers discussed the origin of the world, whether there was one first cause or many; this touched on the complex Aristotelian notion of plural 'intelligences', the causes of planetary movements; and whether the universe was destructible. If knowledge and speculation had collapsed in Europe and Byzantium, they survived further east by the grace of the Persian monarch. The thinkers admired his capacity for abstract thought, even if he lacked their philosophical acuity. But within his realm injustice and crime were as prevalent as anywhere else. Persia at that time was, despite the tales, clearly not Plato's Republic. In person Khusrau was tolerant and enlightened but the disillusion of the seven Athenian philosophers was rapid and they soon begged to be allowed return home. Brought up on high-minded Hellenic paganism they were particularly shocked by the frequency and ease with which Persian men could divorce their wives and remarry. The shah-emperor reluctantly assented to their departure from his court, for he would miss their refined conversation and informed speculation; but first – reflecting a great generosity of spirit – he extracted from his fellow emperor Justinian an agreement that on their return they would be exempted from his anti-philosophical religious laws, and they died eventually in their beds, at peace.[7]

As part of Anushirwan's patronage of scholarship, he re-established a Sasanid university city. Jundishapur (or Gondesapor, 'Shapur's region', about seven miles south-east of the modern Dezful, Iran, due south from Hamadan) had been founded in the mists of antiquity as Genta Shapirta ('the Beautiful Garden') and refounded in 260, following the defeat of the Roman emperor Valerian by Shapur I the year before, when the Persians had allegedly taken Antioch by stealth while the population was at the theatre. Captives (presumably including actors) taken in this ambush were transported east to create within the revived city a cosmopolitan mixture of nationalities. According to Firdawsi, the Persian emperor saw his new city as the reclaimed Antioch of south-west Iran, calling it Vah-az-Andev-i-Shapur, meaning 'Shapur's better than Antioch.' This loose-limbed appellation, indicative of intellectual rivalry, became, along with its original name, pared down to a more manageable Jundishapur. Ten years later it became a university city. With the growing anti-intellectual mood of the Byzantine Empire, reflecting an ever-present fear of heresy, it grew to be the focus for uneasy communities of scientists, doctors and philosophers. In their exile they travelled east with more determination to stay than that shown by the philosophers of the Golden Chain. They came from such Syrian or Mesopotamian centres as Edessa (closed by the emperor in AD 439, almost a century before philosophy was driven from Athens), Kinnesrin, Ras el-Ain and Nisibis. During Anushirwan's reign Jundishapur's relaunch was completed and it became dominated by Syriac-speaking Christians, mostly Nestorians, with a sprinkling of Jacobites (who, despite their very different views on Christ's nature, held learning equally in honour).[8]

The scholars worked in a collegiate-like environment, with an academy, a school of medicine equipped with a hospital, and an observatory. The hospital is said to have been the first that was run entirely on scientific, experimental principles, where diseases were treated by modern pharmacological methods.[9] Medicine was practised without reference to notions about spirits or magic. Here Syriac learning flourished for 200 years, outlasting the collapse of the Sasanian Empire. When Justinian had shut down Greek knowledge and enquiry, he incidentally reduced the significance of the Greek language, which henceforth became largely a language for history, theology and military tactics. (Latin was used for law.) Syriac, with its parent language Aramaic, became the forward-looking language for science and philosophy, as later did Arabic. Hebrew was important too, the 'special reserve' language of the Jewish community, who more usually spoke Aramaic and subsequently Arabic. The enlightened patronage of the immortal-souled Persian emperor, and the competence and scholarship of the Nestorian Christian scholars working in Syriac, enabled much knowledge of the ancients to survive which might otherwise have been lost, in view of the darkness in the West. Except in mathematics, Alexandria had ruled itself out, despite a distinguished intellectual pedigree stretching back to Hellenistic times, because of its fondness for magic and spells. Without the resource of Iran, medicine and astronomy would have advanced much more slowly, and if there had been no enlightened monarchy in sixth-century Iran we might be congratulating ourselves today at just having reached the stage of Robert Boyle and Isaac Newton.

Sasanid Persia was destroyed in AD 641 by the Islamic armies; but the caliphate Persianised itself by locating itself in Iraq in 750, and more precisely in Baghdad in 762. Al-Mansur, the first Abbasid caliph, had a reputation as 'proficient in jurisprudence and fond of philosophy and astronomy'.[10] A court of scholars, physicians and astrologers began to emerge in Baghdad, led by the Nestorian family of Bukht-Yishu from Jundishapur, who for seven generations distinguished themselves as physicians. The reports of al-Mansur commissioning translations of philosophical texts are probably legendary, although it seems likely that he ordered the translation of two Indian texts: one on astronomy known as *Siddhanta,* and the other on mathematics, which introduced the Indian numerals which we know as arabic, but which are known to the Arabs as *Hindi,* and the zero. A collection of fables, recomposed in Arabic from a Sanskrit original, also appeared, known as *Kalilah wa Dimnah,* in which various animals discourse on life, fate and good and evil, and which became popular in medieval England;[11] it was noted by Matthew Paris and versified by John Gower. Harun al-Rashid likewise extended caliphal patronage to learning, especially of medical texts.

During the caliphate of al-Mamun Baghdad grew from being a city which valued knowledge to becoming the seat of a universal civilisation. In 830 the caliph established a House of Wisdom (*Bayt al-Hikmah*), which served as college, library and translation centre. It was almost certainly based on Jundishapur. The first head was Nestorian Christian scholar Hunayn ibn Ishaq. He was an able translator, carefully mining meaning from the best texts available, even writing to the Byzantine emperor, Leo the Armenian, requesting manuscripts. He is reputed to have received a high salary, plus the weight in gold of every book he translated. Pride of place was given to Galen's voluminous medical treatises.[12] Another noted translator was a pagan star-worshipper from Harran (Syria) called Thabit ibn Qurra, who specialised in mathematical texts such as those by Archimedes and Apollonius of Perga. (His familiarity with these works derived naturally from his community's need for accurate observation of heavenly bodies in the cause of worship.) As at Jundishapur, some of the translators were Jewish; one such was a Persian-born astronomer named Mashallah (d. 820).[13] All texts became accessible to the large number of people who had come to speak Arabic, a language which through its fluency and flexibility was uniquely suitable for expressing scientific accuracy.[14] No subject was off limits. Nothing was hidden or inaccessible. Scholars were able to become acquainted with every doctrine, from the Greeks or their rivals, on matters spiritual or secular. The compass of knowledge lay open, and those who sought refreshment there found themselves satisfied and intellectually replete.[15]

If one looks at the actual titles of the texts translated by Hunayn and his colleagues at the House of Wisdom, one can be glad that much was saved but also feel a sense of regret that the world of the ancients was rediscovered in such a pared-down manner. There was nothing from the tragedians and no epic, although a translation of part of the *Iliad* was made but is now lost. No Herodotus or Thucydides. From Plato, the *Republic*, the *Timaeus* and the *Laws* alone were translated. The *Republic* is a magnificent construct, memorable today perhaps for its myths as much as for its arguments about the state; it comprises an ideal of sorts and one can see how philosophers would be drawn to its realisation. But it is also a repressive dialogue in which the liberty of the individual is clamped in a vice of something that approaches totalitarianism, and in which the interests of the state are held to be paramount. (Some of the repressiveness was later retracted by Plato in the *Laws*.)

The appeal of the *Timaeus* (which was also one of the few works of antiquity to be read in the scattered places of literacy in Europe's Dark Ages) lay in its explanation of the origin of the world and the place given by it to a single God, who was however more a kind of demiurge – a craftsman-creator – than the Deity of Abrahamic monotheism. It is hard to read the *Timaeus* today without finding it humourless and crabby, with passages reminiscent of the cranky chatter of a loquacious New Ager. In it, the basic unit of fire is identified as the pyramid, and perfect souls are said to return to their origins in the stars. The dialogue (which is more of a monologue) is dogmatic, overserious and nerdy; it never entertains the possibility that it might be mistaken. It is devoid of the engaging ironic intellectual banter of the other dialogues of Plato, with their lively social settings and astringent use of the Socratic *elenkhos*, the method of proof by which Socrates led his companion into holding two contradictory opinions before he himself indicated the resolution to the philosophical problem in question.

From Aristotle the *Categories, Physics, Metaphysics* and *Magna Moralia* were translated, as well as the great work of logic, the *Prior Analytics*. Here was a solid basis for a system of thought, in which scientific advancement was given the chance to develop with a system of syllogistic logic and within a secure (maybe too secure) metaphysical system. Aristotle's logic remained definitive until the modern era of Frege, Russell and Wittgenstein and is still an important instrument of reasoning. The classical philosopher's explanation of God as the 'unmoved mover' or first cause, a God accessed by reason, rather than Plato's supreme artificer, made his views acceptable to monotheist theologians, although his view that matter had always existed put him at odds with them. When one first encounters Aristotle's system of philosophy it appears unnecessarily complex, a perverse attempt to create difficulty where there was none. But it had the advantage (as Bertrand Russell pointed out) of being a better system than any of the others then extant. Moreover Aristotle was at heart an observer and an empiricist. However complex his views on the various types of substance, on the four classes of causes and on the potentiality of matter and the actuality of form, he created a basis suitable for the development of science.

Al-Mamun's court sponsored scientific practice as well as theory. Accepting – at this early date – that the earth was round, his astronomers measured one degree of its surface. The measurement was carried out near Palmyra and yielded a result of 56.66 miles as a single degree, a result which was out by about 2,877 feet or 950 metres. This figure gave the earth a circumference of 20,400 miles, an underestimate of some 22 per cent.[16]

Learning had travelled from Athens to Jundishapur, and from Jundishapur to Baghdad. It then spread out: from Baghdad it became the province of the whole of the Arabic-speaking world, from Islamic Spain to Central Asia. Despite the adoption of Aristotle within the Islamic world, Islamic theologians tended to hold back from giving their full assent, proclaiming the incompatibility of *kalam* (scholastic philosophy based on belief, or perhaps the rhetoric of faith) with *falsafa* (free philosophy). But theologians were not all-powerful. Free philosophy remained in the arena of thought, and the sciences of astronomy, optics and medicine advanced rapidly (if indirectly) in the early centuries of Islam. Al-Kindi, known as the philosopher of the Arabs, was the first in Islam to seek to reconcile Plato and Aristotle. He was also (as was common at that time) an astrologer, an alchemist, an ophthalmologist and a theorist – from a neo-Pythagorean viewpoint – about music. Music was seen as akin to mathematics and philosophy, owing to the exact divisions of the string that were observed in producing the octave, fifth, fourth and major third. (This was however a banal notion, as sterile and self-referential as trying to concoct a theory of the universe from the seven regular solid figures.) He enlarged on Aristotle's difficult notion of the passive and active intellects (not to be confused with the intelligences; the passive intellect is basically the facility we have for receiving and understanding information, and the active is our capacity for originating and creating new concepts and ideas). It is hard to deny that his focus on this matter led philosophy briefly down an obscure and complex byway. His text on optics was, however, influential, if erroneous.[17]

Al-Kindi was followed by a Turk from Central Asia named al-Farabi, who had been tutored by a Nestorian Christian and had settled in Aleppo. Through the medium of the Arabic language he attempted to reconcile the two classical philosophers, but with a political slant: he sought to combine the thought of Plato's *Republic* with Aristotle's *Politics*. He also made an early attempt at classifying knowledge. His Neoplatonist philosophy posited that the Intelligence and the World-Soul emanated from the One, and the Cosmos proceeded from the thoughts of the World-Soul. Rich, fascinating and consoling ideas; the ultimate cloudy metaphysics, the poetry of contemplation. Like al-Kindi, he was also drawn to theorising on music.[18]

Avicenna (980–1037), from Bukhara, enjoyed an immense reputation in Europe throughout the Middle Ages and in the early-modern period.[19] In his own time he was known equally as a doctor, lawyer and philosopher.[20] His medical text, the *Qanun* (Canon of Medicine), was translated by Gerard of Cremona and printed more than twenty times in the sixteenth century. One cannot overestimate its importance. In 1598 it was even being translated into Scots Gaelic by one Duncan McConacher.

This highly influential work, subdivided into general principles, drugs for treatment, diseases of particular organs, fevers and the use of compound medicines, represented the summit of medical knowledge for six centuries. It is admirable if only for its attempt at organisation and for the spirit of science which pervades it.[21] Avicenna (Ibn Sina) was also distinguished as a philosopher; he fruitlessly read Aristotle's *Metaphysics* forty times until a commentary by al-Farabi opened his mind to its meaning.

One of his philosophical concerns was surprisingly modern: he wondered whether a man suddenly created, found flying in space, could form the notion of existence, without experience or sensory input. Could there be a private, unempirical awareness of self? This is the issue which possessed Descartes and led him to declare that, even if all the evidence of the senses was a hoax and a malicious deception, a person who yet retained the capacity to think would be aware of self. '*Cogito ergo sum*' was a notion that was hacked away by Wittgenstein, who argued forcefully that private languages and private experiences of this type are meaningless philosophical bafflement, and that matters like self-consciousness can only emerge through social interaction and shared language games. Avicenna argued – like Descartes, despite the very different theoretical position – that a person could, on his own, form a notion of existence, since the consciousness of self, which would be present even as he floated untouched and untouching in space, could give him the notion of being.[22] Awareness of public, out-there being would (he claimed) follow from consciousness of a private, in-here self.

His other concerns were more typically scholastic: he distinguished necessary and contingent beings and speculated on the chain of causes, which he concluded stretched back to the first cause, the uncaused being who must be God. Using the notion of God as a necessary being and attaching that idea to the Aristotelian distinction between potentiality and act, he saw God as pure act, which probably means that while all other beings are *becoming*, God is *being*; God has, so to speak, got there, while the rest of us continue to hurry on. From this he deduced the necessary goodness of the Deity. As a scientist he noted the slow process of the evolution of geological forms. Avicenna wrote a number of myths, which explore his understanding of the relation between the soul and the body and mortality. In one of them the mystical theme is that of love, seen as the only power able to guide us to goodness and enable us to escape the bald bleakness of nothingness and materiality.[23] A number of his ideas went on to pervade the thought of St Thomas Aquinas, even though the saintly doctor was compelled by the need to uphold orthodoxy to attack the Islamic philosopher as an infidel.

Medicine returned to the fore in the work of al-Razi or Rhazes, who held the post first of chief physician of the hospital at Rayy (near Tehran), before gaining the same position in Baghdad. He is best remembered for clearly distinguishing the symptoms of measles and smallpox. His text, Latinised, was published in London in 1766, and in English in 1848.[24] He also wrote a vast medical textbook known as *Hawi* or *Continens* ('comprehensive textbook'), detailing the corpus of medical knowledge of the time, which was translated both in Brescia (1486) and Venice (1542). Another scientist who challenged the authoritative myths of the day was abu Ali al-Hasan ibn al-Haytham (known as Alhazen), an Egyptian Arab, who was able to work within the realm of the mad caliph al-Hakim, showing that Fatimid Egypt could encompass scientific rationality alongside religious violence and extremism. Ibn al-Haytham declared that, in the act of vision, light did not, as was hitherto believed, travel from the eye to the object but from the object to the eye. He came to this conclusion on the basis of the observation that objects grow larger or smaller the closer or further away they are from the eye. His correct deduction revolutionised the study of light and optics, making possible the study of perspective and changing for ever the visual arts.[25]

Averroes (1126–98), or Ibn Rushd, was, in terms of the ideas that were passed on to Europe, the most influential philosopher to come from the Islamic world. His background was the law and he was himself a judge, as well as a capable astronomer. Born in Cordoba, he was introduced to the Moroccan court by Ibn Tufayl (see below) and eventually held the post of physician to the self-styled caliph. He has been charged with rationalism and atheism and there is no doubt that, on entering Europe, his ideas became transformed into tremors of intellectual energy, shifting the tectonic plates of Church and permitted knowledge.[26] But his works show a devotion both to faith and reason, in a balanced manner which almost calls to mind the mixture found in the rational piety of an English gentleman in the eighteenth century. He himself admired Aristotle above all – 'this man is a rule in nature, and an example which nature has devised to demonstrate supreme human perfection.'[27] This admiration became absorbed into the intellectual outlook of medieval Christian

Europe, where, to Aristotle's status as 'the philosopher', Averroes was known simply as 'the commentator', a point which was not made in Kenneth Clark's introverted view of Europe's apparent self-creation, *Civilisation*. Averroes sought to interpret the classical philosopher's ideas in their pristine unadorned state; nevertheless Aristotle emerged in his writings in a cloud of Neoplatonic fragrance.

His major philosophical opponent was Avicenna, who he said had misinterpreted Aristotle by separating essence from existence. A thing's essence – that which it most essentially is – cannot be separated from the thing's existence. You cannot have the essence of a fork without a real fork. Avicenna had also said that God was a necessary being. To Averroes this was meaningless, since necessity cannot be an attribute. His views on the soul were very challenging to medieval faith. The individual soul, to Averroes, was a passive intellect, distinct and separate from the 'world active intellect', and as such it perished at death. The metaphysical reasoning is complex and technical here. In life – this too is a surprising concept – the individual, passive, mortal soul was seen as illuminated by the world active intellect, a world soul possessed by all of humanity, from which each member of humanity partakes a portion, as though it were a gigantic piece of flat pitta bread from which each person might take his or her own bite. When, to continue the analogy, an individual can no longer bite and the body dies, the individual soul dies too, and the world active intellect moves its concerns elsewhere. (Perhaps one can understand the notion of the world active intellect in terms of 'the consensus of conscious humanity at any one moment'. William James himself felt drawn to the notion of a 'panpsychic' world-spirit.) Averroes' view of the mortal soul was a development of Aristotle's view of the soul as an entity enmeshed in physicality, but it had travelled a circuitous metaphysical journey.[28]

The doctrine of the mortal soul removed the notion of a 'future state' from the prospects for posthumous humanity and thereby negated the idea of rewards and punishments in a life to come. This idea was socially, as well as theologically, unacceptable, since society might become destabilised if the masses did not fear hell.

Filled with admiration for Aristotle, Averroes sought to reconcile him with Islamic belief. This he did by delimiting, for the first time, the territory covered by religion and that covered by philosophy and science. He became known as the philosopher of 'double truth'. It was claimed that he asserted that religious truths were allowed to be called truths, even if they contradicted philosophical–scientific truths, which likewise might be claimed to be true. Averroes appears not to have been saying that a proposition could be true in theology while a contradictory proposition was true in philosophy. Rather, he was trying to measure out the areas of applicability of religion and philosophy; to draw the boundaries between the two. They dealt, he asserted, with different things. He held strongly that faith was irrelevant to logic, mathematics or science, and that theologians had no business dabbling there. There is a hostility to theologians in his writings, although he favoured religion, insofar as it related to the emotions and the inner life. Only those who continued to confuse the areas of applicability of faith and science could accuse him of saying that a proposition could be true and not true at the same time. Averroes was, however, determined that theology should be subordinate to philosophy, if only because philosophy had to be the distinguishing index between theology and science-and-philosophy. Philosophy held the enviable position of being, from its very nature, both referee and a player in one of the teams.

This view was naturally highly unpopular among theologians; they believed it was their job to act as referee. Eventually in Almohad Morocco, which was a fairly extreme dictatorship where a small community of enlightened philosophers were nevertheless given some scope to think and say what they liked, the study of classical philosophy was banned and Averroes' books were burnt. The orthodox and conformist theological rigorist al-Ghazali attacked him in a work with the title *The Incoherence of the Philosophers*, to which, in the spirit of a first-class literary spat, he responded with a massive work entitled *The Incoherence of the Incoherence*. Averroes' influence waned in the Islamic world as in region after region the vitality of speculation and science was suppressed by political and theological conservatism.

Intellectuality and speculation rapidly burnt low within eastern Islam too, despite the enthusiasm of al-Mamun for knowledge, following the earlier encouragement shown within Sasanid Persia. Eventually the texts that the Islamic philosophers and scientists had worked on and created commentaries about were brought to Europe, where they created an intellectual revolution. But they ceased to be of any but marginal interest in Baghdad and the lands of the eastern caliphate. In the case of al-Mamun it appears that this occurred because he became too devoted to philosophy, speculation and scepticism. He did what no other ruler has ever done: he enforced scepticism. In the year 827 he ordered his people to be doubters and philosophers. Al-Mamun belonged to the doctrinal party known as the Mutazilites, who proclaimed a state intermediate between belief and unbelief.[29] The Mutazilite semi-scepticism echoed the deistical semi-belief, scorned as 'Sadduceist', which had been observed among the Arabs of the peninsula at the time of Muhammad, and in particular the Quraysh, the tribal grouping from which Muhammad sprang. Al-Mamun declared that the Koran was a text created by God, not a book uncreated, alongside God in heaven from eternity. By enforcing belief in non-fundamentalist notions, and by stressing the need for rationality within the conduct of religious faith, and by making adherence to this viewpoint law (with heavy penalties), he made sure that when, with the death of his brother al-Mu'tasim in 842, enforced scepticism had run its course, the reaction in the cause of conservative orthodoxy would be massive.

When, in his turn, the puritanical and reactionary imam of Baghdad Ahmed ibn Hanbal died in 855, not many fewer than a million mourners followed his coffin: such was the popular reaction against the enforcement of doubt amid belief. 'Don't ask *how*' had been the bleak, anti-intellectual rallying-cry of that champion of religious orthodoxy.[30] Thereafter faith came first, and knowledge second, within the Islamic community of the East. The door opened by the early Abbasids had all but closed – a door which had led in the direction of Aristotle, away from fundamental belief. At the time this process amounted to a kind of scepticism, even if only by indicating that there were other ways to truth than through faith. By making a structure for both faith and speculation, a way forward was briefly made for curiosity and knowledge. As for knowledge itself, it was able to withstand the setback; learning had become accessible right across the Islamic world, from Morocco to the Pamirs. Whenever any rulers of the time (such as the early Fatimids of Egypt) showed enlightened patronage of science and philosophy, or whenever a motivated individual could create a space of knowledge and enlightenment, before the dull monotone of conformity, orthodoxy and despotism closed off learning, knowledge could spread out, expand and explore. It was only a matter of time before it would return to Europe.[31]

The final spear-thrust against philosophy and speculation in the Arab world was delivered by the Mongols in their destruction of Baghdad in 1258. The last scientist-philosopher-historian in the capital of the eastern caliphate was Abdullatif (d. 1231). His manuscript recounting time spent in Egypt now resides in the Bodleian Library; it was admired by the English orientalist Edward Pococke, whose son translated part of it, and an impressive French version was printed in Paris in 1810. The end of Baghdad was so total and so catastrophic, reducing a city of learning and civilisation to the zero-state of skull-piled military triumph, that it never really recovered. Historical specialists who have been buoyed up by anti-Arab sentiments have generally dismissed the significance of the destruction of Baghdad, saying that its science and literature had died centuries earlier; such people, besides ignoring individuals like Abdul-Latif, have usually cared little for literacy, scholarship or human death, focusing instead on control, command and empire, and contemptuously taking in their stride ruin and loss.

❖❖❖

Northern Europeans slowly began to explore the world of knowledge. One by one brave souls went to live abroad, learnt Arabic, translated one or more of the great works of the past and made possible the dissemination of science and philosophy. Knowledge was very restricted in Europe until about the year 1000, in the dark age following the death of Charles the Great. Few texts were read apart from Pliny, St Augustine, Boethius and the *Timaeus*. For the most part ignorance and illiteracy triumphed. But individuals, driven by the desire to know, sought better things. They also looked for adventure. A few travelled east to Constantinople but most seekers ventured south to the world of Islam. There was more to relations between the Christian north and the Islamic south than theology and scripture. Philosophy, science and mathematics soon became of equal, and arguably greater, significance than the minutiae of theological debate. Being able to add up, measure things, multiply the value of goods or subdivide estates was as important as anguishing over the condition of one's soul. Philosophy established the mental agenda of the age as much as religion, and in a more stable and systematic manner, since it had universal applicability, which religion did not. From it the branches of science and mathematics were developed, which were prised off and replanted as disciplines in their own right.

In about 990 the monk Gerbert of Auvergne went to Islamic Cordoba to study scientific learning. William of Malmesbury wrote entertainingly of Gerbert and his Arab studies. The English chronicler took a dim view of the Arab world and its science, believing that the 'usual mode of that nation' was to practise 'divinations and incantations'.[32] Nevertheless William admitted that Gerbert 'surpassed Ptolemy in the use of the astrolabe'.[33] Then as now, scientists were seen by arts writers devoid of scientific training or understanding as a step away from the demonic, and Gerbert is credited with the art of calling up spirits from hell. Allegedly escaping on one occasion with a stolen book, the monk is said by the chronicler to have done a deal with Satan on the seashore to secure his captured treasure. He was also reputed to have imprisoned a spirit within a golden humanoid head which he had sculpted, and to have given the animated object pride of place on a shelf in his study. He used to discuss abstruse arithmetical problems with this gilded cephalic homunculus. Sometimes the problems were too complex and the inspirited artefact would give unsatisfactory answers.[34] If we leave aside the entertaining tales, Gerbert can be seen to have revived arithmetic, geometry, astronomy and music throughout the Frankish world, and to have introduced the numerals 1 to 9 into Europe, but without the zero. Calculation was advanced by his introduction of the abacus. In a striking, and maybe grudging, phrase from the 1845 translation of William, 'he gave rules which are scarcely understood even by laborious computers'. A computer of course designated a person, not an object.

On his return to Frank lands, Gerbert constructed a water-clock, similar to that which Harun al-Rashid had sent to Charlemagne, and a hydraulic organ, which seems to have been driven by steam. The young emperor Otto III expressed his support of Gerbert by appointing him archbishop of Ravenna. But the chronicler will have none of it, declaring that his advancement was due to the assistance of the devil, who had clearly instructed him in the black arts, which enabled him to discover buried treasure 'as one crow picks out another crow's eyes'.[35] In 999 Gerbert was elected pope as Sylvester II. Later commentators – perhaps since their own minds were closed, perhaps as representatives of their own vested interests, or perhaps drawing on the consensus of popular myth – continued to contend that, in his capacity as a scientist, Gerbert had had dealings with the devil while in Spain. To such resistant minds, both Islam and science itself were aspects of the forbidden world of spirits. A book published (in 1999) on conditions in Europe in the year 1000 still hinted that Gerbert was a magician, so slowly do myths about scientists die.

Aristotle noted the urge to know within all human beings and the bravery of those who seek knowledge will always outstrip those who would limit it, damn it as satanic, or compel it into systems. The Castilian kings had been reconquering Spain from the Muslims, and in 1085 Toledo, the former capital, became a Castilian city under Alfonso VI, who described himself, with a measure of tolerance, as the 'emperor of the two religions'. The Castilians preserved and honoured the contents of the Mosque Library of Toledo, an act which stands in contrast to the serial violence of the crusaders and their malevolent destruction of the great library of Ibn Ammar at Tripoli. The monarchs of Castile, showing an openness of mind (while still remaining devout Catholics), sponsored intellectual discovery, and a Castilian archbishop, Raymund I (1126–51), became head of a school of translators, the most industrious of whom was Gerard of Cremona (1113–87), who worked systematically on perhaps as many as 100 texts on astronomy, medicine and philosophy, with a number of co-workers who tended to be baptised Jews. A large amount of learning was thereby made available. Words that could not be translated remained in Arabic – as they do today, giving us alcohol, alchemy and cypher, elixir and soda (derived from Arabic *al-suda*, meaning 'a splitting headache').[36]

Adelard of Bath (*fl.* 1100–30), after study at Laon and Tours, travelled on to Castilian Toledo, learnt Arabic, the essential language, and translated three works by al-Khwarizmi: the 'Astronomical Tables', the 'Introduction to the Art of Astronomy', and the 'Algebra'. This last work had been fashioned in practical form: the Central Asian author had written his text with a view to expounding 'what is easiest and most useful in arithmetic, such as men constantly require in cases of inheritance, legacies, partition, law-suits and trade, and in all their dealings with one another, or where the measuring of lands the digging of canals, geometrical computation, and other objects of various sorts and kinds are concerned'. In 1126 Adelard brought his translation of the first two works to western Europe, as well as an Arabic version of Euclid's *Elements*. In 1130 his achievement received public recognition and he was granted 4*s* 6*d* (23p) from the revenues of Wiltshire. This sum may seem small; it is perhaps equivalent to a grant of £200 or $300 today. But a grant of any size for intellectual distinction, paid from an English county treasury, is to be accounted a notable act of public generosity.[37]

Adelard was a brilliant and original man, with a rangy, questing and restless mind which delved within traditions other than his own for solutions to the problems of the age. His image of the intrinsic nature of authority hints at the difficulties experienced by those looking for knowledge. He viewed authority as a halter; that is, as a sensible restraint, but something which should be relaxed to allow the full scope of speculation and knowledge to develop. In explaining natural phenomena, he held that God should be used as an explanation only when all others have been exhausted – an explanation of last resort, so to speak. He also created a plausible attempt to reconcile Plato's idealism with Aristotle's empiricism: how can people or things be at once individual, original, unique, worthy of wonder, and at the same time derivable from antecedents of prime matter and classifiable into genus and species? His theory inclined towards the variety and multifacetedness of Aristotle, although he accepted certain aspects of Plato. He held that Platonic universal forms could not exist except in the world of ideas; Platonic forms for him inhabited the world of art and imagination. Individual objects or people were derivable from Platonic forms only in the sense of being imagined creations; the greater part of their 'thisness' was derived from their Aristotelian natural history. Thus, John Doe as John Doe is a unique self-conscious being and a fully realised person, by virtue of the imaginative creation of his identity, while at the same time as a human being he is a member of a species, as an animal a subordinate genus, and as a substance the most universal genus.[38]

Another Englishman who travelled easily between England and the multiethnic Mediterranean at this time was Thomas Brown. His profession was that of international civil servant rather than philosopher or scientist and he was at home in both England and Norman Sicily. Born in about 1120, he found a job in Palermo as a secretary in 1137, principally as a drafter of legislation. In 1143 he is found working in the royal curia as μαστρο θωμα του βρουνου, 'mastro thoma tou brounou', making a judgment concerning a boundary dispute. In 1149 he adopted an Islamic identity as Kaid Brun, while working in the diwan (or government office) with a secretary called Othman and attaching his '*alama*' (opinion) to a transcript of the records of the bureau. Then he returned to England, apparently to work in the exchequer of Henry II. These differing identities – Latin, Greek and Islamic – were possible to European men of scholarship and ability in the twelfth century, proving that, as with the promotion of science and sense in Castilian Spain, there was a progressive, humane and educated alternative to the whipped-up northern clerico-aristocratic violence of the Crusades.[39]

Islam started to become a field of study. Robert of Ketton (in Lincolnshire) was the first European to translate the Koran (into Latin), in 1143. The work was financed by Peter the Venerable, Abbot of Cluny. The intention seems mainly to have been to study the beliefs of Muslims, with a view to creating the conditions for their eventual conversion; but there may have been a possibility of disinterested curiosity in the studies: the beginnings of an interest in Islam as something worth exploring for its own sake. Peter the Venerable was, in the context of Christian–Islamic relations, one of a select band of honourable Christians of the Middle Ages. He sought to persuade the Muslims by argument rather than by the sword. 'God does not altogether will it,' he memorably declared of religious violence, a quiet response to the clamour at Clermont of '*Deus le volt*'.[40]

Averroes began to be translated and his Aristotelian ideas were taken up with enthusiasm by European thinkers who embraced the new. In about 1215 Michael Scot (d. 1235, probably from Balwearie, Fife) travelled to Spain and Sicily to learn Arabic and study the world.[41] His was a remarkable intellect. At Toledo in 1217, apparently working alongside a Jew called Andrew, he translated into Latin a work on astronomy by the Islamic Andalusian al-Bitruji (a pupil of Ibn Tufayl, known in Latin texts as Alpetragius), which happened to be without scientific merit, but the attempt was a brave one. (Jews found Averroes' ideas disturbing and thrilling. In the eighteenth century Thomas Warton made the point that the growth of knowledge was a beneficial effect of the dispersion of the Jews.[42]) Three years later Michael Scot translated Aristotle's zoological text *Historia Animalium*. In 1220 he is known to have been in Bologna and in the years following he gained the patronage of papal circles, which led to the offer of the archbishopric of Cashel. This he declined, on the grounds that he did not know the Irish language. Travelling on to Sicily, to the splendid court of Frederick II of Hohenstaufen as court astrologer (a post offering more exciting vistas for an intelligent and ambitious Scot than that of an Irish archbishopric), he created Latin versions of a number of Aristotelian works, some from the Arabic and others from the Hebrew. He translated Aristotle's *On the Heavens*, and may have Latinised parts of Aristotle's *Metaphysics*. He is known for certain to have translated some of Averroes' vigorous elucidatory commentaries on the *Metaphysics*. Michael Scot also created a Latin version of another of Aristotle's zoological texts, the *De partibus animalium*, to satisfy Frederick II's great curiosity about the natural world. He also translated Aristotle's *Physics*, and Averroes' commentary on it. Sometimes a note indicated his versions were translated from Greek, presumably to add greater authenticity; for instance, the text in the University Library at Cambridge has a line indicating that the translation of *De partibus animalium* is from Greek. But examination of the text demonstrates that it derives from the Arabic.[43]

There was a curious matter here. A number of Aristotle's works had been known to Europe before Michael Scot's translations in versions from the Greek probably by James of Venice (*c.* 1150). But the philosopher had been seen by the Church as heretical and indeed as we have seen was prohibited. (The *Metaphysics* had existed in a translation from the Greek since the year 1000.) It was only after the exertions of the Scot, who also made influential versions of Averroes' commentaries, that Aristotle became acceptable to the Church. In other words, Aristotle needed an interlocutor (who happened to be a Muslim) before his philosophy and natural history could, despite his views on the mortality of the soul and the eternity of matter, become acceptable to the great doctors of the Catholic Church, whose thought culminated in the grand system of St Thomas Aquinas. The irony of the situation can perhaps be comprehended when it is remembered that thinkers such as Roger Bacon and Albertus Magnus based a considerable part of their thinking on Arab ideas, and that these intellectual developments were occurring at the time when publicly, in the field of the here-and-now – *tode ti*, or *haeccitas*, in Aristotelian terms – papal authority was declaring that the Muslim infidel should be crushed. Roger Bacon, drawing on Arab texts, was the first to distinguish *mathesis* from *matesis*, that is, knowledge from divination. The Catholic Church developed its philosophical thought with the aid of the subtle and compelling teaching of a Muslim but was driven inflexibly by its dogma to campaign against the peoples of that faith.

Frederick II may have sent Michael to Oxford in 1230 as part of the imperial mission to the universities of Europe to disseminate the recently Latinised Aristotle. As in the case of Gerbert, Michael Scot was identified by his contemporaries as a necromancer, and one cannot avoid the fact that he did dabble in divination in a weird and somewhat crazy way, and was far from a simple seeker after truth. Despite possessing an intellect which helped to propel the world to a new category of knowledge, he belonged to the medieval world of magic and strangeness. Scot designed a curious helmet-like contrivance for himself, in order to protect his head from the fate which he had divined as his own: a blow on the skull. Nevertheless he took this device off at a critical and unavoidable moment – in church, during a most sacred moment of the mass, the elevation of the host – and was immediately killed by a falling stone. Dante placed him not far from the central circle of hell. Sir Walter Scott, in *The Lay of the Last Minstrel,* drew an image of him as only a magician, ignoring his learning and high practical intelligence. Coleridge planned a drama on his life, believing it to be more vivid and colourful than that of Faust. He too saw him only as a sorcerer.[44]

There were other bringers of knowledge, and integrators of the East and the West. In around 1180 Daniel of Morley (the modern Morley St Botolph, a village just west of Wymondham) sought to escape the prohibitions of Paris, finding that city 'dominated by law and pretentious ignorance' and so travelled to Castilian Toledo to discover Arab philosophy and science. At about the same time a shadowy character known as Alfred the Englishman (or Alfred of Shareshill, near Wolverhampton) translated Aristotle's *On the Soul* from the Arabic, along with some pseudo-Aristotelian biological texts.[45]

In the developing arena of European thought, the forceful and persuasive argumentation of Latin Averroists played an increasing part, helping to draw a line with early medievalism and look towards early modernity. Their leading thinker was Siger of Brabant.[46] Drawing on their Aristotelian antecedents, Latin Averroists denied personal immortality and a future state. They also believed in the eternity of the world, holding that God had not created it by his fiat. In order to reconcile such notions to the Church's teaching, the Averroists had to juggle adroitly with ideas such as the truth of scientific concepts in a world where theology was still the index of what might be thought. (They were convinced that, whatever the Church might say, the ideas of Aristotle were true.) When challenged, Latin Averroists were apt to declare to unconvinced churchmen, 'Aristotle? I was just reporting his words.' This formula, cunningly uttered, let them off the hook of heresy.

Throughout the period 1210–77 the University of Paris, whose arts faculty held Aristotle in high esteem, was shaken by dissension. Aristotle, as understood by Averroes, was seen as dangerous. His concept of the mortal soul and his denial of a future state had sent shock waves through the university. His astringent scientism was alien to the Church's temper of thought. Jacques de Vitry discouraged the reading of books of natural philosophy. The Church banned Aristotle's scientific texts in 1210 and 1215.[47] They were permitted in 1231, only to be banned again in 1263. Both Albertus Magnus and Thomas Aquinas struggled to assert the primacy of theology, castigating Averroism as satanic while using his methods. But Siger of Brabant demonstrated a way forward, despite the odd obliquity in his thought, for instance his belief in a form of cyclical, astral determinism (a notion popular in the East). He defied the theologians by asserting God's ignorance of particulars, and by denying divine providence. Siger was condemned as an Averroist in 1270, along with his colleague Boethius of Dacia (who believed that man's supreme good consisted in the philosophical contemplation of truth and in virtuous living according to the light of nature). Both men were brought before the Inquisitor of France in 1277, the year of the 'Great Condemnation' at the University of Paris, and subsequently vanished into obscurity, although their ideas proved indestructible. Some of the condemned statements of 1277 give an indication of the power of Latin Averroism, which they had promoted: 'The sayings of the theologians are based on myths.' 'No one knows more for knowing theology.' 'The wise men of the world are the philosophers.'[48]

Having survived the Great Condemnation, Averroism reappeared more powerfully in the fourteenth century. It went on to redefine Aristotle in a fashion closer to his texts than the Church's version of Aristotelian scholasticism. The University of Padua had been founded in 1222 as an offspring of Bologna University. Under the Carrara family the city became noted for its civic humanism. The university rediscovered the classical style and in matters of philosophy and religion it soon showed independence of thought. Averroism became popular and from Padua, rationalist, anti-Church sentiments spread to Venice and Ferrara, creating some of the groundwork for the Renaissance. We find Pietro of Abano (1253–1316) there, a decidedly sceptical thinker and medical practitioner, a follower of Averroes, also known as Peter the Heretic: he disbelieved in providence and denied the existence of the devil. (As an astronomer he formulated the theory that the stars are moving freely in space, not, as hitherto believed, revolving on a sphere.[49]) Marsiglio (or Marsilius) of Padua was a profound social thinker; indeed, his mind was one of the most bold and original of the high Middle Ages. His text *Defensor Pacis* (The Defender of Peace, 1324) entirely rejected papal

73

claims to temporal power. The papacy was used to viewing itself as the arbiter of temporal rulers. It assumed the power to judge and depose them if necessary. Marsiglio said that this posture was devoid of legitimacy, since there was no justification for the intervention of the Church in the affairs of the state. The state was a matter for the people alone. More than that, he argued that the pope and the priesthood should be subject to a council which should include laymen, and that this council should oversee the administration of the sacraments and the preaching of divine law.[50]

The basis of his argument lay in his view of the state as the teleological expression of the fulfilment of man's natural desire for a sufficient life. This argument was carefully Aristotelian, driven forward by the notion of the separation of the divine from the rational, which had been the Andalusian Arab's particular contribution. The job of the state was to impose minimal coercive regulation in the affairs of people; and the populace itself was the only legitimate source of state authority. There could be (according to Marsiglio) no divine law, and no priesthood claiming authority from God to direct the affairs of men. Moreover since preaching and the sacraments affected the lives of men, it was appropriate for lay people to have a say in their administration. With these bold concepts, the secular began to be separated from the priestly, and the souls and bodies of men and women began to be unshackled from the medieval world.[51]

The text of this Latin Averroist became a text of some importance in the reform of the sixteenth century. It is arguable that Erastianism – the theory that the Church should be subordinate to the state – which emerged in the same century, had its origin here, and its descent too was from Averroes.

Padua continued to fashion thinkers whose minds refracted the clear, hard light of Aristotle, in conflict with theologians and contrasting with the hermetic elitism of Platonism of all types. It cannot be denied that Platonism was enormously important during the Renaissance and one of the driving forces within it. It appeared to represent an immense spirit of cultural liberality which is hard to reconcile for anyone reading Plato's views on art as expressed in the *Republic*. The truth is complex. The Platonism of the Renaissance was in nearly every case the Neoplatonism of Plotinus, not the original texts of Plato's dialogues. And the aspect of Plotinus that the thinkers and artists of the Renaissance found particularly congenial, even exciting, was the vision offered of the notion of infinity: not the controlled, limited view of life which they discerned from Aristotle, but one of limitless possibilities, human as well as divine. This was in tune with the temper of the Renaissance. The vistas and prospects held up by Neoplatonism were immense and intoxicating for artists. Nevertheless, even here there were exceptions, one of whom was Pomponazzi.

Pietro Pomponazzi (1462–1525) was a professor of philosophy, first at Padua and then at Bologna. His treatise *On the Immortality of the Soul* (1516) provoked a lively controversy because it took a strongly Aristotelian stance while rejecting the views of Thomas Aquinas. Pomponazzi was subsequently hailed by the French Enlightenment as an early rationalist who had concealed his atheism so as to keep the Church off his trail; but the evidence suggests that this was an exaggerated view. Nevertheless he represented a genuine intellectual descendance from Averroes, even though he rejected Averroes' view of the immortality of the world active soul and the mortality of the individual soul. He concluded that the immortality of the soul cannot be rationally demonstrated; it can only be accepted as an article of faith. In other words, he was delimiting the immortality of the soul away from rational discussion and into faith. As with Averroes, he was keen to set the boundaries between theology and faith, and reason and natural philosophy, and emphasised that the first must not stray into the domain of the second. This opened the way for rationalism and modernism, but it was not either. Pomponazzi remained influential for at least a hundred years. His works circulated widely in manuscript and he only really lost influence when the Aristotelians were supplanted by Galileo.[52]

The influence of Paduan thought even reached England. The stress on constitutionalism and rejection of absolutism can be seen in a work with the ringing title *An Exhortation to styrre all Englyshe men to the defence of their countreye* (1539). The author was Richard Morison, who in 1550 became Henry VIII's ambassador to Charles V. In the early 1530s he had travelled and studied in Padua, where he had developed his ideas. 'What thynge is more beneficial unto mannes life than polytyke order, than mutuall societie of men, knytte together in iustyce, temperancie, modestie and honest lybertie, one to helpe and comforte an other, one to instruct and teache an other, in al thynges, but in especiall in matters belongyng to god, and such as maynteyne this societie?' Papal power stood in opposition to those qualities. Morison even considered the pope to be more spiritually destructive than the Islamic empires. 'The turke suffereth men, taken in warre, to kepe their religion, to serve god, as his lawes woll. The bysshop of Rome, more crueller than Turke or Saracẽ, thinketh his victory worth nothing, except he overthrowe goddes word, except he drive out ryght religion, except he utterly bannyshe Christe.'[53]

Thus, despite the rapid fall in the Islamic west's esteem for his thought, Averroes contributed a radical secular streak to European society, looking toward the post-medieval world of the Renaissance, where human society, science and philosophy could stand alongside religion on equal terms. The new outlook followed naturally from his delimitation of the conceptual universe of science from the conceptual universe of the divine. In Europe, henceforth, religion was just one of many topics; it no longer had the right to claim an overarching authority. This view had been central to Averroes' thought.

Dante is without doubt the great codifier and imaginative illuminator of Christian ideas on philosophy, law, metaphysics and the afterlife, as seen from the high point of the Middle Ages. Yet there are ironies and problems in his work. Perhaps the most significant is that *The Divine Comedy* (*c.*1310–14) appears to have owed part of its origin to various Islamic models. The notion that the profound spiritual epic drew solely on the *Aeneid*, on Lucan's *Pharsalia* and perhaps on a translation of the *Odyssey*, and other European sources, is perhaps open to question. The structure of the poem and the physical layout depicted in the Inferno are remarkably close to Islamic models. Islam is relevant to *The Divine Comedy* in terms both of structure and content.

The philosophical position seen within the *Comedy* is largely a secular, Averroistic construct. Dante believed in a universal secular empire in which, although an emperor held authority from God, the Church should be secondary in the affairs of mankind. As we have seen, the origin of the separation of powers can be found in Averroism, which also had within it the strange and difficult 'pitta bread' belief in a universal human active intellect. This latter, when combined with a Stoic–Aristotelian view that all people are in essence citizens of one city, drew together ideas to create Dante's view of a benevolent cooperative empire. Another underlying Averroistic idea within the *Comedy* was that, where there was dispute, the truths of intellect were superior to the truths of revelation. Aristotle's philosophy was superior to the miraculous. Dante himself placed Averroes and Avicenna in limbo, barely in hell at all; and as if to emphasise his enthusiasm for Ibn Rushd, he also placed the defiantly Averroistic Siger of Brabant in paradise: 'the eternal light of Siger, who, when he taught in the Street of Straw, established unwelcome truths'.[54] The poet placed some words of praise for Siger in the mouth of St Thomas Aquinas, Siger's great opponent, surely an ironically placatory gesture designed to grant orthodoxy to a heterodox progressive who Dante believed deserved it.

The Divine Comedy also shows some structural similarities to Islamic models. About 200 years after the death of Muhammad a number of poetical versions of the Prophet's 'Night Journey' and 'Ascension' (in Arabic, the *Isra* and the *Mi'raj*) circulated. These all originated from the verse in the Koran already noted, which described Muhammad's prayers at Jerusalem. In what is known as Version A of Cycle I, the sleeping Prophet is woken by a man who leads him to the foot of a mountain. He is bidden to climb, but declines to do so until his guide's companionship inspires him to continue. They ascend, and witness six scenes of terrible torture: bodies torn asunder, pierced with arrows, hanging upside down. The punishments are explained when the guide relates the lives of the sufferers. The two travel on, to be enveloped by smoke. They hear confused sounds of pain and anger. (Dante was to write of '*parole di dolore, accenti d'ira*'.) It is Gehenna, and they are urged to pass on. The surroundings change to men at peace and children at play. Three figures meet Muhammad: Zayd ibn Haritha, a former slave who had become Muhammad's adoptive son and who had died at the battle of Muta of September 629; Jaafar, the Prophet's cousin, who had preached Islam in Abyssinia and fallen in the same battle; and Abdallah, a friend of the Prophet. These three welcome the Prophet. Finally Muhammad looks towards heaven and sees Abraham, Moses and Jesus around the throne of God, waiting for the Prophet of Islam to join them.[55]

In another version of these cycles of tales, Muhammad is accompanied by two guides and travels to see similarly powerful visions of the afterlife, but which are stylistically more developed and closer to Dante's. Here we encounter the prototype of Dante's Minos, the steward of hell. There is a similarity in the nature of the punishments: a swimmer in a sea of blood is the usurer, an image very like Dante's.[56] Other Islamic cycles of sacred legends embellish and enrich the notions of the visions of the afterlife, which were clearly of common currency throughout the Islamic world.

It is possible – no more – that Dante knew one or more of these Islamic legends, since translations have been found, and published (in 1949), of two versions of the *Mi'raj*, one in Latin (the *Liber scalae Machometi*) and the other in Old French (*Le Livre de l'eschiele Mahomet*). Both are versions of a lost Castilian version of the *Mi'raj* which Alfonso X had had translated. This lost text was known in the fourteenth century to followers of Dante, and was called the 'Libro della Scala' by Fazio degli Uberti, and 'Helmaerich' (= *al-Mi'raj*) by a Franciscan preacher.[57]

There is also an individual allegorical poem of the tenth century that seems to expound some of the details to which Dante was to give poetic form. It is very unlikely that the poem was an antecedent of *The Divine Comedy*, but it may have shared a common source. Abu-l-Ala al-Ma'ari (973–1057) was a great Arab poet. He has been called 'the philosopher of poets, and the poet of philosophers'.[58] His *Risalat al-Ghufran*, or treatise on pardon, is a subtle attack on moralists who are devoid of a spirit of forgiveness. Against them al-Ma'ari sets the spirit of the mercy of God. The *Risalat al-Ghufran* takes the form of a letter to a literary friend, Ibn al-Qarih of Aleppo, who in his writing had condemned those men of letters who had lived lives of impiety or debauchery. Al-Ma'ari demonstrates, by his self-effacing poetry, that some libertine and pagan poets could be received into paradise. In the poem, Ibn al-Qarih is miraculously taken on a journey into heaven as a reward for his dutiful and pious stance. Here he finds a number of poets, novelists, grammarians, critics and philosophers released from the cares and bitternesses and backbiting hatreds of their lives into friendship and conversation in the peace and harmony of a garden of delight. The pious visitor discusses with each of those whom he had condemned in his writings their works and the divine mercy which had brought them to paradise.

There is a heavenly feast at which two ravishing houris are in attendance. He praises their charms. They laugh and tell him that he already knows them. 'But you are the houris of heaven,' he replies. 'No no,' replies one, 'I am Hamduna of Aleppo – a woman famous as the ugliest woman in the city, repudiated by her husband (a rag-picker) on account of her foul breath.' 'Then who are you?' he asks the other. 'I am Tawfiq the black woman, who works at the desk of the Baghdad library.' Ibn al-Qarih is bewildered and is informed by a passing angel that houris are of two kinds – those created in heaven and those elevated to paradise for their good deeds.

The man of letters expresses a desire to visit hell; his way is barred by a fierce-looking lion. But this is a special lion, and, touched by the divine spirit, the big cat is granted the power of speech and explains that he has been taken into paradise (even if it is the paradise of guarding the gate to hell) as a reward for protecting a cousin of Muhammad on a journey to Egypt.[59] Hell is real, and there are poets in it; the spirit of forgiveness is not all-pervasive. One of the condemned is the great Imru' l-Qays. Hell's occupants live in single cells; there is none of the community of spirits of the upper regions. The traveller is moved to pity. But even here he is able to question his fellow poets on obscure passages in their works.

Returning from hell, the visitor meets Adam and questions him on some verses in Arabic which he was said to have written. Adam, in friendly mood, replies that he did indeed speak Arabic in paradise, but this changed to Syriac when he was expelled on to earth, and he only relearnt Arabic on his return to heaven following his repentance. The verses, from their content, had been composed on earth; so, apparently having forgotten his Syriac, he is unable to help his earthly visitor.

Then, after being addressed by miraculous serpents in a magical garden, Ibn al-Qarih ascends to paradise itself; attended by the loveliest of houris, he finds the dwelling-place of the poets who wrote in an imperfect metre, before he is driven on in a magical carriage to a house of heavenliness which is to be his for eternity.

The Divine Comedy was written on a much larger scale than the work by al-Ma'ari; but there are similarities (notably with the episode of the two women) for a tentative hypothesis to be made that the *Risalat al-Ghufran* may have originated from one of the same poetical springs as Dante's great epic.

The intellectual partnership in medieval times between the Islamic and Christian worlds (one cannot say between East and West, since much of Islamic thought took place in Morocco and Andalusia) ended somewhat ingloriously in the person of Ramon Lull (1235–1315). Lull was above all determined to convert the Muslims and the Jews. As a result of his advocacy of conversion, chairs were created in oriental languages in the universities of Paris, Louvain and Salamanca. However, within his mind there laboured no spirit of disinterested enquiry. Lull devised a forbiddingly complex metaphysico-theological system to back up his claim to the right to convert non-Christians, forcibly if need be. (Descartes witheringly said of his system that it taught you to speak without judgement of things of which you are ignorant.[60]) It was an organic structure quite unlike the Averroistic system, where religion and philosophy were free to go their own ways. Here theology was firmly in control. Moreover – this is often overlooked in Lull by theorists who pronounce on the grandeur of his system – within his writings there were inky blots of hard and malevolent bigotry and hate, which no amount of detailed, admiring, semi-reverent explanation of his complex system can ignore. In his work *On the Interpretation of the Dreams of James II of Aragon,* Lull noted with distaste that all monarchs were attended by Jewish physicians, and even in monasteries the doctors were Jewish. This system was accursed, he said, and must be stamped out.[61] Jews, along with Muslims, had only one option: to be converted. Lull himself met his end while preaching to the Muslims of Tunis. Devoid of tolerance, disinterest and any sort of scientific Aristotelianism, devoted instead to a kind of paranoid and withdrawn techno-Kabbalism, his sense of virtue boosted by bouts of mind-sapping chanting, he showed none of the spirit of humility before knowledge which had led Europeans to reach out to the Islamic world for wisdom. Lull died a martyr's death, which almost appeared to have been willed.

❖❖❖

The impress of Islam on late medieval Europe was ambivalent. On the one hand, the universal faith-centred world of St Augustine had been broken up, as a demonstration and perhaps as an effect of the Averroistic spirit. The state now held the upper hand in political matters, not the bishops. By delimiting the areas of influence of the regnum, or secular power, from the sacerdotium, or priestly power, Averroism opened up a path to the Renaissance within the late-medieval world, although one should be wary of exaggerating the matter. Averroism, unlike Neoplatonism, was not humanistic or cultural. There are no Averroistic paintings or poems. In its utterances it remained scientific and philosophical. Most Renaissance thinkers soundly attacked Aristotelianism and scholasticism; led by their earliest representative, Petrarch, they opted rather for the imaginative power and mystery which they found in the Neoplatonic world view, and rejected the particular, piecemeal and proto-rationalist standpoint of Latin Averroism. The Academy in Florence had a pointedly Platonic echo in its name.

At a popular level, hankerings for the ever-marketable commodity of confrontation remained. In England, Muhammad (or 'Mahound' as he is frequently called) was seen as at best a schismatic; but a schismatic is too pale a thing to set oneself against. More frequently he was one of a trinity of false gods, the others being Apollo (or Apollyon, hence Bunyan's character in *The Pilgrim's Progress*) and Termagant. Both Termagant and Apollo appear to have been survivors from antiquity. Termagant may find her origin in the Old French *tervagant(e)*, in turn derived from the Italian *trivigante*, which may have meant 'wandering under three names', the names in question being those of Selene (the moon), Artemis and Persephone.[62]

The appearance of 'Mahound' as a member of a trinity gives us pause for thought. This is because the central aspect of Islam is the unity of God and the weakest aspect of Christian theology is belief in the Trinity. ('I do wish we did not have it,' as Archbishop Tillotson was to declare in 1694 of the Athanasian Creed.[63]) Muslims and Jews popularly held that Christians believed in three gods and were polytheistic. Hence for the Christians to propose a trinity as an integral part of Islamic belief can hardly fail to look like an example of Freudian transference: the off-loading of something embarrassing or difficult from oneself on to an adversary, who might be a person or a group. 'They have the problem: it's not ours.'

But sometimes, amidst the antagonism, a brilliant flash of truth appeared. Despite William of Malmesbury's claim that the Arabs' main mode of operation lay in performing 'divinations and incantations', and his willingness to believe exotic stories, his summary of the faith of Islam is exemplary, a pithy and accurate sentence done in ten Latin words. Having observed that the Wends and the Letts were the only pagans left in the world, he continues, 'for the Saracens and Turks worship God as Creator, holding that Mahomet is not God but his prophet'.[64] There could be no greater contrast to 'Mahound', or *The Song of Roland*, than this succinct summary.

Within medieval literature and music there is a large Islamic component. Thomas Warton was one of the first to recognise the impact of 'the Arabians' in his *History of English Poetry* (1774–81, with many reprints). Warton, who described the Arabians as 'this wonderful people',[65] emphasised and indeed exaggerated the part they played in restoring learning after the calamity of the barbarian invasions. He believed that Arab literature made its impress on that of Europe long before the Crusades: the Spanish, finding 'a brilliancy of description, a variety of imagery, and an exuberance of invention, hitherto unknown and unfamiliar to the cold and barren conceptions of a western climate, were eagerly caught up' and 'entirely neglected the study of the Latin language'. From Spain such literature spread into France and Italy.[66] In Warton's opinion the notion of courtly love derived from the Arabs: 'This passion they spiritualised into various metaphysical refinements, and filled it with abstracted notions of visionary perfection and felicity. Here too they were perhaps influenced by their neighbours the Saracens, whose philosophy chiefly consisted of fantastic abstractions.'[67] Warton's later editor, Richard Price, points out that the Grail legend of Parzifal almost certainly was (in part) of Arab origin. Wolfram had said that Master Kyot (or Guiot) first discovered a manuscript in Toledo, where its authorship was said to be one Flegetanis, whose father was a Saracen; this stimulated him to further study. (Flegetanis = *al-falak ath-thani*, 'the ruler of the second sphere'.) Eventually Kyot learnt of Titurel and Amfortas, of Herzelunde and Gamuret. Price concludes that the story was partly Arab and partly European. Most of the scene is laid in the East and the names are oriental. (Parzifal travels with Baruk – *mubarak*, 'blessed' – to Baldag, or Baghdad, the letter 'l' being interchangeable with 'gh'.) 'The Saracens are always spoken of with consideration; Christian knights unhesitatingly enrol themselves under the banner of the caliph; no trace of religious animosities is to be found between the followers of crescent and the cross; and the Arab appellations of the seven planets are distinctly enumerated'.[68]

Warton's views have been frequently contested. Opponents of the notion of the transmission of Arabic poetical forms to west European literature (such as metre and rhyme) have declared that literary texts cannot actually identify the path of transmission. But nevertheless there are strong similarities and coincidences between Arabic court poetry and Provençal poetry.[69]

One of the strangest literary echoes in English literature concerns Chaucer's 'parfit gentil knyghte'. In the poet's text he appears as a man of great humility and exquisite values. Yet the text makes it clear that he had participated in the sack of Alexandria in 1365, which was among the most savage episodes in the spectrum of the Crusades. How do we reconcile his virtuous manners and polished understated style with his participation in that act of extreme brutality? There seems to be no answer. Maybe, despite the things that we sense we hold in common today between ourselves and medieval people, there are areas of experience and of values which are completely alien to us. Elsewhere in *The Canterbury Tales* Chaucer gives evidence of the impress of Arab science and knowledge. 'The Squire's Tale' is a relative of the type of popular Islamic tale that was widely current: magical, flighty and fluttery, telling of birds and maidens and Indian kings, the sort of tale that a western European readership found irresistible, which reached its high point in Thomas Moore's *Lalla Rookh*, and was the forerunner of Christmas pantomime. In 'The Squire's Tale' there is a central place for a mirror, with the poet focusing his attention on the artefact, discussing 'the laws of light reflection' with reference to Aristotle and Alhazen (ibn al-Haytham), and demonstrating knowledge of the properties of light.

Chaucer's rougher poetic contemporary, William Langland, showed in *Piers the Plowman* that – like William of Malmesbury – he had a reasonable and unprejudiced grasp of the basic issue of Islamic theology, which is that Muslims worship one God, the same deity as the Christian God. Langland wrote, 'for the Saracens all pray to the same Almighty God, fully believing in him and asking his grace.' He held that 'Pharisees, Saracens, Scribes and Greeks' all believed in God the Father. It was, as he saw it, the job of Christians to advance them in a sequence towards belief 'in Jesus Christ, his only son', and thence on, until the Christian faith became clear to them. He did not realise that this path was not a way to belief but towards the main stumbling block between Christianity and Islam: that to followers of the latter the Trinity represented the division of the Godhead; it reeked of polytheism, and was therefore unacceptable at the deepest level of faith.[70]

Shadowy characterisations can be found which derived from a cruder, more street-level understanding of Islam and which haunted English literature of this time and later. In Chaucer's 'Sir Thopas' the giant Sir Olifaunt swore 'By Termagaunt', and two centuries later the pagan (or paynim) in Spenser's *The Faerie Queene* 'oftentimes by Turmagant and Mahound swore'. In the York Cycle of mystery plays, Pharaoh tells his followers to 'heave theeir hearts to Mahownde', and in the Chester plays, Herod threatens to destroy anyone who does not believe in 'sant mahowne, our god so sweet'. The writers of the cycles of English mystery plays assumed without question that idols of Mahomet were worshipped by his 'pagan' followers. According to one legend, the idols of Egypt fell down with the appearance of the infant Jesus; these, by the type of anachronism which is met in faith and belief, are called 'Mahomets' or 'maumets'. At the crucifixion one of the soldiers declares that not all Jesus's 'mawmentry' shall save him.[71]

Questionable theological writers found idols of Mahound in Spain and the Levant. Here Islam was interchangeable with idolatry, despite the fundamental Islamic opposition to images. The terminology of the late Middle Ages survived in Shakespeare. Hamlet remarks, 'I could have such a fellow whipped for o'er-doing Termagant,'[72] and Edgar in *King Lear* speaks of 'the foul fiend Mahu', that is, Mahound.[73]

Europeans also held to a strange myth that Muhammad's iron coffin remained suspended in the air between two mighty lodestones. This notion has never been current anywhere in the East and probably occurred following confusion with other stories. (A parallel legend tells how the tomb of St Thomas, the apostle to India, stood suspended between four giant magnets.) The notion of Muhammad's tomb was pervasive and is found well into Stuart times, in the famous text depicting the plight of King Charles I on the eve of his execution: *Εικων βασιλικη: The Pourtraicture of His Sacred Maiestie in his Solitudes and Sufferings* (1649). Here we read: 'For thus have they designed and proposed to me a new modelling of soveraignty and kingship . . . that the majesty of the kings of England might hereafter hang like Mahomet's tomb by a magnetique charm between the power and priviledges of the two Houses, in an aiery imagination of regality.'[74] The image is perhaps apt, but it is based on a dismal medieval legend.

If Muhammad's name was often a term of abuse, so too was the term 'Turk'. In polemical literature, the word denoted any Muslim who hailed from the Turkish empire, whether Arab, Albanian or Turk, and it became an all-purpose hostile epithet. In the religious diatribes of the late sixteenth and early seventeenth centuries, the adjective was part of the range of insult. An exiled English Catholic, William Rainolds, wrote a massive 1,000-page volume of theological dialogue bearing the title *Calvino-Turcismus, id est, Calvinisticae Perfidiae cum Mahumetana Collatio* (1597) (Calvin-Turkishness, or a comparison of Calvinistic perfidy with Mohammedanism). In it the author stated that Calvinism was rather worse than Islam; it also accused the Calvinists of adroitly using the threat posed by the Turkish armies for their own ends. A response by the Protestant Matthew Sutcliff was entitled *De Turco-Papismo, hoc est De Turcorum et Papistorum adversus Christi ecclesiam et fidem Conjuratione, eorumque in religione et moribus consensiene et similitudine* (1599) (On Turko-Papism, that is, on the conspiracy of the Turks and the Papists against the Church and faith of Christ, and on their harmony and similarity in religion and customs). Neither of these works makes any real point about Islam.[75]

In *Henry IV, Part I*, Falstaff places his own modest achievements in the field alongside those of 'Turk Gregory', who 'never did such deed in arms as I have done this day'.[76] Sir John was alluding, in a confused manner, to the conquering Pope Gregory VII, who had humiliated the emperor at Canossa. Another writer devised the pun 'Urban the second, the second Turban', to us a foolish jingle in view of Urban II's call to the Crusades in 1095, but again making sense at the time by casting both the pope and the Turk as 'the other', 'bad guys out there', virtually interchangeable, both constituting, to a controlling, semi-paranoid mind unwilling or unable to make distinctions or think in terms of particulars, an 'axis of evil'.[77]

The popular stereotyping was, like any crude anti-foreigner language, a pugnacious defence of popular self-esteem and an assertion of self-righteousness. It was often at variance with high policy. Rulers and governments in succeeding centuries found no difficulty in making alliances with 'infidel' powers. Francis I opened a 'second front' by allying himself with the Ottoman Empire while a prisoner of the emperor Charles V. English policy at the time of Queen Elizabeth I looked to the Turks for a quasi-alliance against Spain. Adventurers sought a trading and diplomatic relationship with Persia, at this time an implacable enemy of Ottoman Turkey. The prejudices of the past grew dim in the course of the active diplomacy of the sixteenth century.

Occasionally, too, in secret intellectual conclaves the trappings of prejudice were abandoned. A serious study of differing religious faiths, made in a comparative context, is to be found in Jean Bodin's *Colloquium Heptaplomeres* (Symposium of the seven wise men on the secrets of the sublime) of 1593, which lay unpublished until 1841 and was not given a full translation in a critical edition until modern times. Here the disputants are Catholic, Lutheran, Calvinist, Jewish, Muslim, natural – that is, undogmatic – theist and sceptical classicist. The text has one foot planted in medieval times, since it takes seriously magic and devils. It also shows unshakeable deference to biblical texts and sees classical philosophy as words rather than methods, nuggets rather than arguments. To a modern mind there is considerably more strangeness in Bodin's *Colloquium* than in Plato's *Republic*. But at the same time the equality of spirit shown in the utterances of the different believers, and the good-naturedness of their disagreements, are remarkable and forward-looking.

In the present context the opinions and beliefs of the Muslim Octavius are of special interest. He is presumably given that name rather than, say, al-Mansur or Abdur-Rahman, so that Bodin cannot be accused of giving voice to the other side. Octavius had been captured by pirates off Sicily and bought as a slave by a Syrian merchant, from whom he learnt Arabic. In Syria he read a book written by a converted Dominican which led him to Islam and to his freedom.[78] Octavius is deeply impressed by the monotheistic beliefs and social conscience of Muslims; they are furthest of all from idolatry, he declares, worshipping one eternal God in a pure spirit, and they also show great generosity to the poor and needy. To strangers they offer 'exquisite dishes, baths and beds' and ask for nothing in return, but rather they themselves give thanks with the words, 'May it be granted to my soul that God loves you.'[79] Octavius also points out the closeness of Islam to Judaism and to natural theism (the belief that God and godliness manifest themselves naturally, without scriptures or revelation). He indicates that Muhammad won over Jews and various Christian communities, by declaring that Christ was not God. Arian Christianity – that is, the faith without a belief in the Athanasian Trinity – is, Octavius holds, the foundation of Islam.[80] And Arianism had been confirmed by eight church councils. He quotes from suras of the Koran on the elevated position of Jesus within Islam.

Bodin grants his Muslim debater considerable freedom. He allows him no combative legends or negative characterisations about 'imposture'. The spirit is of an open-minded eagerness to learn and discuss. This seems to have derived from Bodin's own position, which was closest to that of the undogmatical natural theist Toralba, who would have held that any religion can be classed as right religion, so long as it was performed with uprightness and a search for good.

Such opinions were not yet held by more than a small minority, and if they were held at all, it was in secret. But they were reflected in an oblique way by diplomatists and statesmen. The masses might be told that nothing had changed and assertions of loyalty and devotion to faith were made by rulers, but these affirmations were '*circenses*', circus acts designed to maintain social equilibrium while the leaders occupied themselves with global diplomacy and matters of trade owing less to devout belief than to the interests of empire, state or dynasty. In public affairs, in war and diplomacy, religious affiliation played one part among several. It also sold a deal to the masses. But it could also be overridden.

CHAPTER FOUR

'Almost Continuall Warres'

fter Nicopolis, Sultan Bayazid had been left master of western Asia
and eastern Europe. In a mood of masterful confidence, he
asserted to the prisoners able to raise the ransom for freedom,
such as the *comte* de Nevers, that he was not expecting them to give him
any oath as an expression of peace. He expected them to raise an army
against him and he looked forward to the continuation of the war. But
the crusading survivors could do no more than limp home. The Sultan
went on to conquer Greece, the birthplace of wisdom, which became
territory disputed between Venice and Turkey, awaiting a distant Hellenic
revival. Only Byzantium remained unconquered.

Despite the controlling mastery of the Ottoman ruler, his fortune was to
undergo a swift and total reversal. His empire came close to the point of
crashing to nothing. From a position of commanding the life or death of
thousands at the flick of a whip, the victor of Nicopolis was compelled to
follow the army of a conqueror and was ousted from his palace at Bursa to
endure the painful rigours of an alien baggage-train. Bayazid's conqueror
was not a Christian sovereign. In an event that foreshadowed a serious
future conflict, the effective antagonist of Turkey came from the east.

Almost two centuries earlier, in 1220, the Mongol army of Chingis
Khan – the name means 'universal ruler' – had moved westward from the
treeless, grassy slopes of its original home south of Lake Baikal, swept by
incessant winds, and had occupied the region of Samarkand and Bukhara
(in present-day Uzbekistan). Within a few years this army had
overwhelmed Persia. 'Not one thousandth of the population escaped,'
according to a contemporary chronicle.[1] The speed, violence and vast
distances covered by the Mongols seemed like divine judgement and
Europe quaked in anxiety of their arrival. It was some years before they
were domesticated into a brief tactical alliance with the crusaders in
Palestine. Matthew Paris records that in 1238 'the people of Gothland

and Friesland did not dare to come to Yarmouth for the herring fishery'.[2] (As a result herrings became extraordinarily cheap in England.) In April 1241 a Mongol army destroyed a combined force of Germans, Austrians, Hungarians and Poles at Liegnitz (modern Legnica, Poland). Later that year the Great Khan Ogodei died, and the dynastic dispute that ensued in the Mongol capital of Karakorum saved Europe from further destruction.[3] But the Islamic east was still prey to the Mongols. European visitors to the Great Khan, apparently repressing memories of the encounter at Liegnitz, noted his protection of Christians, though they sensed that the support he offered to differing faiths arose 'from an indiscriminate superstition rather than a special predilection'.[4] In terms of military hunger the Islamic states were physically closer than Europe to the Mongol base and therefore more easily destroyed. In the thirteenth century, Islamic Asia, rather than Europe, absorbed the ferocity of the Mongols.

But, indicating the unpredictability of human affairs, the Mongols, under Ghazan Khan, converted to Islam around the year 1300. Their destructive fury was curbed by the new faith, though not ended. Since they continued to attack the Mamluks of Egypt, and despite the confrontation at Liegnitz, they were seen as potential Christians. Edward I accredited Geoffrey de Langley, with two esquires, to the Persian court of the Islamic Mongols. Travelling via Genoa, Trebizond and Tabriz, this English delegation presented gifts of silver plate, fur garments and carpets, and returned home with a leopard in a cage.[5]

Ghazan Khan was a systematic, cultured and, for the most part, wise governor, although he ordered the destruction of all non-Muslim religious buildings in his capital Qazvin. But the most powerful image of the later Mongols was conveyed by a distant cousin. From about 1380 the conquering violence of Tamerlane – Timur ('iron') the Lame – spread like a tempest of fire through Asia. Here was a conqueror who believed not in calm government but in devastation and in pyramids of skulls. Persia, the Caucasus, India, Iraq and Anatolia were wrecked in a manner hitherto unseen in the annals of those lands. In 1402 he faced the Ottoman sultan Bayazid in battle (the same who had humbled the crusaders at Nicopolis and welcomed the militant hatred of his enemies), now, six years later, grown fat and indolent and with his personal life dominated by an overwhelming desire for gold.

Battle was joined at Angora, which as Ancyra had witnessed Pompey's final defeat of Mithradates in 63 BC. Tamerlane, with forces numerically far superior, 'with much adoe obtained the victorie'.[6] Ottoman Turkey appeared finished, a once-powerful dynasty shattered to the ground like Shelley's Ozymandias. Richard Knolles' description, written as the Elizabethan age darkened into the Jacobean, glimmers with a haunted half-light, though the sombre language is not always accurate in matters of fact:

Behold Baiazet the terrour of the world, and as he thought superior to fortune, in an instant with his state in one battaile overthrowne into the bottome of miserie and dispaire: and that at such time as he thought least, even in the middest of his greatest strength. It was three daies (as they report) before he could be pacified, but as a desperat man, still seeking after death, & calling for it: neither did Tamerlane after he had once spoken with him, at all afterwards courteously use him, but as of a proud man caused small account to be made of him. And to manifest that he knew how to punish the haughtie, made him to be shackled in fetters and chaines of gold, and so to bee shut up in an yron cage made like a grate, in such sort, as that he might on everie side be seene; and so caried him up and downe as he passed through Asia, to be of his owne people scorned and derided. And to his farther disgrace, upon festivall daies used him for a footstoole to tread upon, when he mounted to horse; and at other times scornefully fed him like a dogge with crums fallen from his table. A rare example of the uncertaintie of worldly honour, that he unto whose ambitious mind Asia and Europe, two great parts of the world, were too little, should now be caried up and down cooped up in a little yron cage, like some perilous wild beast. All of which Tamerlane did, not so much for the hatred to the man, as to manifest the just judgement of God against the arrogant folly of the proud. It is reported, that Tamerlane being requested by one of his noble men that might bee bold to speake unto him, to remit some part of his severitie against the person of so great a prince; answered, That he did not use that rigour against him as a king, but rather to punish him as a proud ambitious tyrant, polluted with the blood of his owne brother.[7]

The Mongol warrior was now master of all of Asia Minor, including the Aegean seaboard with its established trading stations. He wrote to Henry IV of England offering him the chance to trade freely at his ports. In reply the English monarch, communicating through the good offices of an English-born Minorite or Friar Preacher, John Greenlaw, known as 'Archbishop John' of Tabriz, congratulated Timur on the victory. Both parties would continue to trade. Bayazid's defeat was 'a great source of consolation and joy to us'.[8] England continued to believe in some sort of an alliance with the Mongols, no doubt reckoning that the potentate who had dethroned the victor of Nicopolis might be an ally. Tamerlane was also closely observed by Henry III of Castile, one of those strange and perceptive monarchs who emerge unaccountably with the vision of a modern-day international statesman, when so often the focus is narrow and parochial. Ruy Gonzalez de Clavijo was despatched from Toledo to Timur's court in 1403. Before travelling on to Samarkand, he and his party went to Khoi in north-west Persia, where they met ambassadors from Egypt, whose gifts for Timur included a giraffe.

Tamerlane's rule over Asia Minor collapsed within half a century; his victory at Angora, like its near contemporary, Henry V's victory at Agincourt, had no lasting significance. The Ottoman Empire reconstituted its collapsed body-mass and, following its victory at Varna in 1444, went on to extinguish the allotment-sized remnant of the Byzantine Empire, whose emperor, despite derisive comments on the 'decadence' of Byzantium offered by some writers, died fighting bravely on the battlements alongside his men, his body in its last state indistinguishable from that of any Greek soldier who died in defence of the homeland on the fateful day of 29 May 1453.

Even in the aftermath of the Ottoman seizure of Constantinople diplomatic moves were afoot to destabilise or even crush the Turks' empire. Uzun Hasan, 'long' or 'tall' Hasan, whose name Marlowe recalled and converted into Usumcasane, was shah of the Akkoyunlu, or White Sheep Turkomans, and effective ruler of much of Persia. In the opinion of the Venetian prince Caterino Zeno, he was a pleasant gentleman who always drank wine with his meals and was fond of amusing himself in a homely manner, but who could be dangerous when too far gone in his cups. He had married Kyra Katerina, a Christian lady from Trebizond, the Pontic realm which was to outlast Byzantium. She was known as Despina, a feminine version of 'despot' usually rendered 'mistress', and a name which might indicate that her presence was more than merely diplomatic or decorative. From his capital at Diyarbekir he despatched a diplomatic mission to Venice in the hope of winning an alliance in support of the emir of Karamania, the region south of Konya, against the Ottoman Turks. Venice was deeply anti-Ottoman at this time, since, following the Ottoman conquest of Constantinople, it had lost its Black Sea trade. Karamanian loyalities wavered between Turkey and Persia, inclining to the Ottomans. The Doge and his councillors sought to bend them towards the east and, in a diplomatic démarche, dispatched two high-ranking representatives to Diyarbekir. An experienced Venetian consular agent procured weapons for Uzun Hasan.[9]

When hostilities reopened in Karamania in 1472, a joint assault by the Turkoman shah and the Venetian navy was launched against the Ottoman Turkish positions in the region. The assault was unsuccessful – Ottoman artillery won the day – but diplomatic relations were strengthened between Venice and Uzun Hasan. In retrospect, little could have been achieved by the pact; the distances were too great and the world outlooks were probably too different. But the engagement reduced Ottoman pressure on Europe, which was feeling severely tested at this time. A number of European courts (including that of Pope Calixtus III) sent embassies to the White Sheep Turkomans in the aftermath of Uzun Hasan's defeat, in vain – for he died shortly after and Venice made peace with the Ottoman Empire. In cultural terms, the contacts between the Most Serene Republic and the White Sheep Turkomans led to the establishment of a colony of Persian metalworkers in a district of Venice, from where their highly finished work spread further into Europe, initially to Nuremberg and Augsburg, and later to England, where the intricate work of Elizabethan goldsmiths displays the influence of Persian craftsmanship.[10] Both Turkoman confederations were swept away by the dynamic Safavids, the founders of early modern Iran, who became the only serious opponents of the Ottomans at the time that the latter were winning copious victories in Europe.

Persia in its modern guise, the state whose lineal descent can be traced to the post-1979 Islamic Republic, was created in the early sixteenth century by Shah Ismail of the Safawi family. ('Safawi' is the adjective of Safi, the name of an ancestor of the dynasty. The term 'Safavid' Persia derives from this name, as does the Elizabethan–Jacobean English word 'Sophy', meaning shah.) Ismail made Shia (correctly 'Shii') Islam the state religion, reflecting a long-held devotion of the Persians for the partisans of Ali. Fired by the passion of religious rivalry, Shia against Sunni, with the battle of Kerbela actively present in their minds, they took up arms against the Sunni Turks, in the manner of the Protestant and Catholic armies which half a century later would tear Europe apart.

In 1502 Ismail defeated the White Sheep Turkomans, who were Sunnite, and from his first capital of Tabriz set about forging a Persian state based on Shiite Islam. Shiism became the defining feature of the state and, apart from during the reign of Nadir Shah, has been the central element in Persia/Iran's continuity ever since.[11]

By proclaiming Shiism as a national religion, Persia under Ismail became a political rather than a geographical entity.[12] As a regional Shiite power, Persia became embroiled in almost constant war throughout the sixteenth and early seventeenth centuries against two neighbouring Sunni Muslim powers: the Uzbeks to the north-east, with their capital at Bukhara, and the Ottoman Turks to the west. On one occasion the Crimean Tatars (who were also Sunni Muslims) joined an alliance against Shiite Persia.

The mutual antagonism between Turk and Persian was known and understood in Elizabethan England. A book on the struggle by the Italian Giovanni Tommaso Minadoi had been translated by Abraham Hartwell the Younger and had appeared in 1595 with the title *The History of the Warres between the Persians and the Turkes*. Minadoi knew about Shiism and compared Persian soldiers favourably to those of the Turks. The hostilities were summed up as 'A warre not onely long & bloudie, but also very commodious and of great oportunitie to the Christian Common-wealth: for that it hath granted leisure to the Champions of Christ to refresh and encrease their forces, being now much weakened by warres both Forreine and Civill'.[13] The significance of the Turko-Persian war for Europe was also noted by the Flemish diplomat and scholar Ogier de Busbecq, whose *Four Epistles* (of 1554–62) constitute a vivid commentary on the Ottoman Empire. In his 'Second Epistle' he remarked, ''Tis only the Persian stands between us and ruin. The Turks would fain be upon us, but he keeps him back; his war with him affords us only a respit, not a deliverance: When he once makes peace with him he will bring all the power of the east upon us, and how ready we are to receive him, I am afraid to speak.'[14] The same struggle was also noted in a work by George Abbot, later archbishop of Canterbury, in *A Briefe Description of the Whole World* of 1599: 'As Papistes and Protestants doe differ in opinion, concerning the same Christ: so doe the Turkes and Persians about their Mahomet: the one pursuing the other as hereticks with most deadly hatred. Insomuch, that there be in this respect, almost continuall warres betweene the Turkes, and the Persians.'[15] The struggle finds echoes in Shakespeare and Milton. In

The Merchant of Venice, we learn that the Prince of Morocco, Portia's suitor and a Sunni Muslim, had taken part in the campaigns. He proffers a scimitar

> That slew the Sophy, and a Persian Prince
> That won three fields of Sultan Solyman.[16]

Milton, describing Satan's flight down into hell in Book X of *Paradise Lost*, also alludes to the Turko-Persian wars:

> As when the Tartar from his Russian foe
> By Astracan over the snowy plains
> Retires, or Bactrian Sophi from the horns
> Of Turkish crescent, leaves all waste beyond
> The realm of Aladule, in his retreat
> To Tauris or Casbeen . . .[17]

'Aladule' was Ala al-Dawla Dhu'l-Qadar of Erzindjan; the name may be romantically mysterious, but in the context of the history of Anatolia, the person was more hard-edged. A Turkoman, he was supported by the Egyptian Mamluks and was an unceasing opponent of the rulers of both Persia and Turkey.

Shah Ismail, in his first outburst of revolutionary energy, seized cities as far west as Diyarbekir and Baghdad. The Ottoman sultan, Bayazid II, still under pressure from Europe, was compelled to sue for peace. From a base at Gilan on the Caspian, Shah Ismail's conquests ranged far over Persia and the Caucasus. He campaigned into Khorasan and stalled the Uzbeks.[18] Manifesting a deep antipathy to his Ottoman neighbour, whose Sunni Islam was unacceptable to his newborn Shia state, he sought allies further west and sent envoys to Egypt and Hungary. This political and military confidence was provocative to Ottoman Turkey. Ismail's acts were an outrage to Bayazid's son Selim (Yavuz – 'the Grim'), who arranged for the murder of his own father and then had himself proclaimed sultan. His first act was to campaign against Shiism within the Ottoman state, massacring or imprisoning 40,000 Shiites in Anatolia. Here Shiism was the predominant faith, and Selim saw its adherents as domestic potential sympathisers with the enemy. He was now set to confront Ismail on the battlefield.[19] After he dispatched a diplomatic note to the Shah couched in an aggressive bombastic style, Ismail wrote back to him declaring that he did not seek war and suggesting that Selim's letter might have been composed under the influence of opium. He sent the royal secretary a box of dope to bring peace and joy. Selim indeed habitually smoked a pipe impregnated with the sublime infusion, but the gift was unwise. The Ottoman Sunni religious authorities (the *ulema*) added weight by declaring that it was a religious duty to kill Ismail. The two armies met in August 1514 at Chaldiran, where the Turks won a decisive victory. The Persians were comprehensively outgunned and Sultan Selim entered Tabriz in triumph. Ismail, alive but injured, was compelled to retire from Tabriz to Qazvin.

Selim the Grim went on to crush Syria and Egypt in 1517, and created the effective fortress state which terrified most of Europe for more than a century and a half: 'the present terrour of the world' in Richard Knolles' memorable phrase.

When the new generation of rulers emerged in both Turkey and Persia, each proved to be as stubborn and warlike as his predecessor. Ismail was succeeded by his son Tahmasp (Milton's 'Bactrian Sophy', and known as 'Shaw Thomas' in English historical documents); and Suleyman the Magnificent is justly known as the conqueror who besieged Vienna and destroyed Hungary as Bayazid had crushed Serbia. Neither sultan nor shah was remotely conciliatory. Within the Ottoman Empire, warfare became the prime profession and the state became to a great extent an instrument for war. Until modern times the Turks saw themselves as the '*ordu millet*', the army community, the people defined by warfare. In the early twentieth century Sir Charles Eliot wrote, 'The Turkish army is not so much a profession, or an institution necessitated by the fears and aims of the government, as the active but still quite normal state of the Turkish nation.'[20]

Tahmasp, resolving to challenge the outcome of Chaldiran, entered into a renewed diplomatic correspondence with Europe, proposing a series of alliances with the Holy Roman Emperor and the King of Hungary. Shah Ismail wrote to Emperor Charles V in 1523. Why are the Christian powers not combining against the Turk, but fighting among themselves? he asked. He urged Charles to mobilise and attack the common foe.[21] He dared the Sultan to attack, by reoccupying Tabriz. Suleyman, having concluded conquests in Belgrade, Tunis and Rhodes, hastened east with his army to campaign through the hard Kurdish winter, in order to crush his Persian opponent. Tabriz was taken, and Baghdad too, although no borders were conclusively fixed. A further round of hostilities in 1548 also failed to produce a definitive settlement, although the Armenian fortress-city of Van was incorporated into the Ottoman Empire. Peace of a kind was declared in 1555 between the two Islamic powers, initiating a truce that lasted for the best part of thirty years.[22]

Perhaps at this moment the modern world of 'Europe and the Middle East' began. But it was an unfamiliar modernity: not that of western Asia entirely represented by the Turkish empire, vanishing eastwards out of sight into a kind of nebulous oriental mirage, chanting a pilgrim song into Central Asia. The realm of the Turks was circumscribed to the east by Safavid Persia. The Ottoman Empire was finite, a creature of warfare, diplomacy and commerce which was beginning to interact with Europe, and which was far from being a dreamworld of images, a Platonic form of 'the other', an unbounded eastern space, the limitless manifestation of an infinite faith.

Within a decade England was active in the area. Anthony Jenkinson was perhaps best described as a kind of mercenary, or freebooter, diplomat. In 1559 he was employed by Tsar Ivan the Terrible as his representative in Bukhara, the Uzbek capital. (Today we might say that he operated the trading and diplomatic franchise offered by the tsar.) Two years later he headed a mission to Persia, acting on behalf of both England and Russia, opening up trade in Shirvan and Baku (today in Azerbaijan) and finding his way to the Persian capital.[23] He returned to Moscow laden with silks, dyed kelims and precious stones for both the tsar and the English Muscovy Company. The northern route to Persia did not last, either for the purposes of exploration or enterprise, since the storms and the pirates on the Caspian Sea made commerce impossible. Trade languished, depleted and seemingly doomed. But in a flash the flexible energy of commercial enterprise reinvigorated the region. The western route into Iran was suddenly and brilliantly opened up. The mood shifted, the colour changed and the Safavid dynasty of Persia, emerging from 100 years of war into a new era of peace and splendour, established a state with authority, power and the indefinable quality of majesty, paralleling that which was so finely projected in Elizabethan England. In Persia, Englishmen would play an original and compelling part.

Persian culture and trade drew diplomats, traders and adventurers, but the expanding web of European alliances and hostilities meant that England gravitated not to the stately pavilioned splendour of Persia but to the geographically closer Ottoman Empire. To Queen Elizabeth I and her court, with the issue of the security of the state uppermost, Ottoman Turkey, with its control of half the Mediterranean, was of greater importance than Persia with its silks and brocades. In the uncertain years immediately preceding the Spanish Armada, England stepped out in a cool saraband, seeking a chaste partnership with Ottoman Turkey. The moment seemed right to engage the Orient in the restrained dance of nations.

CHAPTER FIVE

'The Magnificence of the Queen his Mistress'

O n 14 November 1582 the tall ship *Susan of London* 'departed from Blackewall, bound for the Citie of Constantinople'. Bad weather detained her for a couple of months around England's southern coastline. In January she docked at Cowes on the Isle of Wight, where she took on board William Harborne, son of William Harebrowne, of Great Yarmouth, Norfolk. A stern Calvinist, Harborne was making his second journey to the Ottoman capital, where he was destined to become Queen Elizabeth I's first ambassador to the sultan's court.[1]

England was then approaching the peak of her Elizabethan glory, resplendent in culture, increasingly convinced of her role as an elect nation, the champion of Protestantism and an unwavering opponent of Roman Catholicism. Her ministers maintained a rigorous spy system directed against adherents of that faith, holding them to be agents of foreign power. England's struggle with Spain was soon destined to reach its climax.

Ottoman Turkey for its part was past the noonday of imperial glory. The sun of victory was now in decline. Although there were still conquests to be won, the era of the great triumphs of Selim the Grim and Suleyman the Magnificent was over, and the Ottomans were beginning to taste defeat. The offspring of the sultans were being drafted into the court rather than the army. The conflict with Shiite Persia dragged on, despite episodes of peace.

William Harborne had made an earlier visit to the Ottoman capital in 1578. He had gone as a businessman, employed by Sir Edward Osborne, a leading London merchant, who in the previous decade had been seeking ways of expanding trade with the East. England's trade with the

Levant, briefly flowering in the years 1510–34 (largely owing to the enterprise of the Gonson family) had declined in the mid-century, and France had taken a position of primacy in the region owing to her tacit alliance with Ottoman Turkey. The French alliance with the Muslim power originated with the bitter struggle between Emperor Charles V and Francis I concerning authority and independence. In February 1525 Francis had been defeated at Pavia by the emperor, and held prisoner in Spain. In great secrecy the imprisoned monarch had sent envoys to the Ottoman sultan, imploring the Islamic emperor's confidential assistance. A ruby ring, manifestly of royal French provenance, was spied on the finger of the Ottoman grand vizier. Secret messages begged the Sultan to help free the French king from his Madrid jail and attack Charles V. Suleyman was equivocal in response, but a diplomatic process was set in motion, signalling an end to the politics of confrontation.[2]

On his release Francis I negotiated extraterritorial privileges (or 'capitulations', each of which was listed under a different heading or *capitula*) with the Ottoman Empire in 1536, and invited the Ottoman fleet to base itself at Toulon five years later. These agreements were negotiated between equals and were in no way humiliating for the Muslim empire. A pact, rather than an alliance, grew between the two parties, in which both ignored the dictates of religion. The 'most Christian king' pioneered the commonsense way to international relations, discarding the notion of the 'infidel'. By doing so the French monarch was reconnecting his country with the type of policy embodied in the ambassadorial link established between Charlemagne and Harun al-Rashid, and abandoning the grandiose and ill-conceived policy of the Crusades. The enterprising, practical England of Elizabethan diplomacy could not remain sidelined by this project, and indeed the progressive mood is echoed in the poetry of the time; no Elizabethan poet refers to 'the infidel'.

In some ways Protestantism had an ambiguous relationship with Islam, and this became a further element in England's non-committal attitude towards the Ottoman Empire. Ecclesiastical reformers had sometimes seen Islam, and the advance of the Turkish army, as either a standard by which to measure Christianity or a metaphor for the judgement of God, and sometimes as the exercise of God's judgement itself. 'We western Mahomets,' John Wyclif had bewailed as early as 1380, as his heart turned over the corruption within the Church.[3] Here Islam was seen as successful, courtly, rich and luxurious, while Christianity needed to be a religion of poverty and adversity. Let the prelates, he declared, continue to be 'Muslims'. We, the faithful, will be poor and suffering Christians. Luther's attitude to Islam was open, undogmatic and changeable. On the one hand in 1517 he wrote that it was wrong to fight the Turk, since to do so amounted to challenging God's judgement upon men's sins. But at the time of the siege of Vienna of 1529 he was fully in favour of fighting the Turkish forces. Whence the difference? Almost certainly because latterly the Turkish army was in the German heartland, whereas twelve years earlier it had been occupied with Persia.[4] Even then the Protestant notion that the Turkish army was God's instrument had not finally gone away. Much later, in 1683, at the time of the final Ottoman siege of Vienna, Nathaniel Mather wrote to his brother in New England that it was rumoured that before the winter the Turk would be in Rome, 'the executioner of God's vengeance'.[5] Protestant ambiguity concerning Islam was to be useful for Queen Elizabeth in making overtures to the Turkish empire.

At the same time there were half-hidden currents of thought. In the first place, probably all the Protestant reformers knew, or knew about, Marsiglio of Padua's *Defensor Pacis*, the pared-down, un-Platonic text which manifests a strong vein of Latin Averroism and thereby owes a debt to the Andalusian Islamic philosopher.[6] In the second place, despite the advances of the Turks into Europe, the Christian humanists who were to pioneer the post-Calvin generation were unafraid to name the main Islamic capital city as a place where different religions could coexist.

Traditional Christian theology was facing some very radical questions at this time; indeed there was one issue in relation to which Catholicism and Calvinism united in a spirit of sacred intelligence which led to ecclesiastical murder. The notion of the Holy Trinity, three persons in one God, came under scrutiny in Europe in the sixteenth century; and it was not hard to discern a mood in favour of the unitary concept of God which characterised Islam. In 1553 Michael Servetus (Miguel Serveto y Reves), a brilliant Spanish scholar and physician who had lucidly and cogently disavowed the accepted notion of the Trinity, was burnt at the stake in Geneva in circumstances of particular cruelty after, first, legal process in Catholic Lyon, and then in a grotesque heresy trial instigated by Calvin. Servetus, who read the Bible in the original languages and also published the first account of the pulmonary circulation of the blood, declared that the Trinity was not scriptural. In doing so his spiritual thoughts seem in part to have been drawn back to the glories of Islamic Spain, as he envisaged that some sort of unity – or perhaps community – with the Muslims and Jews of his country of birth, who had not finally been expelled, could be achieved by a Christian disavowal of Trinitarian beliefs.[7] He attacked the forbidding scholastic jargon that the Christians had adopted to bolster the structure of their beliefs. None of it was scriptural – trinity, hypostasis, person, essence, substance. Servetus sought to do away with harsh technicalities in favour of a more personal faith, and in doing so he found, while professing a deep devotion to Jesus, a similarity between his view of the Deity and that of the Jews and Muslims; and he noted 'how much the tradition of the Trinity has been a laughing-stock to the Muslims'. He advised his readers to 'hear what Muhammad says, for more reliance is to be given to one truth which an enemy confesses than to a hundred lies on our own side: Christ is the greatest of prophets, the spirit of God, the power of God'.[8]

Servetus' death at the hands of the Genevans gave a profound shock to the more humane of the reformers. In Basle in 1554, a small book was printed, with the spurious imprint of Magdeburg. One of the authors disguised himself as Martinus Bellius; his real name was Sebastian Castellio. The book, written in response to that dreadful death, was entitled *Concerning heretics, and whether they should be persecuted*. The argument was made that within Christian societies there might just be a case for toleration rather than killing. The text was one of the earliest pleas against devout rigour within Europe. What is interesting in this context is that one of the cases explicitly quoted by the authors of the book was that of the situation in Islamic lands: 'There are in Constantinople Turks, there are Christians, there are also Jews, three nations very different from each other in religion, which however live peaceably amongst each other.'[9] A notion within Islam, it seemed, had something to teach Europe of this date. The *dhimmi* structure of Islam (the word means approximately 'covenanted'), which allowed the different communities of Muslims, Jews and Christians to coexist, might be relevant to religious differences in Europe, where, except on the individual whim of a ruler or a magnate, toleration and coexistence were not yet possible. Toleration was alien to Christian society; it was part of the structure of Islam. Within the Koran itself one finds the statement 'Let there be no compulsion in religion,' although this is one which has infrequently been adhered to.[10]

Opponents of the Trinity were being found elsewhere. In 1569 a group of dissident Lutherans from Heidelberg, led by Pastor Adam Neuser, declared that they disbelieved in the Trinity and put themselves under the protection of Sultan Selim II of Turkey. Sentenced to banishment, Neuser (who was not a heroic figure) eventually landed up in Transylvania, where he converted to Islam.[11]

A more lasting challenge to Trinitarian orthodoxy is traditionally believed to have originated in Italy around the year 1546. A group of learned citizens is said to have met in Vicenza, which was under the sovereignty of Venice, determined to sift truth from falsehood within the Christian religion. They sensed a new mood of rationality and criticism in which the Trinity as proposed in the Athanasian Creed had to go, since it was based on devout faith which had abandoned reason, whereas reason was, they held, a gift of God. (The Athanasian Creed is a misnomer. The Creed is a pious fraud, being in reality a Latin hymn, composed at least a century after the death of Athanasius, whose language was not Latin.) Christianity had, they believed, become encumbered in the early centuries AD with Neoplatonic ideas devoid of sense (such as the wordy outpourings of Pseudo-Dionysius the Areopagite of c. 500, who wrote an influential antirational defence of faith). The reforming Italians sought to strip the faith of the accretions and try to reformulate essential beliefs according to the gospels. Their meeting of minds created a firm foundation, and the group's spiritual descendants, the Unitarians, can be found throughout the world today. Their first leader was Lelio Sozini, or Sozzini, a native of Siena from a distinguished legal family, whose name was Latinised into Laelius Socinus. He and his colleagues resolved to break with 'the idolatry of Rome'. In welcoming reason as a partner to theology, they declared that Jesus was not a person of the Godhead, but had been an ordinary individual specially chosen by God. They denied the Incarnation and saw the Crucifixion as a dreadful and cruel death, but one which only had meaning by evoking compassion in human hearts. They rejected the doctrine of the atonement. Jesus had been sent by God to show people how to live, not to perform an archaic brutal self-sacrifice to appease a jealous god. They held that this latter view was ethically inadequate. Some Socinians held that prayers should be addressed to God alone, and not to Jesus.[12]

These beliefs, which bore a resemblance to the Islamic view of Jesus (although differing views were expressed on his actual status), put them at serious risk from the Inquisition. Some found a home in the liberal intellectual city of Basle, with its fine and brave printing press run by Oporinus (Herbst). Others headed for the Ottoman Empire, ending up in Damascus. A group went to Transylvania, then under the suzerainty of the Ottoman Empire, where toleration was in the process of being secured by law. John Sigismund (Zapolya) of Transylvania, king from 1540 to 1571, was converted to Unitarianism by the preacher Francis (or Ferenc) David, thereby becoming the first and only Unitarian monarch in history. Ferdinand, the Habsburg emperor, sought to crush Transylvania's independence and impose monolithic Catholicism; but the power of the Ottoman army kept him at bay. As an infant in arms John Sigismund had been dandled on the lap of Suleyman the Magnificent. In 1568 the King of Transylvania declared the city of Kolozsvar (Clausenburg or Cluj) to be an entirely Unitarian city.[13]

In passing, one might wonder why the question of the Trinity, dormant for well over a millennium, should suddenly re-emerge as a theological issue in the sixteenth century. Was it part of a plot to undermine the entire Christian Church by robbing it of its most talismanic (if obscure) belief? Was Europe being prepared for an Islamic conquest? These are lively speculations but the truth is probably more simple. Erasmus had been the pioneer of reform and, though he had remained Catholic and Trinitarian, he rejected the 'Trinitarian proof-text', I John 5: 7, as inauthentic. This verse exists in the English Authorised Version, but has been excised from the Revised Version. The word 'Trinity' occurs nowhere in the Bible. It therefore became hard for Erasmus's successors, no longer bound to the authority of Rome, to be Trinitarians, since they were thereby compelled to believe in, and show devotion to, something that lay outside their unique text. This looked like idolatry. Theologians of the reform such as Calvin and Beza, who by contrast accepted Trinitarianism and demanded devotion to the holy three, had taken a questionable leap of faith.

In terms of education and publication, the most important group of anti-Trinitarians was that which, led by Laelius Socinus' nephew Faustus, went first to tolerant Basle (where he met Sebastian Castellio) and then to Poland, at the time the most tolerant Christian country of west or central Europe. Here a remarkable idealistic community of radical, equal and rational Christians became established, where humanity and intellectuality flourished together in a peaceful cooperative society rarely seen in the annals of humankind. Students of all denominations flocked to the Socinian academy at Rakow, which at its greatest extent had 1,000 pupils. (It became known as the 'Sarmatian Athens', a testament to its achievement, which most Poles today, unwilling to share in the fame of a non-Catholic past, carefully avoid.) The community's subsequent history and the Socinian view of Islam relate more to the theological and scientific ferment of the seventeenth century; but here it suffices to recall that serious men were not only questioning the Trinity, a most important issue of Christian theology, they were bringing reason to issues of Christian theology and discovering toleration of those with views other than their own.

The success of Socinus and his followers in creating an anti-Trinitarian tradition was due to their dedicated leadership and to the precepts of the founders, in which reason and progressive moral commitment figured largely. In some respects their teachings resembled the kind of unitarianism preached by Muhammad, with one important difference: the followers of Socinus took the Bible, especially the New Testament, to be literally true. They were intense Biblicalists. Their founder was emphatic in spelling out the Socinians' differences with the Muslims. Jesus's saying in John's gospel (20: 17), 'I ascend unto my Father, and your Father, to my God and to your God,' was quite unacceptable to a Muslim, yet fully believed by Socinus and his followers.[14] At the same time it was undeniable that the clear-headed, mystery-free view of the gospel held by the Socinians, and their emphatic assertion of the oneness of God, put the community in a position in which they could form a bridge between Christianity and Islam.

The intellectual climate was one of hard questions demanding clear answers. The sixteenth century could no longer be part of the unquestioning, dutiful, meek, downtrodden servility of the past. Faith was alert in the sixteenth century. One of the ingredients in Socinianism was Paduan Aristotelianism, the intellectual current derived from Siger of Brabant's Averroism, and hence an interesting rationalist link with an Islamic philosophy. The Socinians believed that the individual soul dies with the body, as had Averroes; they also believed that only faithful souls would be resurrected at the last day. There was nothing mystical or Platonic in their thought, no tenuous groping after The One, or in-turned, guilt-ridden self-dramatisation. Their open rationality is refreshing and healthful. They also sought separation of Church and state, as had the Averroists. Reason, too, might not be just a gift of God, but perhaps was the voice of God. They interpreted scripture in a rationalist, non-miraculous manner, approaching the method of nineteenth-century German theologians, who looked for what actually happened in the gospel narratives. Above all they were anti-Trinitarian: they saw the Trinity as an inexplicable mystery, a piece of out-dated, Neoplatonic scholasticism, and their view of Christianity was that it was a pattern of how to live, not a sacred mystery. (How could Jesus Christ have existed as a person of the Trinity before AD1?) The Athanasian Creed was held to veer off into unintelligibility. Miracles might challenge reason but they could be understood. This Creed was beyond sense altogether. The Socinians' resolve was to believe nothing that could not be understood.

In this rational faith, the gospels were seen as rational documents. Mysticism was something which had been inserted into faith by princes and bishops in order to anaesthetise the moral sense of the masses and to numb their critical faculties concerning injustice and oppression. The Socinians, in their Polish homeland, became a small but distinct light of the Renaissance. The unitarian parallels of their faith with Islamic theology are interesting but should not be overstressed. (What is important is their openness to the Islamic viewpoint and their preference for Ottoman overlordship to Habsburg, which merely crushed them.) They were the brave outriders of the Protestant challenge, dissidents who in denying the Trinity cut a tougher pathway than those of other reformers. Perhaps at this time an element of Trinitarian anxiety can be discerned in the names of the Trinity Colleges founded in Oxford (in 1555, two years after Servetus' martyrdom), Cambridge and Dublin (in 1592, when the Polish Socinian group was showing strong progress in education and publishing), the first and last of which were founded emphatically in honour of the 'most holy and undivided Trinity'.

❖❖❖

William Harborne had been sent in 1578 by Osborne and his partner Richard Staper on a commercial fact-finding mission to Constantinople. He travelled overland through the same tolerant land of Poland, thus avoiding both the Venetian navy and the Inquisition. He passed through Lvov (Leopolis, Lemberg or Lviv), where his brother-in-law lived, and Kamaniets, today in Ukraine but in the sixteenth century a fortified Polish–Ottoman frontier town.[15]

Arriving in Constantinople (the designation 'Istanbul' is inappropriate, since the term had no currency until 1923), Harborne had, after skilful bargaining, gained the trading rights that he and Sir Edward Osborne sought – not least because he was able to offer tin and other war *matériel* to the Turks. There was deemed to be nothing wrong or unusual about arming the Islamic Ottoman Empire, especially if it could be persuaded to attack the Catholic powers of Europe. Trade and warfare overlapped almost imperceptibly. Thereafter English merchants were permitted to trade in Turkey on the same terms as the French and the Venetians. Following Harborne's departure the French ambassador persuaded the Sultan to revoke the concession but the privileges were soon reinstated. Queen Elizabeth granted Letters Patent to the Turkey Company (later the Levant Company) in September 1581, thereby granting royal authority to the enterprises of Osborne, Staper and their associates in trading with the Ottoman Empire.

Francis Walsingham, Queen Elizabeth's spymaster, also turned his attention to the East. In a memorandum entitled 'A consideracon of the Trade into Turkie' (1578), he put forward his view that trading with Turkey had ramifications beyond marketing English goods.[16] England should also seek to market Ottoman goods throughout Europe. Walsingham also saw a benefit to the navy from trading, since otherwise ships' timbers might decay from underuse. The obstacles that he foresaw were that France and Venice would be ruthless in competition, and that the Spanish king would be obstructive, owing to long-standing Hispano-Turkish antagonism. Walsingham predicted that England's enterprise would be opposed 'by fines [finesse] and by Force'. Finesse indicated diplomatic intrigue, and in terms of force he noted the number of Venetian galleys.[17]

The solution was to send 'some apte man' secretly to Constantinople 'to procure an ample safe conducte'. Good ships, well manned, should be chosen to accompany him; 'unles twenty sailes may be set on worke they shall not be of sufficient strength.' There were further economic issues to be considered. If the English traders took with them too many goods and flooded the market, prices would fall and profits suffer. So the English should act as agents for marketing the produce of other, neighbouring countries, though Walsingham put in a caveat that costs should not outweigh potential profits. He was further concerned to help bring to an end the wars between Turkey and 'the Sophy' (the Persian shah), since war depressed trade. England sought peace between the two Islamic powers, although policy tilted in favour of Ottoman Turkey.[18]

Walsingham's memorandum is modern in its outlook. Here too 'the infidel' is absent. This point came to be reflected in a further aspect of Anglo-Ottoman relations, beyond the facts of business. In seeking to secure an Anglo-Ottoman alliance aimed at Spain, Queen Elizabeth's ministers acknowledged a further common aspect of Protestantism and Islam: both shared an opposition to idolatry. She could not disavow the Trinity, but Romish idols were easy to oppose. Sultan Murad initiated the correspondence, calling her majesty 'most sacred Queene, and noble prince of the most mightie worshippers of Jesus, most wise governor of the causes and affaires of the people and family of Nazareth, cloud of most pleasant raine, and sweetest fountaine of noblenesse and vertue, ladie & heire of the perpetuall happinesse & glory of the noble Realme of England (whom all sorts seeke unto and submit themselves) we wish you most prosperous successe'. In the course of her initial compliments, Her Majesty called herself 'the most invincible and most mighty defender of the Christian faith against all kinde of idolatries'.[19] The language was designed to impress the Ottoman sultan and win his support against Spain. The idea grew of a kind of alliance between England and the Ottoman Empire, expressed negatively in terms of the mutual hatred of their faiths for images, although it should be stressed that no deeds at state level came from this understanding. A pasha in the Ottoman capital informed the Austrian ambassador Pezzen that the English were so close to Islam that all that was required was for them to raise a finger and pronounce the *ishad* or confession of faith: a trifle of court gossip, in which there gleamed a sliver of truth.[20] England was happy to see the Islamic Ottoman Empire attacking the Catholic powers of Europe. Therein lay peace for Protestants.

Queen Elizabeth found it necessary to declare to her home audience that she was not showing disloyalty towards Christendom by trading with the Grand Turk; but the declaration was insubstantial. The world had moved on and England was not alone in assessing each power for what it could contribute to security and prosperity. Henry VIII had inclined to a policy of confrontation, although trade with the East flourished during his reign; and no one believed that there had been any devout intention in his absurd crusade of 1511. The Catholic powers had themselves been disunited since the informal alliance between the French king – the Most Christian King – and the Ottoman sultan. The success of Protestantism made crusading seem like a legacy from a superstitious past, a rackety cultish form of idolatry associated with bones and relics; and no

Protestant monarch could follow the pope in a crusading adventure abroad. In 1559 Cecil feared that the pope was about to launch what was termed a 'crusade' against Protestantism.[21]

In the great sea battle of Lepanto of 1571, the conflict in which the Ottomans first tasted a substantial defeat, England took no part, though when news of the victory reached London the bells of St Martin-in-the-Fields were rung, and each ringer was paid 7d for his services.[22] Richard Knolles expressed approbation of the action but his description of it owed nothing to crusading theory or to biblical eschatology, being modelled on a magnificent passage from Thucydides (Book VII). The Elizabethan author, like his Athenian predecessor, captures some of the ambiguity:

> Divers and doubtfull was the whole face of the battell: as fortune offered unto every man his enemie, so he fought; according as every mans disposition put into him courage or fear, or as he met with moe or fewer enemies, so was there here and there sometime victorie, and sometime losse. Many fights were in sundrie places seene mingled together. Some gallies whiles they run to stemme others, are themselves by others stemmed. Some, which you would thinke were flying away, falling by fortune upon one victorious gallie or other, suddenly take them. Othersome as if they had beene of neither part, row up and downe betwixt the battels. The chance of warre in one place lifteth up the vanquished, and in another overthroweth the victorious. All was full of terrour, errour, sorrow, and confusion. And albeit that fortune had not yet determined which way to encline, yet the Christians at length began to appeare much superior both in courage and strength: and the Turkes seemed now rather to defend themselves, than to assaile their enemies.[23]

Lepanto, the classical Naupactus, can however appear like a backward-looking exercise of the Catholic nobility, perhaps even a successful naval equivalent of the Nicopolis crusade: grand, dramatic, full of gesture and expansive sentiment, with a roll-call of names and families but lacking a policy for the longer term, over as soon as it was won and relating more to European family trees than to securing a coherent Mediterranean system. Even in intention Lepanto had only a tenuous link with crusading, since before the battle the pope wrote to the Shah of Persia, Tahmasp, inviting him to join in, 'but the shah cared only for women and money'.[24] A squadron of ships financed by a Shiite Muslim power participating in a Christian semi-crusade would have been a novelty. In 1573 Venice made peace with Ottoman Turkey and recognised the sultan's conquest of Cyprus, which had occurred in the same year as the battle. The following year the Turks retook Tunis, which Spain had seized two years earlier.[25] Nevertheless, whatever the diplomatic aftermath, Lepanto broke the spell of Turkey's naval invincibility. It created a new mood in Europe and in doing so it represented a turning-point.[26]

Catholic Europe, however, should not be held up as some sort of paragon of confrontational virtue at this time vis-à-vis the Ottoman Empire, laying down its life for the virtue and defence of Christianity. The Jesuits rapidly secured a position of power in the Ottoman capital and readily informed the Muslim authorities of rumours which would do damage to non-Catholic Christians. Hard-headed Machiavellian Jesuit collaboration with the Ottoman authorities assured the strangulation of Ecumenical Patriarch Cyril Lukaris in 1638, and thereafter Catholics almost always cared less for other Christian communities than for the power-wielding Muslims.[27]

As the *Susan* sailed towards Constantinople bearing the ambassador, the vessel, seeking a victualling stop, put in at harbour at Majorca. Here the governor had received advance intelligence and tried to lure the crew ashore; a pretence of friendship was made, in the course of which the governor sought to charm Harborne with the gift of an ape. But the plot failed, despite the action of the governor, who, seeing the scheme failing, mounted guns – 'four or five brasse pieces' – to prevent the *Susan* leaving port. The English mariners coolly outwitted their would-be captors and the vessel proceeded on her way.[28]

On 22 March 1583, four months after she had left England, the ship passed Gallipoli. A few days later her crew caught sight of the Castle of the Seven Towers, and on the 29th three galleys escorted the ambassadorial party on its approach to the city of Constantinople. 'Then landed our Ambassadour, and then we discharged foure and twenty pieces, who was received with more than fifty or threescore men on horsebacke.'[29] Harborne arrived on Good Friday, a date which upset almost everyone: the artillery *feu de joie* was heard as the ship was off Seraglio Point, followed by trumpets and drums. All this as the Christians were on their knees at the solemn moment of the Good Friday service. The ambassadorial 'sumptuous feast of meats' which followed was ill attended, even by Turks. But it is doubtful that he was making a Puritan point against an 'idolatrous' date on the Church calendar, since Good Friday is scriptural.[30] 'The ninth of April he presented the great Bassa with sixe clothes, foure cannes of silver double gilt, and one piece of fine holland [linen].'[31] Among the other presents offered to the Sultan was a 'clocke valued at five hundred pounds sterling: over it was a forrest with trees of silver, among which were deere chased with dogs, and men on horsebacke following, men drawing of water, other carrying mine oare on barrowes: on the toppe of the clocke stood a castle and on the castle a mill.'[32] The Sultan entertained the ambassadorial party to a feast, at which the guests were served with 'rice diversely dressed, fritters of the finest fashion and dishes daintily dight with pritty pappe'. This was not supper with satanic legions, but rather a splendid diplomatic reception.[33] The English feasted with the Turks but the pope, Gregory XIII, was, at the same time, echoing the old policy of crusading, seeking to organise a 'Holy League' against the Ottoman Empire. The response of the powers of Europe was negative. There was money to be made from trading with Ottoman Turkey and they were beginning to discover the joys of plotting against each other, with Ottoman Turkey a counter in their subterfuges.[34]

Harborne's status is in a way recognisable from modern diplomatic practice. He acted both as a representative of his sovereign and as a commercial agent. His salary came exclusively from the Levant Company, with the English exchequer contributing nothing. The French and Venetian ambassadors viewed their new rival as a mere commercial agent. Clearly piqued, Harborne riposted in florid Elizabethan style: that he was 'a great noble, greater than any other here, and even if it were not so, they had no right to consider his private position, but only the magnificence of the Queen his mistress'.[35] He busied himself by setting up consulates in Tripoli (today in Lebanon) and Cairo.

In seeking to promote his country's international position, the ambassador sought to encourage a mood which would lead to the conclusion of the war between Turkey and Persia, so that Turkey could focus on the Mediterranean. He also worked to end Murad III's truce with Spain and the pope. The prospect of an Ottoman–English pact was enticing. He reminded the Sultan of the might of Sir Francis Drake's navy, while at the same time stressing that the Queen 'needeth no assistance of other princes, yet shall it [an alliance] be a great encouragement and contentation to her majesty, as a more terror to the King of Spain, they, having like interest, use like endeavour for to abate his power'.[36]

Harborne established an official residence and his moderately successful day-to-day diplomatic activities took the form of freeing the company's ship from seizure by the Bey of Tripoli in Barbary (today in Libya), and in reducing the customs duty for English merchants from 5 per cent to 3 per cent.

Harborne retired after five years and was succeeded by Sir Edward Barton, a fiercely committed Protestant. In his time the post moved towards ending its dependence on the company; he received a salary of £500 from the exchequer, partly because the company was proving to be a mean and irregular payer. Barton continued to try to put obstacles between Ottoman Turkey and Spain, and with the conclusion of a phase of the war with Persia in 1590 he sought to turn the Turkish empire against any power where the Roman faith was successful.[37] He keenly combated Catholicism and Catholic influence in Poland and eastern Europe, often acting without authorisation from his country, going to astonishing lengths to cultivate war between Ottoman Turkey and the 'idolatrous' Catholics. His actions went beyond most known diplomatic practice, either of that time or later. He accompanied the Ottoman army on campaign as it advanced deep into Hungary, being present at the battles against the Habsburg Empire at Erlau (modern Eger, Hungary) and Cerestes (Mezo-Keresztes) in 1596. He justified himself with the words: 'In my small judgment I think it nothing offensive to God to set one of his enemies against the other, the Infidel against the Idolaters, to the end that whilst they were by the ears, God's people [the Protestants] might respite and take strength.'

Barton travelled alongside the Muslim Turks on campaign against the Christian Habsburgs with four gentlemen, twelve servants, an interpreter and three Janissary escorts (all paid for from the Ottoman treasury), with a coach, twenty-one horses, thirty-six baggage camels and their handlers, with requisition slips for daily food and wine: almost an army within an army. But he was in no sense a warrior, for which anyway he was too fat and keen on drink (despite the Calvinism). He took with him twenty-three members of the Habsburg embassy, imprisoned for the last three years, to hand over to the Austrians, and seems keen to have offered mediation over Transylvania. He was perceived to have involved himself too closely and a diplomatic row ensued. The reputation of England became soured. Catholic agents in Moscow related the tales of England's Protestant perfidy to great effect, so much so that Queen Elizabeth felt compelled to send two missions to the Russian capital to explain England's actions. In the second one, which took place in 1600, Sir Richard Lee was sent with orders to declare that the Ottoman Turks had commanded Barton to accompany them on the campaign. The Sultan had indeed 'enjoined' Barton to follow the army; but the ambassador, a mediator and at the same time keen to promote the interests of 'God's People', hardly went unwillingly.[38]

Barton died in 1597 from dysentery in Constantinople and his memorial slab cites his service alongside the Turkish army. Not until David Urquhart can one discover in Ottoman Turkey a diplomat appointed from London who showed such curiously total devotion to the country to which he had been posted.

A few years earlier, in the year of the Armada, diplomats had been abuzz with rumours of Turkish–English collusion: the Venetian ambassador to Rome reported on 16 April: 'The news that the Turkish fleet will come out this year is confirmed from all quarters. It is said that the Queen of England has sent 500,000 crowns to Constantinople.'[39] The Venetian ambassador to Spain wrote on 28 May, 'I have learned from a sure quarter, that they are advised here that the Turkish fleet will take to the sea at the request of the Queen of England.. . . The English ambassador is favorably considered at the Porte, and is in frequent colloquy with the Kapudan Pasha [admiral of the Ottoman fleet].'[40] Intelligence is often faulty, as more recent examples have shown; but such examples demonstrate the manner in which England was viewed as regards Ottoman Turkey, and that the religious distinction was not seen as relevant. Indeed when the pope declared on 3 September that God's work was manifest in the fact that the Turks were too involved in the war with Persia to offer help to England, he himself was in effect declaring that Persia – devoted to Shiite Islam and the Safavid dynasty – was an instrument of the Deity as understood by Catholics.[41] Two years later, when relations with Spain were still raw, despite the defeat of the Armada, the Grand Vizier Sinan Pasha (of Sicilian birth, born Scipione Cicala) declared to the Venetian ambassador that the Queen of England had requested that the Turks supply 200 galleys, for which she would pay all the expenses; and with these and her own fleet she planned to attack the King of Spain. But (declared His Grandeur Sinan) 'we will have nothing to do in those parts. The Queen should send her fleet to join ours, and then something might be done.'[42]

In Europe, the charge of England's near-betrayal of Christendom is echoed in a note by Richard Hakluyt which accompanied his publication of the exploits of mariners and traders. He took refuge in the argument of trade, writing of 'the happy renuing and much increasing of our interrupted trade in all the Levant' and emphasising 'the great and good Christian offices which her Sacred Majestie by her extraordinary favour at that court hath done for the king and kingdome of Poland, and other Christian Princes'.[43] In view of Barton's attempts to undermine Poland, the claim that England had assisted her seems questionable. The unity of Christendom was a device of rhetoric, something to be revealed or obscured as policy or fancy dictated.

The threat from Spain grew less, England felt secure and the subsequent ambassadors acted more for trade than politics. The focus of international intrigue changed as Turkey, no longer a military empire instilling every heart in Europe with terror, took on the appearance of a state where society, politics and the army stagnated, and whose governance alternated between motionless passivity and sudden outbreaks of repression.

England's later ambassadors Henry Lello and Sir Thomas Roe observed the steady decline of Turkey as the internal upheavals of the ruling dynasty provided exotic material for writers of imaginative oriental fiction. The ambassadors – principally the Venetian, French and English – were consumed with feuding amongst each another, quarrels which were as long-winded as they were unprofitable. Great gifts were given, the unchanging means of flattering a potentate and winning favours. The Sultan for his part appeared almost invariably to have understood gifts as tribute; and once they had been offered, they needed to be repeated.[44] One of the most famous gifts was Thomas Dallam's organ, delivered to Sultan Mehmet III in 1599. At the top of this instrument the craftsman had carved a masterpiece of artifice: a holly-bush, set with blackbirds and thrushes. First, the organ played automatically, without human assistance, a five-part song twice over. This was the prelude to an ingenious blending of art and skill: the deftly engineered mechanism proceeded to make the birds 'singe and shake theire wynges'.[45]

The Sultan was so taken by the instrument that he asked Dallam to remain in Constantinople. Dallam, citing a non-existent wife and children, declined.[46] His Imperial Majesty was impressed too by the well-armed English vessel, the *Hector*, which had conveyed Dallam and the organ to Constantinople. ('English vanity in showing off,' grumbled the

Venetian ambassador.) But the growing inertia of Ottoman rule meant that there was no consequent diplomacy. The giving of great gifts suggests the flattery of an inert, largely passive but still important potentate, like the attention (or 'aid') granted to highly rated despotic rulers today. An overwhelming sense of sterility and spiritual exhaustion, of interlocking trivialities, attends the accounts of these occasions of courtly flattery. For all the ingenuity of Dallam's organ, there can be no other response than, 'So what?' It was a mere childish frippery, engineered to stir the dulled, befuddled responses of a decaying court, an affect-free automaton reflecting the inner deadness of official replicants. Sir Thomas Roe was to observe 'a dead silence in the court'.[47] Englishmen continued to play a role in promoting a tougher kind of Ottoman–English trade. Around 1605 Sir Thomas Sherley noted three English-owned shops of 'armes & munitions' open in Constantinople. 'The gayne is very greate,' wrote Sherley of these pioneers of English arms sales to a questionable regime.[48] French, Polish and Venetian trade with the sultan equalled, and even exceeded, that of England, but excluded armaments.

Sir Thomas Roe fulfilled the role of an energetic and statesmanlike English ambassador. He arrived in Constantinople in 1621 and again a vast gift was presented to the Sultan, this time two gigantic candlesticks 'of great value and so rare for workmanship as the like had not been seen'. A certain Thomas Morley had to be present when they were dismantled before shipment and to travel with them, before reassembling them in the Ottoman capital. For some of Roe's time the sultan was the young Osman II, though he was murdered the year after the arrival of the ambassador. Roe's diplomacy stood in contrast to Barton's, and showed even-handedness. Whereas the Elizabethan ambassador had directly nailed his interests to those of the host country, Roe sought to rein in the Sultan's impulsive desires and discouraged him from attacking Poland or the Habsburg Empire. He noted, 'This mighty empire hath past the noon, and is declining apace . . . the gallies which were one pillar of strength and greatness, all rotten and decayed ssithout hope of reparation . . . [the Janissaries] neither are soldiers bred, nor yet bear any reverance or fear; but all are apt to mutiny or dissolution.'[49]

As the empire slipped from greatness, so the ambassadors disappeared into obscurity. Local issues predominated. At the time of the English Civil War a series of comical incidents took place when the

Royalist Sir S. Crowe was supplanted by the Cromwellian Sir John Bendysh. Otherwise ambassadorial life consisted in a round of releasing prisoners taken by pirates, as well as continuing the stately rivalrous game of real tennis with the French and the Venetians.

A more vigorous and interesting unauthorised diplomatic relationship was however occurring with Persia at this time, as Ottoman Turkey ceased to be a great power.

CHAPTER SIX

Shah Abbas and the Sherley Brothers

Engand's diplomatic and commercial venture in the direction of
the Ottoman Empire stood in contrast to a rival policy driven by
the faction surrounding the Earl of Essex. As often in the East,
there was an alternative version. The Essex policy consisted in supporting
a nation which was a committed opponent of Queen Elizabeth's potential
eastern Mediterranean ally. That nation was no continental European
Christian state, quaking in the fear of a renewed assault from the
crescent, but Turkey's rival Islamic state, Persia.

Any Englishman who wanted to know about Persia in the late sixteenth
century would not have had to look far. The great Venetian histories were
available and in English there was Hartwell's translation of Minadoi on
the wars between Turkey and Persia, together with George Abbot's *Briefe
Description*. Busbecq's 'Letters' were available in Latin. *The Merchant of
Venice* echoes Persian–Turkish antipathy.

European interest in Persia had grown slowly in the sixteenth century.
Initially the Portuguese held a virtual monopoly in eastern trade,[1]
following the seizure by D'Albuquerque of Hormuz on the Persian Gulf
in 1507 and the establishment of a trading station there. Only slowly did
the other powers act to challenge their position. In 1561 Anthony
Jenkinson, acting as a freelance diplomat, visited Persia travelling down
the Volga and across a storm-wracked Caspian Sea. He was granted an
audience with Shah Tahmasp before being dismissed from Tabriz amid a
scene of anti-Christian extremism.[2] On this occasion neither the
Venetians nor the Genoese nor the French showed interest in stealing a
march on the disadvantaged English.

The Persian Safavid dynasty reached the zenith of splendour in the reign of Shah Abbas I (1587–1629). This monarch added a new dimension of majesty to Safavid Persia, the state which had been carved out by Ismail and given cautious sustenance by its defensive safekeeper Tahmasp. Under Abbas it blossomed into a civilisation comparable to its contemporaries in Elizabethan England or in Akbar the Great's Mogul court. Shah Abbas could be violent and unpredictable, killing men (including his own son) and maiming them in moods of sudden madness; but at the same time the arts flourished in Persia, the natural Persian talent for the visual arts and manufacturing was encouraged, tolerance was usually shown to religious minorities, and a magnificent new capital city – 'half-heaven' (*nisf-i jihan*) – was built at Isfahan. Dr John Fryer's description of the Chahar Bagh ('Four gardens') of Isfahan gives a glimpse of the culture of the time: 'All the pride of Spahaun was met in the Chaurbaug, and the Grandees were Airing themselves, prancing about with their numerous Trains, striving to outvie each other in Pomp and Generosity. . . . In the Garden itself, variety of Green Trees flourishing, sweet Odors smelling, clear Fountains and Rivers flowing, charm all the senses; nor is there less surprizal at the ravishing Sight of the delicate Summer houses by each Pond's side, built with all the advantages for Recreation and Delight.'[3]

Abbas came to the throne after a dark time for Persia. Ten years of factionalism and invasion had followed Tahmasp's death in 1576. In 1578 a joint invasion of the Shiite state had been launched by the Ottomans and the Crimean Tatars. At one stage the country appeared to be disintegrating along ethnic Persian–Turkoman lines. In 1587 the Sunni Uzbeks conducted a ferocious campaign against eastern Persia. But the young prince Abbas had from the age of about 15 been held as a jewel beyond price by the Shiite chiefs of Persia. In that year they marched on Qazvin and proclaimed him shah, aged 17.[4]

In her critical weakness, Persia made a humiliating peace with the Ottomans, ceding large border territories. Abbas understood he had first to deal with his local internal feudatories, the Qizilbash (literally, 'redheads') and then dispose of the Uzbek threat. Therefore he created a body of troops owing allegiance only to himself, before crushing the Uzbeks. It was not until 1598 that he finally defeated the Uzbek army, freeing Herat, and from a position of strength making pacts with individual Uzbek chiefs along his north-eastern frontier.

It was shortly after this auspicious strengthening of his power, at the dawn of peace and security, that Shah Abbas, in his newly liberated city of Qazvin, received interesting visitors from remote England.

❖❖❖

The Sherley family was perhaps typical of Elizabethan England, even if its members displayed the qualities of the age in an extreme manner. They were buccaneers and opportunists, dedicated to warfare, self-enrichment, art and factionalism as much as the greatest of the time. Sir Thomas Sherley, the father of three remarkable brothers, was a partisan of Robert Dudley, Earl of Leicester, who introduced him into affairs of state. In 1587 he became war treasurer in the Low Countries. His prestige was enhanced at home on being appointed sheriff of Sussex and Surrey. He rebuilt the family house at Wiston, near Bramber in Sussex. Besides their spirited public conduct, the Sherley family had a relationship with money which was recognisable, if exaggeratedly so, to that of many of the time. Periods of great extravagance alternated with times of utter poverty. In 1588 Sir Thomas's goods at Wiston were seized, and in 1603, as King James was being formally led into London, he was arrested for debt and sent to the Fleet prison to serve some months before being released under parliamentary privilege.[5]

His sons sought their fortunes in the furthest corners of the known world. The eldest, also named Thomas (1564–?1630) was the least interesting. He initially committed an offence by marrying Frances Vavasour, thereby incurring the displeasure of Queen Elizabeth I (who disliked both the marriage and the free expression of her courtiers' will) and gaining a spell in the Marshalsea jail. Travelling abroad, he sought to resolve financial embarrassment by privateering, that is, piracy. Initial success made him too ambitious and in an assault on a Greek island (then Ottoman territory), he was arrested and served time in a Turkish jail.[6]

Returning to England, he fared little better, being imprisoned in the Tower for diverting the business of the Levant Company from Constantinople to Venice and Florence. Four years later he was 'confined to the King's Bench' as an insolvent debtor. Wiston fell in ruins and Sherley, demonstrating the triumph of hope over wisdom, married for a second time. His bride, a poor widow, gave him a large family. He remained an MP, eventually dying in obscurity on the Isle of Wight.[7]

His brother Anthony, born in 1565, outshone many of his age with his reckless yet stylish ambition, testing his fortune in the courts of the world to its limit. He was held back by a curious lack of direction and afflicted by a strange ennui which seems to have descended upon him after completing some daring or desperate exploit. He was also incapable of taking second place.

Following his father, he saw service in the Low Countries but unwisely accepted a knighthood from Henri IV of France. On hearing of this Queen Elizabeth is said to have flown into a rage, declaring, 'I will not have my sheep marked with a strange brand, nor suffer them to follow the pipe of a strange shepherd.'[8] Anthony Sherley was briefly imprisoned in the Fleet. One unwise act was followed by another: marriage to Frances Vernon, cousin to the Earl of Essex – a link to the Essex faction, which implicitly brought trouble. The marriage was joyless too.[9]

After a fruitless privateering expedition across the Atlantic, Sherley, desperate for a grandiose idea for action, took the advice of the Earl of Essex, and in 1597 he joined some English volunteers, who included his brother Robert, who had promised support for the Duke of Ferrara against the pope. En route they heard that the matter had been solved. So, as the dread of doing nothing resurfaced and fearful medieval accidie seeped into his soul, he travelled to Venice instead, where there was business for all.[10]

Here, according to Sherley's own account, he received an astonishing commission from Essex. He was to travel to Persia, the newly confident Essex's favoured eastern state, with a double purpose: to persuade the Persian monarch to ally himself with the Christian princes of Europe against the Turks, and to promote trade between England and the East. At some stage, probably in anticipation of the complexity of this assignment, Anthony Sherley converted to Roman Catholicism. It is hard to say when, but it would most likely have been shortly before his departure for Persia.[11]

A ship was fitted out, and in May 1598 Anthony Sherley left for Persia with twenty-four companions. They included his brother Robert, George Manwaring (the 'Marshall'), Abel Pinçon (the steward), six gentlemen attendants, upper and inferior servants (some of whom were Persians) and an interpreter, Michel Angelo Corrai of Aleppo. The voyage was rowdy and antagonistic. A furious row blew up following some disrespectful remarks made by the Italian members of the expedition about Queen Elizabeth. Blows were struck and on reaching the Greek island of Zante Anthony and his party were thrown off and not allowed back on board. Unperturbed,

Roof of the Cappella Palatina, 1132, showing Arab 'stalactiting' decoration, blending with ornate Byzantine mosaic and austere Norman marble. *(Photo: Alinari Archives)*

The Church of the Holy Sepulchre, Jerusalem, engraving by Luigi Mayer, late eighteenth century. (*Stapleton Collection; Bridgeman Library*)

Lawyers working, together yet separately, in Norman Sicily. From left to right: Greek (*notarii Greci*), Arab (*not[arii] Saraceni*) and Latin (*not[arii] Latini*), respectively and appropriately bearded, turbaned and crew-cut. (*Pietro da Eboli, Liber ad Honorem Augusti, Palermo, c. 1195–7, Berne, Burgerbibliothek, cod. 120.II, f. 101r*)

William II of Sicily on his deathbed, 1189; he is attended by an Arab doctor (*Achim [=Hakim] medic[us]*), and an Arab astrologer, who is watching a giant star in the sky, and holding an astrolabe in his left hand. (*Pietro da Eboli, Liber ad Honorem Augusti, Palermo, c. 1195–7, Berne, Burgerbibliothek, cod. 120.II, f. 97r*)

Wooden carving of a deer, damaged, Fatimid, eleventh century, dating from the time when crusaders were sacking and colonising the eastern Mediterranean. *(Christie's Images)*

Sicilian–Arab casket, Norman, twelfth century, decorated with images of animals and arabesques, painted on ivory. *(Staatliche Museum, Berlin. Bridgeman Library)*

Michael Servetus (?1511–53),
visionary scholar, Christian humanist,
discoverer of the lesser circulation of
the blood, upholder of the belief in
One God undivided into Persons;
burnt at the stake at Geneva for
disavowing the Trinity, 27 October
1553. *(From Alexander Ross, Pansebeia,
1664 edition; private collection)*

Edward Pococke (1604–91), first
Laudian Professor of Arabic at Oxford
University, opponent of obscurantist
myths, enthusiast for Arabic learning
and poetry. Image by Silvester
Harding; from the 1806 edition of
Specimen Historiae Arabum.
(Private collection)

Sir Anthony Sherley, portrait
engraving, 1612, Netherlandish. *(From
Samuel Chew,* The Crescent and the
Rose, *Oxford University Press, 1937)*

Lady Mary Wortley Montagu,
attributed to Jonathan Richardson.
(Bridgman Library)

Title page of the Pocockes' Arabic–Latin edition of Ibn Tufayl's *Hayy ibn Yaqzan*, 1671: ownership signature of James Harris of Salisbury, linguistic theorist well disposed towards Islamic culture, friend and librettist of G.F. Handel, correspondent of Henry Fielding. *(Private collection)*

Hayy and Asal, two rational contemplatives, entering a Queen Anne-style mosque, bizarrely adorned with statues of Avicenna and Averroes; surmounted by the legend 'D.O.M.' (*Deo Optimo Maximo* – to God, the Best and Greatest), an invocation suitable to both Christians and Muslims: frontispiece of the 1708 edition of Simon Ockley's translation of Ibn Tufayl's original. The text at the foot can be translated as 'For the invisible things of God become manifest with the creation of the world'. *(Private collection)*

'An Awkward Corner on the Shipka Pass': the contemporary caption to a scene (situated north of Plovdiv, Bulgaria) in the 1877 Russo-Turkish War. *(Private collection)*

The 1683 siege of Vienna, from an image of Ortelius. (*Nineteenth-century reproduction; private collection*)

they hired a vessel to take them first to Crete then Cyprus. At Alexandretta in Syria they sailed up the Orontes river to Antioch and travelled on to Aleppo, the city of the Turkey Merchants. Here they were hospitably received and Anthony was able to borrow a large sum of money. He also assembled a fitting ensemble of gifts intended for the Persian monarch, including pieces of cloth of gold and twelve cups of emeralds. An incidental novelty of the party's stay in Aleppo was their experience of drinking 'a certain kind of drink which they call koffwey'.[12]

After a delay, they travelled to Bira (Birejik) on the Euphrates, where they embarked on boats to Fallujah (Phalouge). Here they took time for a brief glance at the ruins of Babylon, without paying much attention to them. Crossing to Baghdad, luck seemed to desert them for the second time; but again fate showed a favourable hand. The governor of that city confiscated all their goods, including the emerald cups (to the value of 6,000 crowns). Orders arrived from the Ottoman capital that the party should be arrested and sent to the sultan. But, according to Sherley's account, they were saved through the artful generosity of a Florentine, Signor Speciero, who helped them secretly to join a caravan of Persian pilgrims and gave Anthony money and gifts to make good his losses. Manwaring claims that their rescuer was not a Florentine but an Armenian merchant.[13]

Departing stealthily from Baghdad, the party reached Qazvin in early December 1598. Shah Abbas had entered the city in triumph just five months earlier: a free city now, but it no longer sufficed as a capital for his majesty. Already he had decreed that Isfahan, in the heart of old Iran, was to become the jewel of the Safavid dynasty: a city planned to be more magnificent than any in Europe or Asia.

'There we awaited the King,' wrote Abel Pinçon, the steward. Shah Abbas was informed of their presence, then 'ordered us to issue forth two miles outside the gates of the town to do him homage'. As they approached his majesty, Sherley and his brother Robert, and Pinçon, were ordered to dismount in order to kiss the royal feet, 'for it is thus that this prince is accustomed to being saluted'. 'While he stretched out his leg he pretended the whole time to look in another direction.' The party duly kissed the royal boot and then rode fleetly across the camp 'after the manner of the country'. His majesty was dressed in a short tunic, without a robe, decorated with gold brocade, and tight breeches. The turban on his head was adorned with many precious stones and rich plumage. 'In his hand he carried a battle-axe, playing with it, holding it now high, now low, and now and then placing it on his shoulder with rather strange movements.'[14]

Included in the triumphal procession into Qazvin was a display of 20,000 heads of decapitated Uzbeks, 'which appeared to me a hideous spectacle'. More in tune with festivity, there followed a corps of 'young men dressed like women richly decked', who danced wildly to the sound of flutes, strings and drums, accompanying a victory song provided by 'four old women'. Two men danced in the midst of the fray, bearing poles from which hung glittering mirror-glass, and at the end of which there swung lanterns painted with flowers, crowns, laurel leaves and birds. A troop of courtesans, 'riding astride in disorder', was observed in the midst of the crowd, shouting and calling out as if half-mad. Frequently they approached the person of the king to embrace him. Pages followed with wine and cups. The cavalry flanked the party with trumpeters and sackbut-players, playing instruments of extraordinary dimension, 'which gave a bitter and broken sound, very alarming to hear'.[15]

The party moved into the main square of the city, where there were two pavilions. Shah Abbas dismounted and entered one of them, and the European party was led thither. 'There had been prepared a collation of fruits such as pears, melons, raw quinces, pomegranates, oranges, lemons, pistachios, nuts almonds, grapes, sweets and wine.' The visitors were led into the Shah's chamber, 'and there we drank joyously with his majesty, who gave us a very good welcome, showing us by word and deed that our arrival was highly agreeable to him'.[16]

Anthony Sherley and his companions travelled on to Abbas's magnificent new capital at Isfahan, where the parties discussed international issues. Sir Anthony made plain that the purpose of his coming to Persia was to persuade the Shah that an alliance with the European powers would be in his country's interest.[17]

They also discussed military matters. The Shah eagerly talked animatedly on 'our proceeding in our wars, of our usual arms, of the commodity and discommodity of fortresses, of the use of artillery, and of the orders of our government'. He was drawn to the books on fortification that Sherley had brought with him. Anthony Sherley's younger brother Robert, who was to remain in Persia, was to be instrumental in establishing the country's first infantry regiments, when hitherto wars had been fought with irregular loose cavalry.[18] The Sherleys' achievement was summed up some years later by Samuel Purchas, who declared in 1624:

The mighty Ottoman, terror of the Christian world, quaketh of a Sherley-fever, and gives hopes of approaching fates. The prevailing Persian hath learned Sherleian arts of war, and he which before knew not the use of ordnance, hath now 500 pieces of brass, and 6000 musketeers; so that they which at hand with sword were before dreadful to the Turkes, now also in remoter blows and sulphurian arts are grown terrible.[19]

Anthony Sherley, claiming to be an envoy of Queen Elizabeth, even though he was an agent of Essex and acting in opposition to his sovereign's eastern policy, proposed to Shah Abbas that an embassy should be dispatched to the heads of European states, and that it should be a mixed delegation.[20] So a group of about twenty-five was assembled, consisting of twenty Europeans and five Persians, led by Husain Ali Beg. Two Portuguese friars who happened to be present also joined. In the early summer of 1599, this party set out from Isfahan with the fantastic aim of transforming Ottoman eastern Europe, Anatolia, Syria and Africa into the shared realm of Christianity and Shiite Islam. They took with them official letters to the pope, the Habsburg emperor (Rudolf II), the kings of France, Spain, Scotland and Poland, Queen Elizabeth, the signory of Venice and the Duke of Florence. Fifteen Europeans, including Robert Sherley, were left behind in Isfahan as hostages (who were also welcome guests) to guarantee the travellers' return.

They could not travel through Ottoman Turkey, although the interpreter, Corrai, ingeniously made his way across Anatolia to reach Venice. So they set out for Moscow, crossing the Caspian Sea. After momentous and fearful storms, in which the cries of *Agnus Dei* were heard in alternation to desperate calls upon Ali and Muhammad, they reached Astrakhan. There they took to boats, in five galleys each with 100 rowers, until they reached Nizhni Novgorod. Thence, weighed down with luggage containing expensive gifts, they proceeded by sled through a wintry Muscovy, arriving in Moscow itself in November 1599.

The party quarrelled incessantly. One Portuguese friar turned out to be a disreputable conman. He irritated the others by boasting of his seduction of ladies whose frailties he had discovered while hearing their confessions.

In the Kremlin Boris Godunov was tsar. Little is known about the embassy's six-month stay in Moscow, except that Boris treated the English with disrespect and seems to have held them in jail for much of the time.

Boris's hostility might have been encouraged by Jesuit reports in Moscow, for just at this time the Catholics were keenly spreading news of England's faithlessness in supporting Turkey against the Austrian Empire. The embassy itself was a strange creature: not an embassy at all in any real sense, but rather something between a mixed delegation and an international pressure group. The Persians among them were treated with some esteem. Anthony Sherley, after his release, did manage to write to Sir Robert Cecil in June 1600. His skill at writing silvery words was taxed to the full, since he knew that Queen Elizabeth's Levant policy centred on establishing good relations with the Ottoman Empire, not on contemplating wild schemes to bring about its downfall through the combined actions of Europe and Persia. Sherley mentioned the opportunity offered to raise the status of English merchants in Persia. His explanation for going on to Germany rather than returning to England was that his fellow Persians in the embassy party were obligated to carry out the shah's orders. As a tailpiece he airily added that Boris Godunov was seeking a husband for his daughter, and that Her Majesty might cast her eye around for a suitable gentleman 'whom she will vouchsafe to call cousin', and by such an alliance open up trade to India via Russia.[21]

Sir Robert Cecil made clear his sovereign's views in a letter to Robert Lello, English ambassador at Constantinople. 'Hereupon Her Majesty increased her former displeasure towards him.'[22]

Once free they travelled north to Archangel (then called St Nicolas) and took ship to the German port of Emden, which they reached in August 1600. Through Saxony they travelled on to Leipzig. In Prague they were received by Emperor Rudolf, who ordered a reception of 300 mounted citizens and fifteen coaches, a reception 'honourable in the highest degree'. There were talks on trade and armaments but no conclusion was reached, since the status of the embassy was unclear, and also because Sir Anthony had a difficult nature, 'irascible, opinionated, truculent and turbulent'.[23]

On the party travelled, to Munich, Innsbruck, Mantua, Verona, Siena and Rome. In Siena the row between the Persians and the Europeans broke out afresh. The Persians maintained that thirty-two chests of presents were due to be given to the pope, a 'gift of much magnificence'. But there were no chests. Sir Anthony had sold or bartered away the contents in the course of the journey. The cardinal sent by the pope to prepare the party for entry into Rome was compelled to mediate and calm tempers.[24]

In April 1601 the ambassadors made a state entry into Rome, where they were lodged in style in a palazzo. But aspirations towards grandeur were negated by the incessant quarrelling between Sir Anthony Sherley and Husain Ali Beg. They came to blows on the issue of precedence shortly before their planned proud entrance into the holy city.[25] Pope Clement VIII was compelled to grant them audiences on different days. The Englishman was received first. Sherley, showing a mastery of opportunistic untruth, declared that, as regards Shah Abbas, God had 'so touched the heart of his master that he and all his kingdom might be converted'.[26]

While in Rome the party also met Will Kemp, the leading Elizabethan dancer and comedian. The meeting formed the basis of a scene in a play written by John Day and others about the Sherleys, entitled *The Travails of the Three English Brothers*. (John Day had been a student at Caius College, Cambridge, but had been sent down for stealing a book.) Certain scenes show a familiarity between Anthony Sherley and Kemp. Sherley stayed in touch with gossip about the London stage. It is possible that Will Kemp and he were related, since the maiden name of Sherley's mother was Kempe. Sherley's acquaintance with Kemp later formed the basis of a fantasy devised by a certain Reverend F. Scott Surtees, who, in 1888, declared that Anthony Sherley had written Shakespeare's plays. It is however genuinely possible that news of Sherley's activities lay behind the remark of Fabian in *Twelfth Night* (1602): 'I will not give my part of this sport for a pension of thousands from the Sophy!'[27]

At the time Anthony Sherley's fortunes, far from showing evidence of a pension, were declining. Pope Clement VIII was unimpressed by him and he was soon compelled to leave Rome. The rumour mill swirled around him: 'One day ebbs and another day flows with money.' 'He hath done many out of much money, and loud are the lamentations.' Dismissed by the pope, he was forced to assume the cloak of a spy, keeping one step ahead of the agents of Ottoman Turkey, the power against which he had plotted. He never returned to Persia. In the Italian cities misfortunes struck. He was thrown off a bridge in Venice into a canal. He believed himself to be the target of Thomas Wilson, Queen Elizabeth's agent in Rome. An official grand commercial embassy from Persia was received with great pomp in Venice in March 1603, entirely undermining Sherley's status and credibility. He was placed under arrest. 'I am now in the utmost extremity,' he declared.[28]

But fortune relented marginally with the accession of James I. The Stuart monarch had no time for Ottoman Turkey and showed some sympathy for Anthony Sherley, although Cecil advised scepticism. The Englishman was granted a licence 'to remain beyond the seas'. Pointedly he was not permitted to return to England. Peace still eluded him and a new period of wandering was signalled by a final, harshly worded expulsion from Venetian territory in December 1604. After a sojourn in Morocco, where for a couple of years local politics provided a focus for his conspiratorial talents, he moved to Spain and the thread of his life becomes harder to trace. The mixture of opportunism, bravado and fantasy grows more tangled as it loses substance. He quarrelled with his brother Robert in 1611. Sinking deeper into poverty, he still managed to plot and plan in the mid 1620s. The last observation of him alive is dated 1636, after which the trail goes blank.[29]

Robert Sherley had been left as hostage in Persia in 1599. He was aged about 20 and, as an English hostage, had to behave with tact and discretion. But a chance to display his valour came in 1601. In that year Shah Abbas reopened war against the Ottoman Turks, when English relations with the sultan were at their warmest. The Persians were decisively victorious and in one of the engagements – a battle for the Shiite holy city of Kerbela – Robert Sherley was wounded. Soon Robert was commanding the defence of a fortified position dominating a route from east Persia to Isfahan. Robert also married a noble Circassian, Teresa Sanpsonia, who was a relative of one of the Shah's wives. Thomas Fuller commented of her that 'she had more of Ebony than Ivory in her Complexions; yet amiable enough and very valiant'. Van Dyck's portrait of her hardly bears out the ebonied comment, but it shows her vivacity and style.[30]

For years Robert heard no news of his brother Anthony, or of the embassy-delegation. Shah Abbas showed patience towards his well-born hostages despite gaining no actual benefit from the multi-hued embassy. Robert appears to have been under some strain. He wrote anguished letters to his brother: 'I am almost distracted from the thought of anie helpe for my delivery out of this Countrye' (1605); 'Brother, for Gods sake, eather perform, or not promis any thinge!' (1606).[31]

But then fortune changed. A group of Carmelite missionaries arrived in Isfahan and the Shah showed an interest in them. The precise nature of Shah Abbas's attitude to Christianity is disputed, but on this occasion he showed favour and permitted them to build a church of Jesu e Maria in Isfahan. Robert Sherley and his wife astutely arranged to be received into the Roman Catholic Church.[32]

Now, as if touched by a talisman, Robert Sherley gained a magnificent appointment. He was to be the ambassador of His Majesty the Shah to the courts of Europe, a fine post for an English buccaneer. In contrast to the engagement of his brother, Robert's task was more narrowly defined and purposeful; and not being part of a delegation, he would be free of the follies and vanities of others, if only to pursue his own.

Shah Abbas gave Robert Sherley appropriate letters. To James I, the Shah – the letter is given in a contemporary translation – noted that the Carmelites 'treated with us in the Christian Princes behalfes, that the Turcke ought to be assaulted by dyv[er]s wayes, to the end he might be wholly ruynated, wee of this syde and they [i.e. the European princes] of the other, And for us we have not fayled in what might appertaine to us, And nowe wee are likewyse readye wth a potent army; That way wch might be of more p[re]iudice to assault him on that syde, wee haue untill nowe referred to their best deliberacions, But nowe wee have written to them that they come by twoe wayes, wch is to say, by Aleppo and elsewhere as they shall haue best comodity, and wee will goe uppon Diarbecca and Natolia; Thus we determyne (by God's help) to ruyne hym, and to blott out his name, soe shall the Christians and o[u]r Confynes be unyted, and as Neighbors growe stronge in freindshippe.'[33]

Robert Sherley left Persia on 12 February 1608 according to Sir Thomas Glover, who as English ambassador in Constantinople was shadowing Sherley's moves in the interests of the Levant Company; for despite the change in policy towards the Turks brought about by James's accession, Anglo-Levantine commercial realities dictated an attitude hostile to anti-Turkish undertakings such as the Sherleys'.[34]

He travelled, as had his brother and their party some nine years earlier, across the Caspian Sea, then through southern Russia and to the Polish capital Krakow. A strange pamphlet by Thomas Middleton the dramatist (author of *Women Beware Women*) gives a fulsome description of Robert's activities, taking as its starting point his reception by King Sigismund III. Middleton designated the ambassador as Mercury, the messenger of the gods. Persia itself appeared as the great empire of antiquity and late antiquity, which elsewhere provided a convenient fictional disguise for Shah Abbas's empire.[35]

Again in the footsteps of his brother, he visited the emperor in Prague. There was grandeur, esteem and flattery; Rudolf knighted the envoy, but nothing of consequence was accomplished. Despite its clearer focus, the embassy was daily growing to resemble his brother's. Travelling on to

Florence, he impressed all by the quality and fantastic colour of the Persian silks he wore; but, added the Venetian envoy in an aside, 'He gets the stuff but does not pay.'[36]

He achieved a stunning entry into Rome in September 1609, accompanied by a party of eighteen, eight of whom wore turbans like himself. In contrast to his brother's quarrel over precedence, Sir Robert glided in, his way smoothed by the success of the Carmelites in Persia. His Holiness received him in the Hall of Signatures, in the presence of twelve cardinals. Sir Robert caused more than a ripple among Vatican observers by appearing in oriental robes, with his turban adorned by a crucifix – a turban which he removed in the presence of the pope, whose foot he kissed. The crucifix-adorned turban was not hastily forgotten. Did Robert Sherley belong to the East or the West? Was he one of theirs, or one of us? Was he a cultural traitor?[37]

The familiar plan was outlined, of an alliance between Persia and Europe against Turkey. Everything was most amicable, letters were exchanged, an apostolic blessing given. The next day he went sightseeing around the holy city but nothing of true consequence was traded. The new embassy was fading. The younger brother, too, travelled on to Spain.[38] His plans shifted; they ceased to revolve around international strategic thinking, dealing instead with the more humble matters of regulating Persian trade with Spain through Hormuz. The negotiations were stalled by the King of Spain, so Robert turned his attention to his natural sovereign, King James. Anthony, living in near-poverty in Madrid, forbidden to return to England, raged against his brother for planning a return to England and sought to persuade the Spanish minister to stop him. Robert feared violence and communicated his anxiety to the English agent, Francis Cottington, who calmed his nerves, and assured him of the possibility of secret departure from Spain. The moment of disquiet passed and in June 1611 Sir Robert Sherley left Spain for England.[39]

How would Robert Sherley be received in England? He was an envoy of a foreign power and through his connection with his brother Anthony he might be seen as an outlaw. But he had helped weaken the Ottoman threat to Europe. This had brought him a measure of popularity. Sir William Alexander, the Earl of Stirling, was, in his copious epic *Doomesday*, to write, 'Twixt Turkes and Christians now no Trumpets sound,' on account of the Persian conquests.[40] Whatever disloyalty the Sherleys might have shown to their monarch and to their country's commerce, in the wider context of the future of Europe they had brought respite from a fearsome invader from the east, whose final assault on Vienna was still to come. The Ottoman Empire might have been the unspoken ally of England against Spain, but in the hands of competent sultans or astute grand viziers, it was a threat to the whole of Europe. If England saw itself just as an island, Sherley could be seen as a traitor; but if it saw itself as part of Europe, his role had been beneficial.

Robert Sherley's plans for a Persian alliance were not taken seriously in England, although interest was shown in the possibility of trade with Persia. The turbanned Englishman awaited a royal summons, staying at Wiston, the home he had set out from as a young man twelve years earlier, now crumbling and dilapidated. Its occupants, to whom the world had seemed so full of opportunity at the time of Elizabeth, were now either half-dead, in prison or in poverty. His father was alive, but heavily in debt. Thomas the Younger, having been in jail both in Turkey and England, was also without money; Anthony Sherley was eking out a life in cussed obscurity in Madrid. But the exoticism of Robert Sherley's Circassian wife brought cheer to the gossips, wits and dramatists.

He finally gained an audience with King James at Hampton Court on 1 October 1611.[41] Robert Sherley threw himself down before his lawful sovereign and begged forgiveness for having accepted office under a foreign ruler. James was gracious and forgiving. Before the audience took place there was said to be anxiety about the garb of diplomacy, and no one knows whether Robert Sherley wore his robes and turban, or European dress. It seems likely that James allowed him to be robed as an oriental, on condition that he doffed his turban at a critical moment. In this way eastern and western sensibilities would have been satisfied and the issue of cultural treachery circumvented.

Robert remained for about eighteen months in England. There were difficulties but he had the pleasure of Teresa giving birth to a son. Henry, Prince of Wales, agreed to stand godfather, and Robert named his son Henry in his honour. Robert wrote to the prince, in his individual, if crabbed and unlettered, style:

> Most renownede Prince. The great honnors and favors it hathe pleased your highnes to use towards me, hathe imbowldede me to write thes fewe lyns, wch shal be to beseeche your highnes to Cristen a son wch God hate given me. Your highnes in this shal make your servant happy, whos whole londginge is to doe your highnes som segnniolated servis, worthy to be esteemed in your Prinsly brestt. I

have not the pen of Sissero, yett wontt I not means to sownde your highnesses worthy prayses in to the ears of forran nattions, and migtey Prinses; and I assure myselfe, your highborne Sperritt thirstes after fame, the period of greate Prinses ambisions; and further, I will ever be your highnes' most humbele and observant servant.

Robart Sherley[42]

His business dealings in London were fruitless. The main issue was the export of silk from Persia. Silk was a royal monopoly, and of great importance. There were three options. One was to maintain the trade along its present route, through Ottoman lands (a route which brought a healthy profit to the Levant Company). The other possibilities were to divert it along the Caspian–Volga route through Russia, or else to send it south, through the Persian Gulf, the Indian Ocean and round Africa. This third option, to send it through territory which was controlled by the Portuguese, was only practicable if a treaty could be made with Spain.[43]

The route through Russia and the Caspian was unpopular with the merchants. Complex negotiations took place, with the participation of Sir Thomas Roe, former ambassador in Constantinople. Roe's view of Sherley was that 'as hee is dishonest, so is hee subtile'. But such sentiments could just be the prejudice of one whose task had been to build up good relations with Turkey being brought face-to-face with one dedicated to opposing such a pact. The negotiations were to end somewhat summarily and to the surprise of seasoned negotiators like Roe, with the Portuguese being ousted from Hormuz in 1622 by an English naval assault, thus initiating 350 years of British control or semi-control of the Persian Gulf.[44]

Robert's efforts to interest the merchants in Persian silks failed too. The material was held to be not up to standard. The English agent in Spain noted that some of Robert's former Spanish friends were now inclined 'to give him the name of Cosener and of a Counterfeit'. He was rumoured to be distributing papal indulgences.[45]

He still had the regard and friendship of King James. His Majesty, uninterested in the Turkish trade, took seriously the offer of Shah Abbas for the right of entry into Persian ports for English shipping in the event of a new conflict with Spain.

Robert sailed back to Persia in January 1613. The long voyage was largely uneventful and the party finally landed at Lari Bandar at the mouth of the Indus. They were given a hostile reception by Portuguese settlers, now in the last decade of their commercial supremacy. Travelling on to Surat, they were graciously received by the Great Mogul Jahangir. Jahangir tried to persuade Sherley to leave the employ of the Shah and offered him a large salary to work for him, but Sir Robert declined. He left, with gifts of elephants and 'huge massie Coines'.[46] Sir Robert respectfully presented the elephants to Shah Abbas.

Shah Abbas still put some trust in his ambassador, despite the fact that he had very little to show for his efforts. So there was no alternative to his setting out for Europe again, to try to accomplish the goal of an alliance.

We hear of Robert Sherley next in Madrid in 1617. Here he remained for five years. Francis Cottington noted that 'The two brothers are much fallen out.' At the same time the East India Company had become seriously interested in the Persian trade. One of their agents, Richard Steele, had been in discussion with Sherley in Isfahan in 1615; and now two more agents were in discussion with the Shah in Sherley's absence. Their negotiations were opposed by the Portuguese, but since they were on the point of being excluded from the scene, their objections carried no weight.

Sir Robert and Lady Sherley drifted again across Europe, like ageing celebrities, now Rome, now London. John Chamberlain commented in January 1624, 'Sir Robert Sherley with his Persian wife is come hither again, out of the clouds, I think, for I cannot learn where he hath been all this while.'[47] Again he had an audience with King James and again the turban was an issue: to remove it would be an offence to the Shah, and not to remove it would create an offence to His Majesty. There is evidence of a compromise. Sir John Finnett noted that Sherley removed his turban, laid it at the king's feet, and donned it again. He also bowed low, touching the ground first with his right hand and then with his head.[48]

The discussions, which were now entirely about trade, appear to have made headway. But they foundered on the unwillingness of the Levant Company and the East India Company to reduce the trade of Turkey, or to undertake an enterprise into Persia.

Difficulty, caution: Robert Sherley's path was as stony as a track in Khorasan. It now moved towards ruin. King James died and the negotiations ended, though Sherley did gain an audience with King Charles for a few 'words of condoling compliment'. But then his life became a savage farce. A rival Persian ambassador, allegedly sent by Shah Abbas but in fact appointed 'through the intrigues of the East India Company' appeared in London.[49] His name was Naqd Ali Beg, and through him the Company worked with ruthless determination to discredit Sherley. Its board enthusiastically patronised Naqd Ali. Sir Robert, summoning all the self-respect he could in humiliating circumstances, visited the new envoy and deferred to him in the belief that he was a true envoy of the Shah. As Sherley approached him, Naqd Ali 'snatched his letters from him, toare them, and gave him a blow on the face with his Fist'. Robert Sherley, too polite to respond, was shattered by the experience.[50]

There was a scandal at court. Later, when Naqd Ali was admitted to the royal presence, he behaved arrogantly and insolently to King Charles, scarcely bowing, and turning his back when dismissed.[51]

The Lords in Council were compelled to send both envoys back to Persia, to allow the Shah to decide who was the fraud. At the same time an English ambassador, Sir Dodmore Cotton, was sent to Isfahan, escorted by Thomas Herbert. The two rival Persian envoys could not travel together, so, supervised by the East India Company, two ships were fitted out: a new ship was provided for Naqd Ali, the *Mary*, whereas Sherley and Cotton were compelled to cross the seas in an elderly vessel, the *Star*, in accommodation which was described as 'kennels'. An allowance for wine on the journey was granted to Naqd Ali, but not to Sherley and Cotton. In this way the East India merchants got their revenge on the Sherley brothers.[52] The long and tedious journey ended with landfall at Swally, near Surat, where events took a further dramatic turn: Naqd Ali committed suicide, by swallowing an overdose of opium, in fear of owning up in the presence of the Shah to the Company-created fraud.[53]

Sherley himself reached the Shah at his summer retreat in the middle of 1628. Here was not the young visionary ruler of thirty years earlier, but an ageing, brutalised tyrant, who had murdered his eldest son and blinded his youngest. Sherley was carrying a letter from King Charles, which explained the diplomatic embarrassment and which showed evident sympathy for Robert Sherley; but an agent at court showed it only briefly to the Shah, then hid it. The sly hand of the East India Company was again suspected. The upshot was that Shah Abbas suddenly and angrily turned on Sir Robert, ordering him 'to depart his kingdome, as old and troublesome'. It was a crushing blow and rather bears out Sir Thomas Roe's estimate of Shah Abbas: 'The disposition of the King is to bee very familiar with strangers if they be in Cash. In hope to gett, no man can escape him; when he hath suckd them, hee will not knowe them.'[54]

Robert Sherley was destroyed by the Shah's command, and two weeks later he died at Qazvin, ironically the scene of the first great meeting between Shah Abbas and the Sherley brothers in 1599. Thomas Herbert penned an epitaph:

Hee was the greatest traveller of his time, and no man hath eaten more salt than he, none had more relisht the mutabilities of Fortune. He had a heart as free as any man: his patience was more Philosophicall than his Intellect, haveing small acquaintance with the Muses: many Cities he saw, many hills climb'd over, and tasted many severall waters; yet Athens, Parnassus, Hippocrene were strangers to him, his Notion prompted him to other employments: hee had tasted of sundry Princes favours . . . and from the Persian Monarch had enricht himselfe by many meriting services: but obtained least. . .when he best deserved, and most expected it. Ranck mee with those that honour him: and in that he wants the guilded trophees and hyeroglyphicks of honour to illustrate his wretched Sepulchre (his vertue can out-brave those bubbles of vanities, *Facta ducis vivunt* [the deeds of the great man live]: and till some will do it better) accept this *Ultima amoris expressio* from him, who so long traveld with him, that so much honour'd him.

> After land-sweats, and many a storme by Sea,
> This hillock aged Sherleys rest must be.
> He well had view'd Armes, men, and fashions strange
> In divers lands. Desire so makes us range.
> But turning course, whilst th' Persian Tyrant he
> With well dispatched charge hop'd glad would be;
> See Fortunes scorn! under this Doore he lyes,
> Who living, had no place to rest his eyes.
> With what sad thoughts, mans mind long hopes do twine,
> Learn by anothers losse, but not by thine.[55]

Was there any deeper meaning or significance in the lives of Anthony and Robert Sherley, beyond the familiar features of a buccaneering spirit, a bold opportunism and a ceaseless capacity to dice with fate?

Their labours did not fashion an English policy towards Persia. In this field, it was the principles of Queen Elizabeth which were to hold sway. England never found it profitable or expedient to be a friend of Persia, except in a very minor way. There was never anything essential in Anglo-Persian dealings as there was in the Anglo-Turkish relationship.

But in the wider world of European diplomacy, there were some brief moments when their association with Persia reduced the Ottoman threat to Europe. The Sherleys may have been bad Englishmen, but they were good Europeans, for which England must be grateful too.

Was there a romantic attachment to the East? Were the Sherley brothers the first Englishmen to be drawn to the East, by the demands of a harsh and unforgiving landscape, or by an ancient and self-sufficient culture? This is doubtful. There was nothing dreamy or rhapsodic in the attitude of either brother. In their lives and in their correspondence they give the impression of doing a job that they had set themselves, with what determination and cunning that they could summon. Anthony Sherley believed that he had spotted a niche in the market of international diplomacy and aimed to fill it. His brother followed him; but being younger, and having spent more time in Persia, he grew up to be more focused and to some extent, though still capable of deception, less devious than his brother. The Sherley brothers were no more than freelance diplomats, both fluent on the world stage, the younger possessing a fraction more inner conviction. Robert Sherley, besides reforming the Persian army and thereby weakening the Turks' ability to wage war on Europe, was also a man of two worlds, a faithful servant of the Shah and a man whose deference to his natural sovereign was also honourable. He proved that one can be at home in the East and in the West, and that anxiety about cultural treachery is an issue only for those with experience of one culture, or none.

The vision of an actual alliance between Persia and Europe to crush Turkey was unrealisable and the world leaders with whom the brothers dealt understood that. If the Sherleys had limited themselves to reforming the Persian army and improving the quality of the trade of Persia, they might have achieved more. Their impatience and boredom, and a streak of ambitious madness, drove them to seek what was out of reach, and the bait of grand alliances led them into the realms of fantasy. Ultimately, despite the vast distances and high ambitions, they left little mark, and there was no romance in their careers. The desert sands swept over their achievements. There was no poetry in their lives except of the fickleness of fortune. Perhaps they briefly experienced the intoxication of the East, which draws wild spirits; but most likely, beneath the gloss of adventure, there lay the simple lure of self-enrichment.

CHAPTER SEVEN

Stuart Learning and the Improvement of Human Reason

Despite the persistence of medieval invective in England, by the late sixteenth and early seventeenth centuries the Islamic world had begun to be understood in a non-polemical manner. George Abbot, later archbishop of Canterbury, had introduced a rational element, comparing the differences between Sunni and Shia to those between 'Papistes and Protestants'.[1] Others, too, began to allow reason to play a part.

The clergy, as the educated class, were in the position to be among the first to talk sense about oriental history and the faiths of the region. Many of them were naturally concerned principally to refute the 'errors' of Islam. Refutation – more properly confutation – of the Koran was the guiding principle of Sir Thomas Adams when he endowed a chair of Arabic studies at Cambridge in 1632.[2] Abraham Wheelock, the first holder of the post (for which he was himself largely responsible for gaining funding), was a dedicated confuter. But besides as acting as the domain of controversialists and propagandists, the Church also found refuge for honest scholars. Some ministers were relatively open-minded about Eastern matters and Islam, while others were simply curious.

Another point which drew the clergy to an interest in the East was its linguistic importance. Christians of all views needed to improve the accuracy of biblical texts and some Arabic versions were recognised as being textually significant. The best text of Tatian's *Diatessaron*, an early synthesis of all four gospels, was that in Arabic. This language was also a living Semitic language and bible texts in it often cast light on early Syriac versions. It also illuminated the Hebrew of the Old Testament. When in the early thirteenth century Hebrew grammar began to be written schematically and systematically (by David Kimche, or Qimhi), the model was Arabic grammar.[3] To know Hebrew properly one had to study Arabic. Some knowledge of Aramaic was necessary too – the language Christ spoke, which is spoken even today in a few places in the Levant. Parts of the Old Testament are written not in Hebrew but in Aramaic (then known as Chaldee). The most important section of the Old Testament in that language is a passage of the book of Daniel (2: 4 to 7: 28). Here the text starts with a speech given by a group of Chaldeans in their own tongue. Although the text ultimately reverts to Hebrew, the Aramaic is not abandoned for several chapters after the end of the Chaldeans' speech. It is as though a somewhat somnolent scribe had got into a comfortable groove while using Aramaic, with which he felt at ease, and had forgotten to return to the official language. In the book of Ezra, there are two passages in Aramaic. In Jeremiah a verse is written in the same language. The biblical paraphrases known as targums were texts in Aramaic. Hence the need for a knowledge of the language. Nevertheless, although serious scholars realised that, in order to resolve biblical textual issues, languages other than Hebrew needed to be studied, some clerics, especially devout fundamentalists like John Owen, believed that all biblical criticism was wrong in principle, since it called into question the providential nature of the text and cast doubt on its divine origin.

Arabic was seen as having a kind of junior complementarity to Hebrew. Hebrew was understood to be the patriarch of languages and the first study of serious Biblical scholars. Aramaic, also Semitic, was, so to speak, the elder son in this linguistic family, since it had found its way into the Bible. Arabic was a lesser daughter. Scholars of the history of language, such as John Selden, also found a place for Phoenician. Later linguistic researches have shown up the flaws in this early classification. No one then knew of Akkadian, the parent Semitic language. Written Phoenician antedates Hebrew. But the classification gave a position to Arabic studies. At the same time, Arabic also had a strong practical value, in view of the fact that since the ninth century it had been a language of science, mathematics and astronomy, and it was also used in commerce and diplomacy from the Canary Islands to East Asia. The opportunities offered by the Levant Company gave it a practical edge.

Lancelot Andrewes, who eventually became bishop of Winchester, was a man of great learning and broad horizons. By 1576 he had mastered fifteen languages, which included Hebrew and Arabic, and although none of his Arabic work survives, he supported the efforts of later scholars. In about 1585, perhaps earlier, he had commissioned an Arabic dictionary, and ten years later the first pages were delivered. Andrewes corresponded with scholars all over Europe and most particularly with those in the Netherlands. He saw a real value in oriental studies, as did one of his correspondents, the great French scholar installed at Leiden University, J.J. Scaliger. Scaliger noted the importance of studying Arabic in a letter of 1607. Andrewes, in his comprehension of the importance of Eastern study, added a living ecclesiastical dimension, which went beyond the preparation of texts or polemical antagonism. He began to consider the possibility of forging a link between Anglicanism and Eastern Orthodoxy. The power of this idea grew subsequently and was to reach a definitive form in the following decades.[4]

The principle was to rediscover an authentic tradition for the moderate English Church. The Anglican Church would then become the nucleus of a worldwide centrist church which would lead the way to the reunification of the Christian Church. Church unity was a receding mirage in continental Europe, where the parties were separating into ever more extreme positions: the Catholics, following the Council of Trent, had adopted a position of uncompromising authoritarian isolation, and the Calvinists, having murdered Michael Servetus, were equally convinced of the divine correctitude of their theology. Within Anglicanism the High Church party sought to rediscover traditions which would link the English Church with the primal roots of Christianity. Those who felt the need for tradition in church matters sought a secure basis for its moderation, tolerance and wisdom. Englishmen like Andrewes (or Irishmen like James Ussher) looked to the East, seeking shared ideals in the writings of the early Greek patristic fathers; they searched for possible connections not only with the Orthodox Church based in Constantinople, but with Arab and Aramaic Christianity too. A number of Greek authors were preserved only in Arabic translation and the theology of the Arab Christians of Syria–Lebanon appeared untarnished by either superstition on the one hand or factionalism on the other. William Bedwell, the 'father of Arabic studies' in England, who had studied in Leiden, noted, 'The writings of the Arabs say nothing about purgatory, about the impious sacrifice of the mass, about the primacy of Peter and the apostles, about meritorious justification . . . Here superstition, indeed suspicion, is far off.'[5]

Andrewes' idea of forging links between the Anglican and Eastern Orthodox Churches was taken up and extended by William Laud, who, together with his sovereign Charles I, was a committed proponent of the idea of propinquity, and perhaps eventual intercommunion, with the Orthodox Church. King and bishop understood Andrewes' principle: that the Church of England had to be part of the worldwide church, and not remain simply an individual, localised reformed church. It was the sacred vessel with (to borrow a phrase from Rose Macaulay) 'the most truth' in it. Laud sought to steer a liturgical course which avoided the extremes. His theology had located the origin, the inner authenticity, of the English Church in the preaching of St Augustine of Canterbury and the early archbishops of the premier English see, and perhaps in the earlier Celtic church, rather than in the life and example of Thomas Cranmer. Now he looked to the Greek Church, separated from Rome since the Eastern Schism of 1054, as an ancient, natural and unforgotten theological ally. Rome, which had dismissed the Anglican Church as schismatic, could from the vantage point of an Orthodox–Anglican union be seen as itself the victim of schism. Contacts were made with Cyril Lukaris, the Ecumenical Patriarch in Constantinople, a complex figure who ultimately faced a bleak and terrible conspiracy, a man of new and impulsive vision who (whatever his theology – for strange allegations of forged documents hang over the life of this unusual Eastern cleric) sought to make imaginative theological contacts with the wider Christian world.[6]

In 1624, a wandering German scholar appeared in Oxford, the city to which Laud was devoted. Matthias Pasor had escaped the ravages of the Thirty Years War, fleeing from the great German university city of Heidelberg first to Leiden, before crossing the sea to find intellectual respite along the banks of the Isis and Cherwell. Typically of scholars of that time, he was a man of many accomplishments, being a linguist (who taught Hebrew), a mathematician and a philosopher. He was not the first student of the orient to appear in Oxford: the Coptic scholar Joseph Abudacnus (Yusuf abu Dhaqan) had briefly appeared there in 1610–13. But Pasor's impression on the university was deeper and more lasting. He was also keen to explore further study, and some months later he left for Paris, to learn Aramaic and Arabic from a Lebanese Maronite called Gabriel Sionita, or Jibril al-Sahyuni. After a year or so he returned to Oxford and, with a lectureship in Hebrew at New College, started to give classes in four oriental languages. He wrote no books, on the grounds, first, that enough good books had already been written and he did not wish to burden his students with further study, and second, that booksellers should not have to risk debt on his behalf. He seems to have become restless again and in 1629 he left Oxford for Holland to take up professorships in philosophy and mathematics at Groningen University.[7]

The oriental learning of scholars like Pasor paralleled the approach to the East of Lancelot Andrewes and William Laud. Their work was creating a discreet revolution which would lead to serious scholarship and accurate knowledge rather than strenuous polemic and antagonistic unreason. The new mood found a resonance in the writing of a few poets. One such was Sir William Alexander, the Earl of Stirling, who had been tutor to Henry, Prince of Wales (the youthful godfather, sadly deceased, to Robert Sherley's son Henry) and whom we have already met recording the peace brought to Europe from the cessation of Ottoman hostilities. His expansive poem *Doomes-day* (1614–37) has been described by one critic as a 'vast morass of . . . dead-level sacred epic' in which 'a few flowers gleam'. In this context, it is notable that he gave his readers a couplet that declared that

> The spirituall plague which poysons many Lands
> Is not the Turke, nor Mahomet his Saint.[8]

Stirling located anti-Christ within the Church and the community, not without. He refused to see the bad as the other, the thing out there, the projected image, the transferred object. He observed it within his own tribe. This was a change from the medieval attitude. Despite the verbosity, Stirling helped to encourage a new mood of empirically based knowledge and understanding.

In Oxford, one of Matthias Pasor's most capable students was Edward Pococke. He had been born in 1604 in Oxford, where his father was a fellow of Magdalen College. He went to school in Thame, before gaining a scholarship to Corpus Christi College. In addition to the usual Latin, Greek and Hebrew, he learnt some Arabic from Pasor. More Arabic study was gained in about 1628 from William Bedwell in Tottenham. He was ordained in 1629 and was soon engaging in further biblical study. His work caught the eye of the Dutch scholar G.J. Vossius, who enabled him to make his first break into print.[9]

Like any serious linguist, Pococke realised that he had to gain experience in the field and was successful in applying for the post of chaplain to the Turkey Merchants at Aleppo, Syria. He stayed in Aleppo from 1630 to 1634.[10] This city was a centre of both business and learning, and the Aleppines still today pride themselves on their good sense. They have a saying, *'el-Halabi chelebi'* – the Aleppine is a gentleman. Pococke met a number of Arabs he liked here and who were drawn to his own humane and intelligent personality. One was his Muslim Arabic teacher, his 'old sheich' Fathallah, who 'did not doubt but to meet you in paradise', he was informed by a mutual acquaintance.[11] His posting enabled him to gain a rich knowledge of the language – although he was homesick, declaring 'My chief solace is the remembrance of my friends . . . I think that he that hath once been out of England, if he get home, will not easily be persuaded to leave it again.'[12] But nevertheless, as the English consul told the great jurist (and Arabist) John Selden, Pococke had 'made Arabb his mistresse' and his devotion to her was great. As well as attaining linguistic proficiency, he also managed to acquire a fine collection of manuscripts, which are now housed in the Bodleian Library.[13]

It was as a buyer of manuscripts while he was working in Aleppo that Pococke attracted the attention of William Laud, then bishop of London. Laud was a man of contrary qualities. He exercised great power and influence with King Charles; despite believing that the Anglican Church should be moderate in its theology, he enforced clerical orthodoxy with sternness and rigour, edging into brutality. He also had a passion for enlarging and extending learning and a personal near-obsession for collecting. Oxford University, of which he had been chancellor since 1630, grew magnificent under his tutelage. He enriched his old college, St John's, with the Renaissance splendour of Canterbury Quadrangle. Laud understood the need for a good university library and a competent printing press. Of the 1,300 manuscripts that he gave to the Bodleian Library, about a quarter are oriental. No one knows what drove Laud to his fascination with the East. Perhaps, like a number of more recent Englishmen, he felt mysteriously drawn to its history and culture, and found its siren-call irresistible. Maybe his view of the destiny of Anglican Christianity, to be encouraged into a form of association with the Eastern Orthodox Church, led him to meditate upon the East, and to believe that a great question, or puzzle, needed to be unlocked there. He ached for manuscripts, imposing a kind of manuscript-tax on ships operating for the Levant Company. He was rewarded with numerous texts and oriental coins from the scholar-chaplain and exulted with the thrill of possession characteristic of the avid collector. When in 1634 Laud contemplated establishing a professorship of Arabic at Oxford, it was natural to offer the post to Edward Pococke.[14]

Pococke took up the post in 1636. To Royalists and indeed to almost anyone with an historical sense, this is a year filled with a strangely emotive power, which can still today take hold of the imagination, like the recollection of a final perfect week of summer enjoyed within a walled garden. It was the high point of the personal rule of Charles I. The country was at peace and prosperous. In August of that year Laud, as Chancellor of the University, entertained His Majesty to a week-long festival in Oxford with such delights as the city of learning could offer. In one of the many private gardens of Christ Church, Laud accompanied the King and Queen to several dramatic performances, one of which was of a play with an Eastern theme written by William Cartwright and entitled *The Royal Slave.* The scenery was designed by Inigo Jones and the music composed by Henry Lawes.

The action of Cartwright's play is set in ancient Persia, and Ephesia (western Turkey today). Ephesus has been conquered by Persia. From the Ephesian captives, the Persian King Arsamnes selects one man, who he decrees is to be king for three full days, robed in the majesty of monarchy and granted its limitless privileges, before being ceremonially put to death. However, the prisoner selected, Cratander, turns out to be a high-minded philosopher of a Stoic disposition, quite unlike the other captives, who are noisome fools. (The prisoner-king was played by Richard Busby, later famous as Master of Westminster School, where John Locke and John Dryden were numbered among distinguished pupils.[15] Busby himself was to introduce Arabic lessons into the school curriculum and appears to have written but not published an Arabic grammar. A saying grew up of the pupils in the 1650s: '*Qui puer huc Anglus venerat, exit Arabs*' – the boy who has come here as an Englishman leaves as an Arab.[16]) As king, Cratander bears himself with noble and frugal self-denial. Music is silenced; ladies of ease are dismissed. His fellow prisoners riot and conspire to murder their three-day king but he thwarts their plot. He is offered a chance to flee from Persia but declines, pointing to his oath and his duty. The Persian queen grows fascinated by his high nobility. The time for Cratander's execution nears. He is brought to the Temple of the Sun. The priests prepare to sacrifice him but the sun is eclipsed and a downpour of rain extinguishes the fires of sacrifice. Heaven is clearly displeased with the prospect of the death of a man of such nobility. He is spared and appointed satrap to the Ephesians, who in turn are granted a measure of autonomy within the Persian Empire.[17]

This fable, centring on the notions of kingship, authority, oaths and duty upheld even to the point of death, would have stirred the imagination of all present. It exercises a powerful appeal on the historical sense today. One is drawn to details such as the royal change of mind and the demonstration of clemency and flexibility. The idea of an actor playing the part of a king facing death before a king whose mortal fate we know contains a mythic potency. In January 1649 Busby was a master at prayer only a couple of hundred steps away from the melancholy scene.

There is a further point, which related to Eastern matters. Safavid Persia at this date could sometimes entertain beliefs as superstitious as those current at the time of Herodotus. Shiite Islam had not destroyed an underlay of folk belief. In 1591 Shah Abbas was told by his astrologers that it was extremely unlucky for him to remain on the throne at that date. He had to undertake a temporary abdication in order to avert a nameless threat. This he did, and a non-Muslim, probably a Nestorian Christian named Yusufi, was proclaimed king in his place. Yusufi was crowned and for three days held all the power and privileges of kingship. Then he was dethroned and put to death and Shah Abbas resumed his reign. At this date historical fact was less forgiving than dramatic fable. It is fair to assume that, through the presence of the Sherleys and other Englishmen at Shah Abbas's court, this detail had gained currency and had eventually reached playwrights in London, such as Cartwright.[18]

In the same month as the play's performance at Christ Church, Pococke took up his position as Laudian professor.[19] Only a fragment of his inaugural lecture has survived; this dealt not with problematic issues of theology and textual criticism but with 'the conspicuous honour' accorded to poets among the ancient Arabs.[20] It also explored some of the proverbs of Ali, Muhammad's son-in-law. (Two examples of these: 'Opportunity is swift of flight, slow of return'; 'Men are more like the time they live in than they are like their fathers.'[21]) The professorship entailed lecturing for one hour every Wednesday morning at 9.00 a.m. during Lent, and during the vacations, and all students were compelled to attend under penalty of fine. (This schedule cannot fail to seem odd today.)

Despite the care and attention which Laud lavished on his university, it would seem that his counsel was divided about the future of the Arabic professorship. For no sooner had he appointed Pococke to the post than he sent him off again to the East for further study and to collect more manuscripts. It may have been that Laud was lured to further manuscript acquisition by John Greaves, a fellow of Merton College who was also professor of geometry at Gresham College, London. Or perhaps a mooted plan for Pococke to write an oriental history, to be dedicated to Laud and which needed further study in the East, was too great a temptation for the prospective dedicatee to resist.[22]

Pococke travelled to Constantinople in the company of John Greaves, whose younger brother Thomas, who had learnt Arabic from Pococke, became deputy professor in his absence. For three years the two resided in the Ottoman capital, staying in the house of the English ambassador, Sir Peter Wych. Here Pococke formed a strong friendship, with the enigmatic Cyril Lukaris. He was present at the notable occasion on which the patriarch presented himself at the chapel of the English embassy for the christening of the ambassador's baby son, for whom the patriarch stood godfather, and who was named Cyril in his honour. This event seemed to be embryonic of the desired understanding between the Anglican and Orthodox Churches. Pococke also became friendly with the Ottoman Jewish notable and scholar Jacob Romano, who gave him an interest in Judeo-Arabic (that is, Arabic written in Hebrew letters) and in the thought of Maimonides. Romano may also have interested Pococke in an important Arabic philosophical novel that he was later to translate. But in comparison with Aleppo, the Ottoman capital was an intellectual backwater. Pococke was disappointed to find almost no learned Turks. He hoped to visit Mount Athos, but the peremptory execution of Patriarch Cyril ruled the expedition out and ended any talk of closer relations between the Churches.[23]

Pococke was still in the Ottoman Empire in 1640. The situation in England was sliding towards civil war. In March an old Oxfordshire family friend, Charles Fettiplace, urged him to return to England while Laud could still help him. He delayed until August and then travelled slowly through Europe, stopping to discuss with Hugo Grotius a translation into Arabic that he was preparing of his *On the Truth of the Christian Religion*.[24] Pococke admired this book, which summed up many of his own beliefs. His Arabic version appeared in 1660, funded by Robert Boyle. Grotius wrote of Islam in a manner which indicated he did not feel threatened by it, even though his book was a text designed for Christian conversion. He held that 'by the just permission of God, Mahomet planted in Arabia a new religion'.[25] Grotius believed that theologians had destroyed the unity and the accessibility of Christianity. His text ignores the Trinity, the great stumbling block between Christianity and its fellow monotheisms. He also held that reason and scepticism were important and even fundamental ingredients of Christian belief.[26]

These views were being developed in England at the time by Lord Falkland and the Great Tew Circle. (Abraham Cowley, a member of the circle, wrote a memorable sonnet to Reason, and in another poem he acknowledged the debt owed to Islam for transmitting the texts of Aristotle.) John Aubrey called Falkland 'the first Socinian' in England, indicating his penchant for reason and sense, and his rejection of incomprehensible mysteries such as the Trinity. (Whether he was actually a follower of the ideas of Socinus is open to doubt.)[27] In his *Discourse of Infallibility*, a medieval-type disputation between a Catholic and a rational Protestant, similar in structure to Chillingworth's *The Religion of Protestants*, not published till 1645 but circulating in manuscript in his lifetime, Falkland boldly declares, 'For my part I profess myself not only to be an anti-Trinitarian, but a Turk [i.e. Muslim], whensoever more reason appears to me for that, then for the contrary, and so sure would you; for the pretended infallibility of your [Roman] church could no longer hold you, if you thought you saw reason to beleeve it fallible, as you must do, if weighed, more reason appeared of her adversaries side.'[28]

Edward Pococke, out of the country, was never a member of the Great Tew Circle, but the views expressed by its members were largely similar to his own. He too held that the way forward for the faith was for it to consort with reason and knowledge in a spirit of brotherhood. Grotius, Pococke, Boyle, Falkland and Cowley were all people who saw faith in a larger context, whether of emerging science or in a world filled with many faiths and many people who might be good whatever their faith. They believed in opening out aspects of belief, in making them comprehensible, even if that meant jettisoning theological jargon and mysteries.

Pococke returned to England in 1641 on the eve of the Civil War. Archbishop Laud had been impeached and was held in the Tower. Pococke insisted on seeing his patron, once so powerful, now 'shut up in prison, there to expect the bitter effects of the malice of his enemies, and the madness of the people'.[29] The visitor passed on a message from Grotius, urging him to escape. But Laud, now aged nearly 70, declined the offer, pointing out that if he fled to France it would confirm his enemies' suspicion that he was a secret papist, and that if he went to

Holland he would fall victim to the rage of the Puritans. Laud in prison was still capable of a magnanimous gesture: he endowed the chair of Arabic that he had founded with funds to secure its future. Rents from land in Berkshire were set aside to provide perpetual funding. He also presented further oriental manuscripts to the Bodleian.[30]

During the Civil War Pococke suffered for his connection with Laud. He prudently gained a living in the countryside, at some distance from the dangerous circles of the university city. In 1643 his Oxford college obtained for him the rectorship of Childrey, a village a mile or so west of Wantage, and there he carried out his clerical duties without any of his flock being aware of his distinction. 'Our parson is one Mr Pococke, a plain honest man, but, master . . . he is no Latiner,' declared one of his parishioners.[31] Oxford maintained its position as Royalist capital until 1646, although it was occupied by Parliamentary forces for a month in September 1642. As a garrison city, taking on the appearance of a barracks, it was not conducive to serious or sustained work. Pococke's sympathies were unquestionably Royalist, but his true loyalty lay with scholarship. He paid fewer visits to the city, preferring to work unhindered in the village. Nevertheless, he fell foul of Parliament, which deprived him of pay due to him as professor and seized the property that Laud had designated to fund the Arabic chair.[32] Not all of his parishioners held him in affection and respect. Although they accepted that he carried out his duties in a conscientious and devout manner, he was criticised for lacking the fervour and enthusiasms of the times. His preaching was condemned for its lack of 'boisterous action'.[33] It seems that he had no time for the servile, self-righteous zeal known as 'unction'. To some of his flock he became a target. In these rough times, he recalled the humanity of the people of Syria and Turkey, where his conversation on sacred topics had led non-Christian peoples to hold him in honour.[34]

Pococke found a fellow spirit in John Selden, another man of considerable oriental learning (but less knowledgeable than Pococke) and a distinguished Parliamentary lawyer. Here was a man who might appear as a political opponent. But Selden was a man of broad human sympathy, endowed with what his political opponent Clarendon called 'wonderful and prodigious abilities and excellencies'. Grotius, who differed with him on legal grounds, praised him too, calling him 'the glory of the English nation'.[35] Pococke and Selden were in fact devoted friends, the former correcting the latter's fractured Arabic, and Selden upholding Pococke's case when his fellow Parliamentarians showed zealotry. Selden had shown an interest in Arabic as early as 1614; his largest work, an original, even brilliant, comparative study of the pre-Christian faiths and fertility cults of Syria (*De Diis Syris*, 1617, much reprinted), used Arabic sources, as did his incomplete study of the tenth-century patriarch of Alexandria, Eutychius, 1642. The latter work was finished by Pococke in the next decade, and was to receive a magisterial put-down by Gibbon, as 'a pompous edition of an indifferent work, translated by Pocock to gratify the Presbyterian prejudices of his friend Selden'.

Selden, the Parliamentary lawyer, together with Gerard Langbaine, Provost of Queen's College, made sure that the lands which funded the Laudian professorship were restored. At the same time the ferment of ideas which characterised the times spread directly to Pococke's work. He started work on the translation of the twelfth-century Arabic text which he had probably come across in Constantinople, and which focused on an issue as relevant in the seventeenth as in the twelfth century: the authority of reason against revelation. Pages of an English translation of this text date from the year in which his patron, Archbishop Laud, was executed in the Tower.

As Parliamentary forces prepared to oust the King from his Oxford headquarters, so conditions grew dangerous for Pococke. Soldiers were quartered on his country rectory, an infliction which was all the greater since in 1646 he married Mary Burdett, 'a very prudent and virtuous gentlewoman'.[36] The professor was declared a 'malignant', a word frequently employed at the time, with a sinister totalitarian ring. This was intolerable to his friends, who intervened with General Fairfax with the result that he was left alone.

The appointment of Parliamentary 'Visitors' to 'reform' Oxford and seek out 'malignants' made it clear that the pressure would continue. Pococke seems to have dealt with their visits largely by failing to turn up to their summons, only going so far as to answer affirmatively the question, 'Do you submit to the authority of Parliament in this present Visitation?'[37] His situation appeared to have improved when in 1648 he was appointed (by the King, then a prisoner in Carisbrooke Castle) to a new Regius professorship of Hebrew, with a canonry at Christ Church. But was it wise to accept a position from a king in captivity, even if none but His Majesty could confer it? John Selden, in his capacity as a Parliamentary burgess or regulator of the university, persuaded his committee to endorse the appointment. Pococke's position was for the time secure, even though he was denied the ecclesiastical appointment.

Parliamentary Visitors took their tasks seriously in Oxford, making a close examination of scholarship, checking it for its correctness in accordance with the spirit of the times.[38] Following the King's execution, the situation became more precarious, notwithstanding continuing help from Selden, and from John Greaves, who was supportive, despite losing his astronomy professorship and being banished from the city. Pococke continued to play mouse-and-cat with the authorities, failing to sign an 'engagement' of 1649 (an oath of loyalty to the Commonwealth, abjuring King and House of Lords). The regulating committee seems briefly to have lost its nerve. Pococke declared, 'I have learnt, and made it the unalterable principle of my soul, to keep peace, as far as in me lies, with all men; to pay due reverence and obedience to the higher powers, and to avoid all things that are foreign to my profession or studies; but to do anything that may ever so little molest the quiet of my conscience would be more grievous than the loss, not only of my fortunes, but even of my life.'[39] The committee came back as if reinvigorated the following year. In December 1650 they ejected Pococke from Christ Church and drew up a vote to expel him from his professorships. His fortune appeared to have run out.

But the university drew back from its ideological pursuit, realising what the loss of Pococke would mean. He was one of its great assets, but now on the point of expulsion merely because he did not conform to the current posture. A petition was drawn up by the vice-chancellor and many heads of colleges in support of him. It was strongly supported by Selden and it requested that 'the late vote, as to the Arabic lecture, at least' should be suspended, since Pococke was 'a great ornament to this university'. Almost all the signatories were men who had been appointed by the Parliamentary Visitors.[40] The authorities relented and Pococke held on to the Arabic and Hebrew professorships until the Restoration.

Amid the uncertainty of ejection, Pococke was still able to produce a masterpiece of Near Eastern learning. In 1650 there appeared his *Specimen Historiae Arabum*, ('A Portion of the History of the Arabs'), a translation of part of a work on the dynasties of Arab history by the twelfth-century Syriac bishop Abulfaraj, who was also known as Barhebraeus.[41] Pococke had been studying this text for more than a decade. The published work was dedicated to John Selden, and the dedication was made, in the style typical of Arabic works, not with a grand tombstone inscription following the title page, but with a modest declaration at the end of the preface. What was remarkable about this volume was not so much the critical edition of the text (which covered only fifteen pages of Arabic, facing an equal number of pages of Latin translation), but rather Pococke's notes, which in 357 pages explored Islamic (and pre-Islamic) history, literature and culture for the first time in a serious and rational manner. His text naturally vindicated the Arabs from the medieval charge of idolatry, and he set down simply the beliefs and duties of Muslims.[42] In the words of the modern Islamic scholar P.M. Holt: 'Profoundly erudite in content and uncontroversial in tone, Pococke's notes show the emergence of the scholarly study of Islam from the distortions of medieval polemic.'[43] For about two hundred years this text remained a key European work for the serious study of Islamic history.

Pococke ends the work with a telling biblical quotation. After pointing out that whatever one's opinion of their religion, the Arabs were, in terms of human wisdom, in no way inferior to his readers in mental flexibility or acumen, he concludes with a verse – naturally given in the original Greek – from the Epistle to the Romans (11: 20), which the King James Bible translates as 'Do not be high-minded, but fear.'[44] Today the meaning is better rendered as: Do not be arrogant, but stand in awe. It is as though the Laudian professor had looked to the past (and possibly foreseen future centuries of patronising arrogance extended by the West towards Islam and the Arabs) and advised anyone who could read his text to seek knowledge and show a measure of humility before a great culture. Pococke's admonition is as relevant today as it was in 1650.

The controversies of the day were reflected in his text. The idea was prevalent among the Puritans that it was not right to have fluency in many languages; this was connected to the notion that too much linguistic knowledge, like too much knowledge in general, was apt to lead to loss of belief. Pococke would have none of this. Writing about the Abbasids, he commented:

> The first to reveal himself as one who cherished the noble arts was their second leader Abu Jaafar al-Mansur, who, to his skill in the law, in which he excelled, added the study of Philosophy and above all Astronomy. But it was their seventh leader al-Mamun who raised these disciplines to the heights they subsequently attained. He it was who, in his passionate devotion to these subjects, and paying them their due honour, through the efforts of emissaries brought together

from the Royal Libraries the most important writings of Greece, so that he might explore them in his own home, and, by offering rewards, enticed experienced translators to render them into the Arabic tongue. He exhorted others to read them, and personally attended the disquisitions of learned men, making his own enthusiastic contributions; in short he left no stone unturned in his promotion of all the fine arts. Efforts worthy of a Prince! Thus it came about that in a short time knowledge of them spread throughout all the east and west, wherever the Arabic tongue had extended and their religion had been disseminated by the sword.[45]

Notes by Pococke on the Islamic sects and their dogmatic disputes could be read by a careful reader as relevant to current English disputes on religious authority and the status of sacred text. Pococke also quotes the orthodox and devout Islamic expositor al-Ghazali on the questionable views of some mystical Sufi enthusiasts who had ceased to cultivate the soil on account of their claim that they had achieved a mystical union with God.[46] Simon Ockley's 1708 translation of this passage makes clear its relevance to the passions of the times. 'People ran on to such a degree (*of madness you may be sure*) as to pretend to an union with God and a sight of him without the interposition of any veil, and familiarly discourse with him. . . which sort of speeches have occasion'd great mischiefs among the common people; so that some country fellows, laying aside their husbandry, have pretended to the same things: for men are naturally pleased with such discourses, as give them a liberty to neglect their business, and withal promise them purity of mind, and the attainment of strange degrees and proprieties. Now the most stupid wretches in nature may pretend to this, and have in their mouths such false and deceitful expressions. And if any one denies what they say, they immediately tell you that this unbelief of yours follows from learning and logic, and that learning is a veil, and logic labour of the brain, but that these things which they affirm are discovered only inwardly by the light of the truth.'[47]

Fresh troubles broke out in the parish. Extreme members of the Childrey congregation sought to have Pococke thrown out under a new act which ejected 'ignorant, scandalous, insufficient and negligent ministers'. The case carried on for some months in Abingdon. He was again saved by colleagues, regardless of faction. The Puritan vice-chancellor, Dr John Owen, warned the commissioners of the 'infinite contempt and reproach which would certainly fall upon them, when it should be said, that they had turned out a man for insufficiency, whom all the learned, not of England only but of all Europe, justly admired for his vast knowledge and extraordinary accomplishments'.[48] The charge was dropped; learning and friendship again dispelled the clouds of ideological hatred and popular bigotry.

A further book he and his son were working on was relevant, sometimes directly and sometimes obliquely, to the disputes and conflicts of the mid- and late seventeenth century. This was the philosophical romance that Jacob Romano may have drawn his attention to, and of which a few pages were translated in 1645. (It had been rendered into Hebrew by Moses of Narbonne in 1349.) The full text was not published until 1671, more than a decade after the Restoration.[49] Even then it only appeared in Arabic and Latin. Pococke supervised the work, giving much of the task of translation to his son, Edward Pococke junior, at Christ Church, who lay somewhat in the shadow of his father. The text itself was by Ibn Tufayl and entitled *Hayy ibn Yaqzan* ('the Living One, son of the Vigilant'). Ibn Tufayl had been born in Guadix (Wadi Ash – one of the few places in Europe where it is possible for the traveller today to be given accommodation in a cave) in Andalusia and had risen to be chief physician at the Almohad court of Sultan Yusuf at Marrakesh. He was instrumental in introducing Ibn Rushd (Averroes) to the court and in promoting his work. He died at a great age, in 1189. Ibn Tufayl has been described as a Neoplatonic thinker, and the title, with its implication of an active intellect deriving from a higher entity, swims in the sweet waters of Neoplatonism; here the 'Living One', Soul, is the offspring of the unsleeping Mind or Intelligence, both of which find their ultimate home in The One, the ultimate unity of all things. In Ibn Tufayl's text, the hero is keen to point out that his observations lead him towards The One.

But the content of *Hayy ibn Yaqzan* veers away from the scented night-song of speculative Neoplatonic metaphysics in the direction of the consecutive practical thought of Aristotle, in laying down a programme of observation and description and in learning from mistakes. Something approaching the scientific method is found here. Edward Pococke – perhaps the elder – gave the published translation a radically different title from that of its Arabic original. He called it *Philosophus Autodidactus*, the self-taught philosopher (or 'the lover of wisdom who is an autodidact'), a title which seems to herald the new world of John Locke, empirical philosophy, trusting our own senses and selves (rather than the authority of others), taking responsibility for our own lives and departing from the creaky scholastic complexities and handed-down obscurities of the past. The title alone indicates the empowering of the autodidact, the banishment of class and hierarchies, and the diffusion of knowledge to all. In *Philosophus Autodidactus* the human mind is shown gaining its ideas from observation and reflection, and not from any innate faculty. As Simon Ockley, the first person to translate the work directly from Arabic into English, noted in his preface, the purpose of the work was 'to shew how Human Capacity, unassisted by any External Help, may, by due application, attain to the Knowledge of Natural Things'.[50] From there one travels, according to the author, to supernatural things, after the natural world has been understood aright.

In its attitude to the divine, *Philosophus Autodidactus* was provocative, for Ibn Tufayl's text made it clear that anyone could attain knowledge of God and harmony with the natural world without the intervention of higher authorities. No expositors of holy law, no miracles, no revelation, no saints, no hierarchies, no bishops, no clergy, no sacraments, no ceremonies, no holy books or sacred law were necessary; reason and reflection alone sufficed to lead humankind to knowledge of the natural world and to knowledge of God. This was brilliantly subversive. It is not surprising that the Quakers seized on *Philosophus Autodidactus*, and that one of their leaders, George Keith, was the first to make an English translation (in 1674) from the Pocockes' Latin version.

In view of the influence of the tale and the philosophical implications that it carried, it is worth exploring the Self-taught Philosopher in greater detail. Besides, the story has (despite questionable moments) a certain charm to it. In 1708 Ockley completed his translation from the Arabic text and this is the version quoted here.

We are transported to an island in the Indian Ocean, where there is a child, alone. (The wild child, the son of nature, was a concept set to become a major preoccupation of the eighteenth century. *Hayy ibn Yaqzan*, the tale of an unferal feral child, contains an early account of child development and influenced Rousseau's *Emile*.) How did he come to be here? Ibn Tufayl gives two possible explanations, suggesting the dual tease of 'There was, and there was not', with which some fairy tales begin. One is that the infant was born through spontaneous generation, owing to the island's position close to the equator and through the chance fermentation of 'a certain Mass of Earth'. A fantastic description follows, redolent of weird and complex alchemy, filled with prodigious seethings of the earth's crust, which George Keith, the Quaker translator, dismissed as a 'meer fabulous report'. It tells how a bubble arose, inwardly divided by a thin partition, one part of which was 'full of Spirituous and Aerial Substance'. From this contrivance eventually a baby emerged. (It is possible to find here a curious parallel with the final part of Bernard Shaw's *Back to Methuselah.*) This strange, almost alchemical, explanation may have been a device to keep the reader alert, but it also served to describe the functions of some of the organs of the body; and it attempted to explain the belief that God, as a kind of primal physicist, created man in his own image.[51] The other explanation, rational to us, is that, following a marital dispute within a high-born family (like that between Leontes and Hermione in *The Winter's Tale*), the new-born offspring of the quarrelling partners was cast out from the community either towards another shore or to a watery grave, launched out across the waves within a tiny wooden casket (or 'ark') to seek fortune and encounter fate wherever Lady Chance might lead.

Fortune was on this occasion kind: the 'ark' with its tiny cargo was cast up that very night on the neighbouring island in 'a little shady grove, thick set with trees, where he was secured from both wind and sun; when the tide ebb'd, the ark was left there, and the wind rising blew an heap of sand together between the ark and the sea, sufficient to secure him from any future danger of such another flood.'[52]

The timbers of the casket had grown weak in the waves. The boy was hungry and cried. At that moment a roe deer was wandering by, searching for her young (which had been devoured by an eagle), and, hearing the voice, approached the ark, which she battered with her hoofs. Then she saw him; 'as soon as she saw him she shew'd the same natural affection to him as if he had been her own, suckled him and took care of him.' The roe 'liv'd in good pasture so that she was fat and had, such plenty of milk, that she was very well able to maintain the child; she took great care of him, and never left him, but when hunger forc'd her; and he grew so well acquainted with her, that if at any time she staid away from him a little longer than ordinary, he'd cry pitifully, and she, as soon as she heard him, came running instantly; besides all this, he enjoy'd this happiness, that there was no beast of prey in the whole island.'[53]

He learnt to walk and teeth appeared.

'He always followed the roe, and she shew'd all the tenderness to him imaginable; and us'd to carry him to places where fruit trees grew, and fed him with the ripest and sweetest fruits which fell from the trees; and for nuts or such like, she us'd to break the shell with her teeth, and give him the kernel; still suckling him as often as he pleas'd, and when he was thirsty she shew'd him the way to the water. If the sun shin'd too hot and scorch'd him, she shaded him; if he was cold she cherish'd him and kept him warm; and when night came she brought him home to his old place, and covered him partly with her own body, and partly with some feathers which were left in the ark . . .'[54]

Together they roamed with a herd of deer and the boy learnt to imitate their voices and the sounds of other birds and beasts. He learnt to distinguish between the different calls of the deer – when they needed help, when they called their mates, when they signalled to indicate their proximity or distance. For (adds Ibn Tufayl) 'you must know that the brute beasts have different sounds to express these different things.'[55] 'Thus he contracted such an acquaintance with the wild beasts, that they were not afraid of him, nor he of them.'[56]

Soon he was observing other differences: that the animals had built-in defences, whereas he was naked and defenceless, slow and weak by comparison. In any dispute he came off worst. He saw he was different from his fellow fawns.[57] They rapidly grew to be vigorous and swift and they had horns. In responding to the calls of nature, they hid their deposits beneath their tails, and their private parts were more concealed than his own.

He was different, he despaired at his difference and he was now aged seven. So he plucked the leaves off a tree to cover himself before and behind and learnt to use the bough of a tree for attack and defence. He also noticed that the other animals avoided dead creatures; so when he came across a dead eagle, he stripped off the feathers and wrapped himself in the skin. This kept him warm, and discouraged other beasts except for 'the Roe, his Nurse, which never left him, nor he, her; and when she grew Old and Feeble, he us'd to lead her where there was the best Food, and pluck the best Fruits for her, and gave her them to eat'.[58]

Then the roe, weakening, eventually died. 'When the Boy perceiv'd her in this Condition, he was ready to dye for Grief. He call'd her with the same voice which she us'd to answer to, and made what Noise he could, but there was no Motion, no Alteration.' There was no concept within him of death as an end; Ibn Tufayl makes the point that he was searching for 'that part w[h]ere the defect was, that he might remove it, and she return to her former State, of Life and Vigour'.[59]

He then behaved to her corpse in what appears to be an unreverential and unfilial manner. But it made sense within the context of the (to us) primitive Aristotelian view of sensation and perception which the author advances. He noticed that if he closed his eyes, stopped his ears or held his nostrils, the senses of seeing, hearing and smelling would cease. With the dead roe deer there was no obstruction. He was not driven to conclude (as we would be) that sensation had for her ended, and that eyes, ears and nostrils were necessarily connected with the sensory process. To him, the true connection between the thing sensed and the person sensing it lay deep within the body: 'the disaffected part lay in the Breast.'

So, searching for the key to life, he cut open her body, giving himself an anatomy lesson in the process: discovering lungs and heart. When he came across one of the cavities beside the heart he believed that he found the centre of sensation. This belief, strange as it is, was hardly less odd than Descartes's assertion that the pineal gland was the seat of the soul, which was activated by a flow of animal spirits.

The boy mused upon his departed adoptive mother, the dead roe. How was existence tied to corporeality? Why did Being forsake body?[60] Being had left her and all that was left was body. Now that Being had fled, the carcass required disposal. He observed a fight between two ravens, in which when one had been killed, the other dug a pit for its corpse. This action taught him to perform the same deed for his mother.

The young lad was troubled by a crisis of identity: the other deer had a family resemblance to his mother, so he kept to their company, while searching all around him for the appearance of something a bit more like himself. Other creatures had creatures similar to themselves for company; why didn't he?

A fire broke out on the island. Boldness led him to it and he stretched out his hand, only to be rudely burned. He grabbed a stick, put it into the fire and carried it flaming home to his hut, where it gave him light and heat. On noting that the flames went upwards, he concluded that fire was a celestial substance. He learnt to feed the fire, sometimes quickly, sometimes slowly. Once he put some fish on it and 'as soon as e're he smelt the Steam, it rais'd his appetite, so that he had a Mind to Taste of them'.[61]

Fire was warm; his mother had been warm. So he concluded that they shared the same substance. A somewhat barbarous experiment confirmed him in this opinion.[62] 'Moist Vapour' came to be understood as the key to existence; on its departure, death ensued.

His naturalist enquiries led him to observe the arrangement, situation and rough extent of the animal kingdom and to understand how they connected with one another. But his classification was of a very rudimentary type, indeed it hardly existed. Despite pointing out the variety of the animal kingdom, he found it to be 'One' in regard of the animal spirits which were diffused from the heart of all creatures. ('One' seems to refer to some Neoplatonic point of convergence; although it could also be taken to mean a single community of which all the various individuals were members.) Indeed, there was but one animal spirit; this, when it came in contact with the eye, caused sight to occur, and with the ear, hearing, and so forth. The nerves directed the animal spirits to whichever part of the body was required; and when the animal spirits could no longer reach a part of the body, action ceased.[63]

Now the lad had reached his twenty-first birthday. He made clothes and shoes and learnt how to construct a dwelling from observing swallows building their nests. He set up a storehouse and tamed birds of prey for hawking. He taught himself to ride the horses whose wildness he had curbed.[64]

In philosophical musings he explored the nature of things, or 'bodies' in Aristotelian terminology – the different kinds of animals, plants, minerals and several sorts of stones, earth, water, exhalations, ice, snow, hail, smoke, hoar frost, flame and heat: a somewhat indiscriminate list, from which he concluded that plurality was their essence, but at the same time they accounted as 'One'. (The text seems to be struggling to say, What do things have in common, and what distinguishes them? – although the desire to make philosophical points negated serious classification.) The fact that animals shared matters of sensation and nutrition, and the capacity to move at will, indicated to him an underlying unity, making a case for the Neoplatonic 'One'. ('He looked upon the whole species of living creatures, to be all One.'[65]) The same was true for plants, and for animals and plants together. Inanimate bodies were also subsumed as 'one', 'tho' multiplied and diversified in some certain respects'.

He explored heaviness and lightness, and heat and cold. 'He saw that Water was rarefied into Vapours, and Vapours again Condens'd into

Water; and that such things as were Burn't, were turn'd into Coals, Ashes, Flame and Smoak, and if in its Ascent it was intercepted by an Arch of Stone or the like, it thickned there and was like other Gross, Earthly Substances.' A discussion follows on body and form. The capacity of bodies to change leads him to consider the two sorts of soul (or 'animating principle'): for animals, the sensitive soul, and for plants, the vegetative soul.[66] He mused upon the concept of body and extension, and realised that material objects had to have some sort of maker.[67] They were 'beholden to some efficient cause'. (In Aristotelian terminology, an efficient cause is something that brings about an effect, but which is unrelated to the purpose or end embedded in the item.) His thoughts began to turn to the idea of a voluntary agent, not subject to physical corruption.

He interrupts this train of thought to cleave his mind to the stars, which he reasoned were finite, not infinite, noting that 'the notion of an infinite body was absurd and impossible'. Speculations move on to the world in general; he 'debated with himself, whether it did exist in Time, after it had not been; and came to Be, out of nothing; or whether it had been from Eternity'.[68] This was problematic, since infinite existence seemed 'press'd with no less Difficulties than that of Infinite Extension'. Yet if the world were 'produc'd a-new, unless it was suppos'd there was Time before it; whereas Time was one of those things that belonged to the world, and was inseparable from it; and therefore the World could not be suppos'd to be later than Time.' Time interrelated with the physical universe. There was no time without physical existence.

From the notion of a thing created, he understood that a creator was needed. The agent who created the world must be 'such an one as cannot be apprehended by the senses'; for if he could be, he would be Body, and if body, already part of the world, which would lead to an infinite regress.[69] So he arrived at the notion of God, infinitely powerful, who created the heaven, the earth and the stars: a 'voluntary agent of infinite perfection'. Considering the variety of animals, he concluded that the creator was 'supereminently Bountiful and exceedingly gracious'.[70] He, as perfect, gave us the notion of imperfection. At the age now of 35, Hayy ibn Yaqzan, through a process of deductive reasoning alone, had arrived at the knowledge of God: an absolute being of necessary existence. For the thinker, perfection and happiness lay only in contemplation of this being.[71] He also concluded that his own soul was immortal ('that his Real Essence could not be dissolv'd'), since it was by means of it that he had apprehended that Absolute Being of necessary Existence.[72] Only mankind was capable of knowledge of this being.[73]

Considering himself, he concluded that he was part brute beast, part a mirror of the heavenly bodies and part a likeness of the necessarily self-existent being.[74] He resolved to explore further his likeness to the third similarity, austerely eating and drinking only such as was necessary for his survival.[75]

A problem arose. How should he eat, since consumption of the plants and animals (created by the necessarily self-existent being) would hinder their perfection and 'deprive them of that End for which they were design'd'; a course of action which would be 'an opposition to the working of the Supream Agent', thereby working against his own desire for proximity with that being? Might it be best to abstain from eating altogether? 'This would not do . . . of two Evils he resolved to chuse the least, and do that which contain'd in it the least opposition to the Creator.' Within these guidelines he decided to eat only the pulp of ripe fruits and to preserve the seeds. His rule was to harvest only those plants 'that there was greatest Plenty of, and which increased fastest', and 'to pull up nothing by the Roots, nor spoil the seed: And if none of these things could be had, he would take some living Creature, or eat Eggs; but when he took any Animal, he chose that sort of which there was the greatest Plenty, so as not totally to destroy any Species.'[76]

The basics of his existence were worked out: he had built a shelter and planned an ethical and ecologically sound diet. This mirrored his similarity to the beasts, within his knowledge of the necessary self-existent being. Now he sought a threefold imitation of the stars, by which he meant undertaking deeds not entirely dedicated to his immediate circumstances. He would make it easy for plants to grow, transplanting those that were situated too close to one another or deprived of the sun. He would water plants in danger of drying up. In the animal kingdom, he would rescue hunted beasts and those 'entangled in a Snare', or any that was 'prick'd with Thorns or that had gotten any thing hurtful fallen into its Eyes or Ears, or was hungry or thirsty'. If a stream was dammed up, thereby preventing access to water for plant or animal, he took care to remove the obstruction.[77] This environmentally aware, altruistic dimension to existence was felt to draw its inspiration from a first imitation of the heavens.

The secondary imitation consisted in keeping himself 'clean from all manner of Dirt and Nastiness', washing himself, keeping his nails and teeth clean, and the secret parts of his body, and applying sweet herbs, as well as perfuming himself with 'Odors'. He would keep his clothes clean, and change them often 'so that he was all over extreamly clean and fragrant'.[78] It is hard to avoid comparing this attitude to cleanliness with Jacques de Vitry's contemporary hell-threatening strictures against the crusaders taking baths, the French cardinal's notion that uncleanliness was next to godliness. Hayy would also take exercise by walking in a circular motion around the island. (This idea was playfully ridiculed by Pope; see below.)

The third category of imitation of the stars was made up of his contemplation of the necessarily self-existent being. This meant a determined turning-away from the material world of sense, a separation from the mundane; going into a cave, where he could fully concentrate on the attributes of the being. With severe spiritual exercises he excluded all thoughts and aspects of daily life.[79]

This blended in to his final similarity, when he discovered the manner in which he was like to God. He began to think that 'he that has the Knowledge of this Essence, has the Essence itself'.[80] He felt he was a portion of God; but this was dismissed as an arrogant illusion, illusory because he was still using the categories of sensible objects which were irrelevant in the context of the Divine. He attempted to give the reader some idea of the contemplation of God, after bluntly saying, 'And now, don't expect that I should give thee a description of that, which the Heart of Man cannot conceive.' He struggled to give a meaning to his contemplation: 'like the Image of the Sun which appears in a well-polish'd Looking-glass, which is neither the sun nor the Looking-glass, and yet not distinct from them'.[81] Further glasses may reflect this essence down a chain of being, leading to the lower world of sense. This image was steeped in Neoplatonism. His spiritual exercises led him to remain for ever-longer periods in a state of inner exaltation. God himself was both multiplicity and singularity; this was the significance of his paradoxical earlier conclusions about 'One' and 'many' within the natural world.

Then he received a visitor from a neighbouring island.[82] Here there lived a sect of high-minded philosophers, whose elevated ideas had brought them to the notice of the king there and to his subjects. Two members of the sect were particularly distinguished: Asal (or Absal) and Salaman. Asal was a mystic, and Salaman of a more down-to-earth mentality. Asal's temperament was retiring and contemplative, whereas Salaman preferred conversation. The two had fallen out. Asal, having heard of Hayy's island, resolved to seek asylum there. A ship was fitted and on arrival he continued his spiritual exercises, conversing with God in a manner which gave him 'the greatest Pleasure imaginable, and the most entire Tranquillity of Mind'. For some time, neither Hayy nor Asal knew of the existence of the other. At length, they caught sight of each another. Asal guessed that Hayy was a spiritual seeker, but Hayy could not imagine what his visitor was, so unlike was the apparition to any of the creatures he had seen.[83]

They approached one another warily, Asal keeping his distance from Hayy, whose long hair made him look like a wild prophet. Asal panicked, but Hayy was faster and stronger and managed to grab his visitor, who, held captive by the unkempt but not self-neglectful figure, 'began to pacifie him with stroaking him'. Hayy could not understand Asal's use of words. In his turn he treated Asal like an unpredictable animal: he 'stroak'd his Head, and both Sides of his Neck'. Eventually Asal's anxiety subsided.

Asal, who was fluent in many languages, tried speaking to Hayy in every tongue he knew. It was to no avail, although Hayy perceived that Asal was well disposed towards him. The visitor made signs to Hayy to eat some of the food which he had brought with him; this Hayy did and after a bout of conscience about breaking the contemplative vows, friendship developed between the two.

Asal taught him to speak by ostensive definition, 'first, by shewing him particular things and pronouncing their Names, and repeating them often, and perswading him to speak them; which he did, applying every Word to the Thing by it signified, till he had taught him all the Nouns, and so improved him by degrees, that he could speak in a very short time'.[84]

Asal questioned Hayy about his origins, of which he knew nothing, and then about his mode of life. Asal was amazed at the depth of his spiritual knowledge and was convinced that what Hayy had discovered by a process of deductive reasoning was the actual law of God as laid down in the Koran. Reason agreed with revelation. He looked upon his host with admiration and respect.

Hayy asked his visitor about his own life. Asal described his island, the sect and the Islamic faith, and the message of Muhammad, all of which Hayy found to be in agreement with his own conclusions. He also accepted the external observances of Islam (prayer, alms, fasting and pilgrimage). But he wondered why Muhammad used parables to describe sacred matters; and he also puzzled over there being no greater prohibition against gaining riches and over-consuming food, things which diverted the mind from the path of God. All the accoutrements of social life similarly seemed pointless to him. Ibn Tufayl makes the point that Hayy believed that all men were endowed with a straightforward temper and a penetrating understanding; he 'was not aware how blockish and stupid they were, how ill-advis'd, and inconstant in their Resolutions; insomuch, that they are like Brute Beasts, nay, more apt to wander out of the way'. Hayy felt it his duty to visit mankind and when a ship docked at the island, they embarked for Asal's native isle.[85]

On disembarking, Asal's friends crowded round them and heard the tale of Hayy. He began to instruct the sect on the matter of approaching higher things. But as soon as he 'began to raise his discours above External things a little', his hearers lost interest and grew secretly angry with him (while still behaving politely). They sought knowledge of truth after the common way, like the rest of the world. He soon despaired of teaching them anything, because they were unwilling to receive what he had to say. So too with the rest of humanity: 'the Desire of getting more, kept them employ'd till they came to their Graves.' Disputing with them only made them more obstinate.[86] Their level of spiritual enlightenment remained universally low. They only wanted novelties.

So he sent a message to Salaman and his friends, apologising for his high-minded discourse; he said that the people were right to stay within their conception of the law, and in their performance of the external rites of religion. Keep the faith of your fathers and don't try anything seriously new was his advice, rather similar to that of Spinoza to his landlady. 'For both he and his friend Asal knew that this tractable, but defective sort of Men, had no other way in the World to escape, but only by this means; and that if they should be rais'd above this to curious Speculations, it would be worse with them, and they would not be able to attain the Degree of the Blessed, but would fluctuate and be toss'd up and down, and make a bad End.' In their present state they would be happy and not come to any harm; so it was best that they should stay that way.[87] So Hayy ibn Yaqzan and his friend Asal sailed away from the world of mankind in order to continue their contemplation; 'Hai Ebn Yokdhan endeavour'd to attain to this lofty Station, by the same means he had sought it at first, till he recover'd it; and Asal followed his Steps, till he came near him, or wanted but very little of it; and thus they continu'd serving God in this Island till they died.'[88] Two rational philosophers, one a man of the spirit and the other more attuned to the mundane, thus found harmony with the world and its guiding principle, and with each other.

Thus ends the compelling fable of the Living One, son of the Wakeful One, reborn in 1671 as the self-taught philosopher, hinting at a new intellectual era of observation and self-reliance. But before looking at the reception accorded to the Pocockes' translation, it is necessary briefly to look at the fable's origins.

Aspects of *Hayy ibn Yaqzan* reach far back to the medieval world. It used to be thought that the original of the story, written in Greek and known as 'Barlaam and Ioasaph', had been written by St John of Damascus in his Palestinian monastery. But the story unquestionably comes from further east, having started life as a parable of the enlightenment of the Bodhisattva, or Buddha-elect.

An earlier Arabic version of *Hayy ibn Yaqzan* can be discerned in the ninth-century Georgian story of Barlaam and Josaphat, a romance known as the *Balavariani* or the *Wisdom of Balahvar*. (Another Arabic version of about the same date is known as the *Book of Bilawhar and Budhasaf*.) The Georgian tale in turn derived from India, where it had represented a version of the education of Gautama Buddha, the Bodhisattva prince, in his journey towards enlightenment. When Gautama was born miraculously to King Suddhodana and Queen Maya, the astrologers predicted that he would forsake the world. The king his father did all in his power to prevent his son's self-hermitisation, but he learnt of human suffering all the same, and at the same time understood how to surmount it. The tale was one of enlightenment. Buddhist elements survive clearly in the Georgian version. Here, a miraculous son in born to the childless King Abenes, who is named Iodasaph, or Budhasaf. At his birth an astrologer predicts that he will be great, but not in the materialistic context of the world of royal gifts, courtly trifles and stifling excess. King Abenes attempts to defy this prediction by bringing up his son in surroundings only of luxury, pandering to the boy's every whim and sealing him from the reality and raw pain of everyday life. Iodasaph learns nevertheless of suffering and death. The king rages in fury, having failed to keep his son from the shadow-side of life. Then a hermit named Balahvar arrives from Ceylon (Sri Lanka or Sarandib) to reveal to Iodasaph the path to eternal salvation, which consists in renunciation. (Here the Georgian version is heavy with notions of Christian doctrine and practice.) King Abenes, the Salaman-type figure encumbered with the traditional trappings of royalty, is left in materialistic frustration on the mainland and at the end of the tale Iodasaph–Asal goes to share with Balahvar–Hayy a life of renunciation and sanctity. The Georgian version is said to have had some influence on the Albigensians. Barlaam and Iodasaph also had a more conventional theological fate: they are today venerated as saints in the calendars of both the Catholic and Orthodox Churches.[89]

None of the earlier versions has the unique quality of Ibn Tufayl's version, which consists in Hayy's reflectiveness and rational striving. Herein lies the originality of the Islamic philosopher, who merely uses the lineaments of the ancient story to make his own points. Some sixty years before Ibn Tufayl, Avicenna had produced a dialogue entitled the *Account of Hayy ibn Yaqzan*, which has some striking and beautiful passages in it, but which embodies a philosophical vision so obscure that the text's incidental pleasures are negated, since the whole is top-heavy with speculative Neoplatonism and futile abstractions.

However significant its antecedents, the effects of *Philosophus Autodidactus* were arguably greater. Quakers and deists derived strength for their positions from Ibn Tufayl's fable; and with its stress on the capacity of human reason, and its rejection of given authority, it is not hard to see it as revolutionary, even if the precise nature of its revolution remains elusive.

Part of its unusualness would appear to derive from the fiction's view of man as originating as an equal with the animals: not so much a lord of creation, but a creature who could be taught by deer and birds, and who was to some extent – initially at least – their closest companion, sharing their life. Hayy is not godlike or made in the image of God from the start. He is not created by a bolt of lightning from the forked fingers of God. Not until near the end of his career does he walk with the divine. It takes him a long time, fraught with trials and errors, to become anything approximating to the image of his Maker.

Maybe part of its ambiguous heritage is also implicit in the work itself: although it is imbued with the Aristotelian scholastic tradition current in the Islamic world, and although that tradition had at its heart an appeal to authority and the unquestioned acceptance of the methods of thinking of the past ('matter is the principle of potentiality, and form the principle of actuality'), yet *Hayy ibn Yaqzan* is a text denying the authority of authority, placing reason and reflection in its place. The position of authority was a topical issue in the 1670s, with philosophy, science, government and religion all searching for new rational bases. Simon Ockley, upholding the Anglican faith, felt that he had to make clear in the appendix to his translation that there was nothing heretical or tending towards 'enthusiasm' in the text he had translated. Nevertheless religious outsiders felt that *Philosophus Autodidactus* gave support to their dissident views and it seems certain that the text encouraged further the diversity of religious discussion in late-seventeenth-century England. A case could be made today for seeing the text as an early statement of the point of view of those who declare that they are religious, but prefer to remain separate from organised religion. The English people, anti-authoritarian by instinct in matters of faith, relishing dissidence, preferring a natural dawn-chorus harmony of differing voices to the grey single note of obedience, thoughtfully stubborn when told to step in line concerning belief, sensitive to the hinterland of faith and usually unwilling to go for the brash allurements of the 'born again', briefly found a kindred spirit in the Arabian self-taught philosopher.

CHAPTER EIGHT

Islam and Europe in the Eighteenth Century

During the Commonwealth Edward Pococke was not idle as a professor, despite the workload of his parish. He produced an edition of Maimonides, in Arabic written in Hebrew script, and laboured on the completion of Selden's text of the Alexandrian patriarch, which was later to receive the put-down from Gibbon. His main occupation was work on the 'English Polyglot', the edition of the Bible in twelve languages and nine volumes, published by the Royalist Brian Walton in 1657, under the protection of Cromwell himself, who exempted from duty the imported paper used in its production. Pococke contributed a long note on Arabic versions of the Pentateuch. And, by way of complete contrast, he published, in 1659, a pamphlet entitled *The Nature of the drink Kauhi, or Coffe, and the Berry of which it is made. Described by an Arabian Physitian.* The Arabic and English texts were printed on opposite pages:

> When it is dried and throughly boyled, it allayes the ebullition of the blood, is good against the small poxe and measles, and bloudy pimples; yet causeth vertiginous headheach, and maketh lean much, occasioneth waking, and the Emirods [haemorrhoids], and asswageth lust, and sometimes breeds melancholly. He that would drink it for livelinesse sake, and to discusse slothfulnesse, and the other properties we have mentioned, let him use much sweet meates with it, and oyle of pistaccioes, and butter. Some drink it with milk, but it is an error, and such as may bring in danger of leprosy.[1]

At the Restoration Edward Pococke presented King Charles II with the celebratory Oxford verses and gained a residency at Christ Church, having had rooms at Balliol during the Commonwealth. He left the rectory in Childrey, but not before he had planted in its garden a cedar, which later grew to be a magnificent tree, from a seed gathered in Syria. After translating Grotius's book *On the Truth of the Christian Religion* into Arabic, in 1661 he brought out an edition (with Latin translation) of an Arabic poem of the thirteenth century, Husain ibn Ali's *Lamiyyat al-Ajam* ('The Traveller's L-verses'), also known as *Carmen Tograi* (the Song of the Tughra), an improving and moral text considered suitable for students.[2]

As a preface to the worthy poem, Pococke adds a vivid and impetuous essay on poetry and the Arabic language, shot through with enthusiasm. The language, he declares, is notable for its expressiveness and great clarity; it can clearly express an idea succinctly, while still manifesting elegance and suavity when other tongues would require plodding circumlocutions. The careful speaker of Arabic works at it as a craftsman with his tools. The language holds a vast number of synonyms: 500 terms for 'lion'; 200 for 'serpent'. 'Calamity' can be expressed in 400 ways; the very list of words was itself a calamity![3]

Pococke recounts the rush of joy that would be found in pre-Islamic times within a family on the discovery of a poetic talent: all would hasten to congratulate the individual's tribe, and the women would beat drums and celebrate as if taking part in a wedding procession.[4] The creation of linguistic artefacts was accounted a prime accomplishment; clear and pure language was admired above all else. Rivalry was intense. After the rule of the sword among the Arabs – Pococke was always stern in his account of the Islamic conquests – poetry, rhetoric, philosophy and medicine emerged at the court of the Abbasids. Especially he singled out, as in his earlier book, the rule of the seventh caliph, al-Mamun, 'who was ardent in his pursuit of these noble studies and accorded them their due honour, they attained such a zenith that regions which had been previously deemed Barbaric were now the sole market place of *belles-lettres*.'[5] A language which had formerly been the domain of theology and poetry now became essential to all who aspired to higher learning; and the Arabs yielded nothing to the Greeks in application and acuity. Pococke quotes his contemporary Henry Savile in saying that 'the practical skills of the Arabs surpassed those of the Greeks in numberless ways'; and John Bainbridge applauded the astronomic skill of easterners. We know comparatively little about the Arab philosophers since we have poor translators.[6] Now, it was for poets and lovers of language to 'unbar for themselves the gates to the beautiful gardens of the Arabs, and pluck their exquisitely fragrant blooms'.[7]

Pococke also derided medieval-type myths, such as that the tomb of Muhammad was suspended in mid-air by large magnets, or that the word 'Saracen' indicated descent from Sarah. (It is a version of the name of a Sinaitic Bedouin tribe, which later came to denote all Arabs.) In the realm of theology, the Arabic language is important for the study of the Rabbinical writings on the Old Testament.[8] Hebrew grammar and poetry are, Pococke asserts, borrowed from the Arabs. The Arabic versions of the entire Bible are useful since the language is that of significant communities of early Christians. Pococke ends his fine eulogy by indicating how much work remains to be done in revealing the qualities of the Arabic language and the civilisation that it enfolds.

This vivid and instinctive warm tribute to language and poetry has been little noticed. Edward Said, in his book *Orientalism,* dismisses the work of Pococke (whose name he misspells), along with that of other pioneers of Islamic and Middle Eastern scholarship, as 'too narrowly grammatical, lexicographical, geographical or the like'.[9] One can only wish that Said's work had been half as vivid, open, sensuous, discriminating and clear, and as informed with true knowledge, accurately reflecting original sources, as Pococke's.

Two years later Pococke produced a full edition of the historical text upon which the notes of 1650 were based. European scholarship was now in possession of a reasonably complete and objective history of the Islamic peoples. Pococke died in Oxford, full of age and honours, in 1691, perhaps the greatest scholar of the time. He probably could have been elevated to a bishopric, had he sought one. But he loved learning and hated faction, and his temperament was non-judgemental. He valued the people around him for their knowledge and friendship, not for their orthodoxy of faith. His passion for seedlings is further shown in the fig-tree, Arbor Pocockiana, which was recorded as growing in one of Christ Church's several private gardens two centuries later. (It may have been the first fig-tree to be cultivated in England.) There is still a fine plane tree, of considerable antiquity, in 'Pococke's Garden'.

The *Philosophus Autodidactus*, on which father and son had worked, had appeared in 1671. It constituted an original addition to the intellectual fare of the time. Pope admired it; Gibbon knew it. But an unsolved mystery is its possible effect on John Locke, and whether it contributed in any way to the production of the *Essay concerning Human Understanding* (1690), the cornerstone text of the foremost British philosophical tradition, empiricism, whose practitioners have included Berkeley, Hume, Mill, Russell and Ayer, and which as its name suggests is based on the central notion of knowledge gained through experience.

The year 1671, the date of publication of the *Philosophus Autodidactus*, was when Locke began examining the nature of human understanding, having hitherto concerned himself with public affairs and political philosophy. At some date in that year Locke held a meeting with 'five or six' friends at Exeter House in the Strand (London) to discuss matters concerning knowledge and its acquisition. On 17 July Pococke's translation was given a review in the Philosophical Transactions of the Royal Society by the Society's secretary, Henry Oldenburg.[10] It is unlikely that Locke would have missed this notice. It is possible that the new notions concerning the nature of reason and the evidence of the senses in gaining knowledge merely coalesced fortuitously at the same time in the same place. It is more likely, but 'not proven', that *Philosophus Autodidactus* exercised a subtle influence on the direction of Locke's thinking while he was preparing the *Essay*. Thus it seems a degree more than possible that Ibn Tufayl's thought played some part in the establishment of the tradition of British empiricism, and in the creation of the modern British world initiated by Locke and the Whigs.

There are naturally wide discrepancies between Ibn Tufayl's method and Locke's. Hayy ibn Yaqzan understands perception in a bafflingly complex scholastic manner; he also exhibits a lack of rigour and gives only a small (though real) place for scientific experimentation. But if one foot is planted in the past, the other is tentatively finding the solid ground of the future. Reason and reflection, those Lockean qualities, are given central places in the Arab text.

Perhaps the most important similarity lies in the notion that knowledge is built up bit by bit, by association of ideas. This is one of Locke's central notions. The knowledgeable mind does not just leap into the world fully charged with primary and universal truths. It starts off as a *tabula rasa* (a blank tablet). The fundamental aspect of Locke's method (which approximated to that of Ibn Tufayl) was to examine the origins of ideas and the ways in which the understanding came to be filled with them.

Passages in *Hayy* show further methodological similarities to Locke's *Essay*. Just as the Andalusian hero based his knowledge on his senses and built up his knowledge of the world gradually, so (for example) Locke wrote, 'All those sublime thoughts which tower above the clouds, and reach as high as heaven itself, take their rise and footing here; in all that great extent wherein the mind wanders in those remote speculations it may seem to be elevated with, it stirs not one jot beyond those ideas which sense or reflection have offered for its contemplation.'[11] Both authors agree that we inevitably use reason, even when we are engaging in spiritual matters, since reason is used even in the decision taken to accept revelation as true. Specific details found in Locke echo Hayy: 'If a colony of young Children should be placed in an island where no Fire was, they would certainly neither have any Notion or Name for it.'[12] In other places Ibn Tufayl's text is consonant with Locke's philosophy, principally, in the notion that there are no innate ideas within the human being. Locke noted how a child acquires ideas: 'It is *by degrees* he comes to be furnished with them.'[13] Hayy's habit of reflection finds an echo in Locke. Locke, in agreement with Hayy, did not hold that the senses alone produced knowledge; we know what we know because here too we apply reason to the input of our senses. The Arab's method of observation was Locke's, as also was the English philosopher's willingness to make compromises when close adherence to theory would have led to absurdity. (For example, Hayy decided not to starve himself in the cause of allowing plants and animals to achieve their full potential.)

But there is no reference to Locke's having read Pococke's translation, and the philosopher's library did not contain a copy of it. Nevertheless it would have entailed a major act of deception to keep Locke from the *Philosophus Autodidactus*, since Locke and Pococke moved in such similar circles. Locke was a close friend of both Edward Pococke senior and junior, and paid a warm tribute to the elder Pococke after the latter died in 1691; he would have known the Laudian professor (who was twenty-eight years his senior) at Christ Church in the years following 1660, when Pococke was back at the college, and for five years Locke was a fairly frequent visitor. Locke said of his senior colleague, 'I know not any one in the university whom I would more willingly consult.'[14] Pococke, declared the philosopher, 'had often the silence of a learner, where he had the knowledge of a master'.[15] Locke left Oxford in 1665 to work for his patron, the 1st Earl of Shaftesbury, but still returned from time to time. He was also tutor to the younger Pococke, who was an undergraduate at Christ Church from 1662 to 1665. Pococke junior would have taken his MA in 1668, the year he would reasonably have started work on the translation of *Hayy ibn Yaqzan*.[16]

The Pocockes' translation briefly became a European bestseller. In Paris Francis Vernon, brother of the English secretary of state James Vernon, was acting as a cultural ambassador and could not keep up with demand. All the professors of the Sorbonne sought copies. He gave his last copy to Christian Huyghens, the Dutch mathematician and astronomer who had been made an FRS ten years earlier and had now settled in France. The work was translated into Dutch in 1672; in England, George Keith's version of 1674 was the first of three English translations in the period 1674–1708. (The second English version, undertaken by George Ashwell in 1686, was a rare and compelling example of English spiritual-pastoral, imbued with quiet ecstasy, with passages reminiscent of Thomas Traherne. Ashwell's language is alert to the unique sylvan qualities of English, calling to mind a painting by an English landscape artist.) German translations appeared in 1726 and 1783, the latter of which, by J.G. Eichhorn, was given the significant title *Der Naturmensch*. The French, after the initial enthusiasm, appear to have grown tired of it; there was no French translation until modern times and Voltaire himself expressed a strong dislike of the work ('nonsense from one end to the other'[17]). However, since part of Voltaire's project was to emphasise the gulf between medieval philosophy and scientific reason, a twelfth-century text was unlikely to appeal to him.[18]

Alexander Pope was drawn to aspects of the philosophical romance. One modern commentator, Shelly Ekhtiar, has suggested that Pope's isolation as a Catholic in a Protestant country led to his identification with the solitary Hayy on his island. The *Essay on Man* contains a passage which teasingly refers to some of Hayy's more obsessive qualities:

> Go, soar with Plato to th'empyreal sphere,
> To the first good, first perfect and first fair;
> Or tread the mazy round his follow'rs trod,
> And quitting sense call imitating God;
> As Eastern priests in giddy circles run
> And turn their heads to imitate the Sun.
> Go, teach Eternal Wisdom how to rule –
> Then drop into thyself, and be a fool![19]

Hayy's 'giddy circles' are perhaps perplexing; but circular motion was a favourite topic of the Arabs, maybe reaching back to notions found in Plato's *Timaeus*,[20] where, since the concept of momentum was absent, movement was seen as only possible by the agency of a perpetual

circularity of motion. The idea may reflect the circularity of the heavenly
bodies; perhaps there is a reference to the circuitous walking which is part
of the *haj* ritual. Circularity has already appeared as an aspect in Siger of
Brabant's Averroism. Moving in a circle is a common feature to ritual and
can represent a wider archetype of faith or life. The medieval English
loved processions, for which large churches, such as that at Blythburgh,
were suited. Today we enjoy walking or jogging round the local park.
Maybe there is a part in us which stays ignorant of the concept of
momentum. We subliminally believe that if we stop, everything will stop.

Pope also noted the passage in Ibn Tufayl's text which called for the
humane treatment of animals. The poet observed, 'I remember an
Arabian author who has written a treatise to show how far a man,
supposed to have subsisted on a desert island, without any instruction, or
so much as the sight of any other man, may, by the pure light of nature,
attain the knowledge of philosophy and virtue. One of the first things he
[Ibn Tufayl] makes him [Hayy] observe is that universal benevolence of
Nature in the protection and preservation of its creatures. In imitation of
which, the first act of virtue he thinks his self-taught philosopher would
of course fall into is, to relieve and assist all the animals about him in
their wants and distresses.' The 'universal benevolence of nature' was
somewhat optimistic; but one cannot question the significance of Ibn
Tufayl's text in reinforcing Pope's courageous and solitary campaign
against the prevalent habits of cruelty to animals.[21]

Several imitations attest to the brief fame of *Hayy ibn Yaqzan*. One was
called the *History of Josephus, an Indian Prince* (1696). An anonymous
History of Autonous was offered to the public in 1736. In his
autobiography Edward Gibbon recalls that his tutor in Putney, John
Kirkby, wrote a book in 1745 entitled *The Life of Automathes* (the self-
taught one), which 'aspires to the honours of a philosophical fiction . . .
It is the story of a youth, the son of a shipwrecked exile, who lives alone
on a desert island from infancy to the age of manhood. A hind is his
nurse; he inherits a cottage, with many useful and curious instruments . . . .'.
Automathes becomes a 'self-taught though speechless philosopher, who
had investigated with success his own mind, the natural world, the
abstract sciences, and the great principles of morality and religion'. But,
'The author is not entitled to the merit of invention, since he has
blended the English story of Robinson Crusoe with the Arabian romance
of Hai Ebn Yokhdan, which he might have read in the Latin version of
Pocock.'[22] Gibbon himself was a warm admirer of the work of the elder

Pococke and made extensive use of it in *The Decline and Fall of the Roman Empire.*

There is speculation over whether *Robinson Crusoe* (1719) was influenced by *Hayy ibn Yaqzan,* but there is little, except the idea of a man fending for himself, to connect the two. As Gibbon noted, the two may blend together, but they hardly overlap. Defoe's novel is more highly worked, literary and interesting, but lacks the philosophical dimension of *Hayy,* and the sense of the deep connection between reflection and the development of awareness. *Hayy ibn Yaqzan* can however be claimed as the first work of 'desert island' fiction.

❖❖❖

Despite the excitement manifested from about 1680 to 1710 in *Hayy,* and the 'Arabick' interest of philosophers, 'natural philosophers' (the term for scientists) and dissident theologians, any serious interest in the East thereafter all but vanished. Arabic texts had been valued by mathematicians, astronomers and physicists at the outset of the quest for scientific knowledge; but with the momentous appearance of Newton, Locke and Boyle, the significance of the East diminished. Religion itself underwent a transformation. The strife of the seventeenth century was quietened by Glorious Revolution of 1688 and the arrival of the Whigs, so that the nature and origin of sacred texts were no longer matters of urgent importance. Religious anguish evaporated. Few now bothered with oriental languages, as the comfort of the coffee-house took over from religious strife. William Warburton, Bishop of Gloucester and editor of Pope, was a sociable ironist who had no time for foreign studies. In the journey from faith to fashion, eastern matters were largely abandoned.

Some remained faithful to scholarship and held to the tradition and standards of Edward Pococke These were exceptions, as the educational conditions found at the Oxford of Gibbon's youth, steeped in 'dull and deep potations', became the norm. Simon Ockley, capable but destitute in Cambridge, was one of the last true oriental scholars, though his inability to manage his affairs led to his imprisonment in Cambridge for debt, and a consequent early death – though not before he had made the first translation of Ibn Tufayl from Arabic into English and written a remarkable if sometimes faulty two-volume work of serious history entitled *The History of the Saracens,* which was used by Gibbon. In Ockley's opinion, the Arabs restored to Europe 'things of universal necessity, the fear of God, the regulation of our appetites, prudent oeconomy, decency and sobriety of behaviour'.[23]

Another learned writer who wrote with clarity and objectivity about Islam was Dr Henry Stubbe (or Stubbes). During the Civil War he had served with the Parliamentary army in Scotland, though in 1660 he took the oath of allegiance. He had the misfortune of being burdened with a quarrelsome and unforgiving temperament, bearing grudges across the decades. His work was not published in his lifetime, owing to fear of the censors, and his own political dissidence. During the 1670s he was writing a text on 'The Rise and Progress of Mahometanism', which, despite not reaching the press until 1911, gained a surreptitious fame as it circulated in manuscript. Stubbe's own religious views edged away from Trinitarian orthodoxy in the direction of an understanding of Jesus not as a person infused with the divine spirit to whom prayers should be addressed, but – in the manner, as he saw it, of the early Christians – as the Messiah whose second coming would establish universal peace and truth. Only later, he held, was Jesus prayed to, and seen as the Son of God. Belief in the Holy Spirit as God came even later. Stubbe's views shaded into the Islamic view of Jesus, in which he was seen as a prophet, born of a virgin and the greatest after Muhammad, but not divine.[24]

Here, enriched and strengthened and given definition, were views quite similar to those of the Socinians, now dispersed by the Jesuits from their cooperative commonwealth in Poland. We have seen how opponents of belief in the Trinity had fled to Basle, Poland and the Netherlands; Faustus Socinus had thought it prudent to set up his community of rational believers in tolerant Poland. They settled in Rakow (north-east of Krakow), where the summary of their beliefs was published in the *Racovian Confession* (1605). (A later edition, with a dedication to King James I, was dispatched by them to London, seeking the approval of the Protestant monarch, a task in which they were not successful.) A fine Socinian civilisation blossomed in Poland, with its 300 churches and an academy with pupils sent from families all over Europe, including Catholic ones. Indeed it can be said that the growth in central Europe of Socinianism, dominant within what was known as the Minor Church in Poland, represented one of those few times when humanity has reclaimed the Garden of Eden, creating a society of work, equality, education, progress, classlessness, human harmony, tolerance, Christian socialism and peace, which continued until 1638 when the destruction of the community by the Jesuits began.[25]

Around 1660 the Socinians were finally outsted from Poland, driven out by the renewed zeal of the Catholic Church. Most of them thereupon trekked four hundred miles south-east to Kolozsvar, or Clausenburg (today Cluj, Romania) in Transylvania, where anti-Trinitarians had been a substantial community for eight decades. In the early seventeenth century Transylvania achieved a unique position under the Calvinist Gabor Bethlen. During the Thirty Years War Protestant Transylvania, under Ottoman suzerainty and opposing the Catholic Habsburgs, constituted one of the few parts of continental Europe where the reformed religion survived. Gabor Bethlen was provided with an army by courtesy of the Ottoman sultan, Ahmed I. It is undeniable that the survival of minority communities in Transylvania was made possible by its being beyond the reach of the Habsburg Emperor.

Thinkers did not miss the theological parallels betwen Socinianism and Islam. In the decades since the re-emergence of anti-Trinitarian belief in the mid-sixteenth century, such views had spread widely in Europe, something which was helped by the Socinians' acceptance of rationalism and the scientific revolution, shown in their opposition to the 'incomprehensible' doctrine of the Trinity. The seeds sown by radical dissent had borne fruit. But their survival was made hard both by the success of the Counter-Reformation, and the determination of the Reformers (led by Calvin) to keep the formula for the Trinity.

In England, dissenters expressed disbelief in the Trinity in the reigns of Queen Elizabeth and King James I. Under both monarchs such views were severely suppressed; those concerned were put to death, though James 'politicly preferred that heretics . . . should silently and privately waste themselves away in prison, rather than to grace them and amuze others with the solemnity of a public execution'.[26] The systematic theoretical anti-Trinitarian views of the Socinians seem to have reached England in the 1640s (probably following the beginning of the dispersal of the community from their Polish homeland by the Jesuits) and this theology became identified with a brave and outspoken Gloucestershire schoolmaster, John Bidle.

In England in the 1640s Bidle, the radical anti-Trinitarian, attacked the language of 'trinunities, coessentialities, modalities, eternal generations, eternal processions, incarnations, hypostatical unions and the like monstrous terms, fitter for conjurers then Christians'.[27] Bidle realised that clear thought about faith was impossible without clear language. In his committed assertion of the unity of God, he was firmly opposed to the doctrine of the Trinity, and refused, with fine English stubbornness, to accept what the magistrate might determine should be his religious belief. Bidle also taught his pupil Thomas Firmin that almsgiving to the poor was not enough: you had to make personal enquiries into their condition and undertake proper economic measures to end distress. 'This was one of Mr Bidle's lessons, that tis a duty not only to relieve, but to visit the sick and poor; because they are hereby encouraged and comforted, and we come hereby to know of what nature and degree their straits are.'[28] The visible connection between active practical charity and Unitarianism, in which the introverted, self-concerned realm of speculative metaphysics and dreamy Neoplatonism was abandoned, was clearly shown in Bidle's life.

Socinianism has been accused of leading to deism. Both denied magic and mysteries. But deism (which will be further discussed below) did not treat the scriptures as sacred; it saw Christianity as one form of faith among many. The Socinians were devout and learned, and loved the gospel. They were personally opposed to the dwindling of faith into practical scepticism. But in their opposition to mysteries, the two shared a certain outlook and looked with a measure of favour on the plainness and simplicity of the theology of Islam. Islam was still a live issue among thinkers and had not yet been domesticated in the republic of letters by a 'western' sense of superiority.

The first English translation of the Koran appeared in 1649 and was reprinted in 1688. Since Islam itself is strongly anti-Trinitarian, it is likely that the availability of the text gave an impetus to the spread of scepticism concerning the Trinity in the latter decades of the seventeenth century. (The word 'Unitarian' is not found in England before 1682.) Deistical sentiments occur occasionally in the Koran, especially in Sura 2, translated (incorrectly) in the first English translation thus: 'All those that shall believe[,] Christians, Jews or Samaritans, such as shall believe in God at the day of Judgment, and do good works, shall be recompensed by their Lord, and be free from fear, and affliction, at the day of the resurrection.'[29] Only a few Englishmen actually became Muslims, but resistance to the notion of a triune God continued and this sentiment found a focus in this text. The 1649 version was made from the French and is very imperfect; but its words provided a significant and appropriate language for encountering the divine:

In whatsoever place thou art, whether thou teach what is contained in the Alcoran, or whether thou labour, I am always present, nothing is concealed from thy Lord, of whatsoever is in Heaven or Earth; be it great or little, all is written in the intelligible Book, that explaineth all things. There needeth no fear for such as recommend themselves to God, they shall be exempt from the pains of Hell. The true believers who have his fear before their eyes, shall suffer no torments in the other World; it is declared to them on Earth, that they shall have all content, the word of God admits of no alteration; they shall enjoy perfection of felicity in Paradise. Afflict not thy self for the words of the impious; vertue proceedeth from God, he understandeth, and knoweth all things; whatsoever is in Heaven and in Earth appertaineth to him: They who worship idols follow but their opinions, and are lyars; God hath created the night for repose, and the day for labour; such as hear his word, find therein marks of his Omnipotency. They have said, Do ye believe that God hath a Son? Praised be God, he is most rich, and hath no need of any person.[30]

Here were words of religious comfort, and although they lacked the majesty of the King James Bible, they approached the unity of the Supreme Being with an authentic religious resonance.

The theologically orthodox fought back for the idea of the Trinity. Edward Stillingfleet (Bishop of Worcester) and Charles Leslie were among its most firm defenders. But the interesting point is that, so far as Stillingfleet is concerned, his 1697 *Discourse in Vindication of the Trinity*, written in opposition to both the Socinians and John Locke's epochal *Essay*, was the final fling of the old Aristotelian philosophy. It was the articulation of scholasticism, in opposition to the new anti-metaphysical philosophy of empiricism, where notions like 'substance' were in retreat. Stillingfleet yearned to validate the lumbering terminology of the past. But John Locke (and – dare one say it – John Bidle) had discarded it as meaningless.

The Socinians were sometimes viewed suspiciously as Muslims in disguise. A number of monitory, theologically orthodox books, with titles such as *Historical and Critical Reflections on Mahometanism and Socinianism*, showed a fear of the convergence of the two theologies. Socinianism might be the back door for the entry of the Turks into Europe. There was indeed a parallel between Islam and Socinianism, but without a sinister plot. Richard Baxter, the prolific Puritan author, summarised the situation from his theological standpoint. In his *Cure of Church Divisions* of 1670, he classed Socinians with 'Mahometans, who confess Christ to be a great Teacher, but deny him to be the Priest and sacrifice for sin'.[31] Baxter missed the key point, made by Socinus himself: that there were statements in the gospels about Jesus going to his Father which no Muslim could accept. Nevertheless, just as Muhammad had sought to prise superstitious accretions off monotheism in the seventh century, so now the Socinians had come to a roughly similar position approximately ten centuries later. And however much the movement was suppressed or demonised, the number of its adherents such as Henry Stubbe grew, although the latter's tetchy, cantankerous, donnish temperament was at odds with the optimistic, practical and scientific attitude which their liberated faith gave to the Unitarians. Stubbe would have felt out of place in the classless community of cooperative work established in Rakow.

An extraordinary point of coincidence between Socinianism – now beginning to be called Unitarianism – and Islam occurred in August 1682. An ambassador from the Moroccan sultanate, Ahmed ben Ahmed, had arrived in London in January of that year for the purpose of negotiating the status of Tangier. (In the course of the discussions he had presented two lions to Charles II. He was also a popular figure, and had become an associate member of the young Royal Society.)[32] As his diplomatic mission drew to a close, two leading Unitarian ministers approached His Excellency and attempted to present him with an 'Epistle Dedicatory'.[33] The parties were formally introduced to one another by Sir Charles Cotterell, Charles II's master of ceremonies. The document – in fact an address or manifesto – set out the points of agreement between Unitarianism and Islam which were seen as basic, even fundamental. The text took as its background an earlier discussion concerning the basic theological positions of Christians and Muslims, which had occurred in 1610. The participants then had been an ambassador from Morocco, Ahmed ben Abdallah, a Dutch Protestant (Count Maurice) and a Portuguese Catholic (Don Emanuel, who styled himself Prince of Portugal). Following this meeting the Moroccan had written to give his views to the Christians; these consisted of the usual Muslim view of the singularity of God, with special places granted to Jesus and to Mary. The discussion was held in a rational spirit of seriousness and friendship. It seemed an auspicious basis for the new meeting.[34]

The Epistle Dedicatory re-emphasised the belief in an 'Only Sovran God, who hath no distinction or plurality in persons'. The aim seems to have been to 'form an alliance with the Mahometan prince for the more effectual propagation of Unitarian principles'.[35] Its presenters complained about the 'rash severity' of the clergy,[36] and hinted at seeking the protection of the Moroccan sultan.

The Unitarians expressed the desire to place on record 'in what articles we, the Unitarian Christians of all others, do solely concur with you Mahumetans'. They pointed out that on some important points they 'drew nigher' to Islam than to their fellow Christians.[37] They and the Muslims both struggled to proclaim the faith of the One Supreme God, without personalities or pluralities. After expounding the history of Unitarian belief, they set out the facts of the present-day worldwide dispersal of non-Trinitarians. The only places where they were not numerous was western and northern Europe 'by reason of the inhumanity of the clergy'. The delegation offered some books – Unitarianism is a strongly literate, book-conscious faith – apologising for the 'philosophical plainness and freedom that is part of our profession', but offering them nevertheless.[38] Concluding their declaration, they focused on their internationalism and on the practical and optimistic aspects of religion. Unitarians have preferred to stress the dignity and worth of humanity and never placed much emphasis on 'fallen man', or dwelt long on 'sin', let alone 'original sin'. Their project was 'a union with all mankind', and the core of their belief was in the 'harmonious and relative rectitude . . . placed in the reason of man'.[39]

Despite the good intentions, the Epistle Dedicatory was not accepted. It touched on religion as practised and understood in Islamic countries. The Unitarians' offer to 'discover unto you' the 'weak places that are found in the platform of your religion' – anti-Trinitarians have always believed in going straight to the point – led to the rejection of the document in its entirety. For some reason, perhaps because the discussion was taking place in a public forum, although an open discussion of sensitive theological points had been acceptable in 1610, it was now off limits.

A piece of legislation gave a symbolic, though not actual, boost to English Unitarians. In 1689 the Toleration Act was passed, which, although it specifically excluded them, gave them the sense that the possibility of freedom for their forbidden faith might not be far off. The Conventicle Acts had laid down that they might meet only in a very restricted manner. From 1691 a large number of Unitarian pamphlets were printed, mostly anonymously, and all of them funded by Bidle's former pupil, the hard-working wealthy philanthropist Thomas Firmin, a man who does not deserve the oblivion he has gained.

The Unitarians continued to hold unprejudiced views about Islam. Stephen Nye, author of *A Brief History of Unitarianism,* wrote of the need to purge Christianity of its contradictory and impossible doctrines.[40] Look, he said, at the ground that Christianity has already lost to Islam. According to 'divers historians', Muhammad's own design in 'pretending himself to be a prophet' was only 'to restore the belief in the unity of God, which at that time was extirpated among the eastern Christians by the doctrines of the Trinity and the Incarnation'. Nye wrote:

> They will have it that Mahomet meant not his religion should be esteemed a new religion, but only the restitution of the true intent of the Christian religion. They affirm moreover that the Mahometan learned men call themselves the true disciples of the Messias or Christ: intimated thereby that Christians are apostates from the most essential parts of the doctrine of the Messias; such as the unity of God, and that he is to be worshipp'd without images or pictures, in spirit and in truth. But whatsoever the design of Mahomet was, 'tis certain Mahometism has prevailed over greater numbers and more nations than at the day profess Christianity: nay, it has worn Christianity out of great part of Europe, most of Asia, and all of Roman Africa; not by force and the sword, for the Mahometans grant liberty of religion to the conquered provinces of Christians, but by that one truth in the Alchoran, the unity of God.

Nye continued by affirming that the naturalness of belief in the unity of God, and the 'unreconcilable inconsistence' of belief in the Trinity with that belief, make it impossible ever to win back Muslims, whether Turks, Moors or Persians. The Trinity will perpetually block attempts to convert Muslims or Jews. Such peoples suppose that all Christians must believe in the Trinity, 'and from thence conclude that modern Christianity is no better than paganism or heathenism'.

A further open-minded view of Islam was seen in the case of Arthur Bury, Rector (that is, principal) of Exeter College, Oxford. In 1690 he published a pamphlet entitled *The Naked Gospel,* which was an attempt to pare down the Christian faith to its essentials and to strip off scholastical and Neoplatonic accretions. He found no place for the Trinity or for image worship, calling the first polytheism and the second idolatry. His attitude towards Islam was by contrast engaged. Although critical of Muhammad, he declared that the Prophet 'professed all the articles of the Christian faith'.[41] Muhammad believed himself to be not an apostate but a reformer, he observed. And he had been given 'occasion and encouragement' to be a reformer by the 'Christian doctors', the disputatious and obscure Church Fathers who had piled philosophical speculation on the straightforwardness of the gospel and who had left a legacy not of love, peace and joy, but hate, tribulation and strife. To Bury, reason was the voice of God.[42]

Islam was being given a hearing at Oxford, eighty years before Gibbon offered his famous irony that, had not the Muslims been beaten at the battle of Tours, 'the interpretation of the Koran would now be taught in the schools of Oxford, and her pulpits might declaim to a circumcised people the sanctity and truth of the revelation of Mahomet'.[43] Oxford's official response to Bury was fierce. The Visitor, the Bishop of Exeter, was summoned, and lodged at Christ Church. He declared that he would undertake a visitation of Exeter College and set off one summer morning processing in full solemn ecclesiastical attire. Exeter's gates were slammed in his face. After a token resistance he broke in and declared Bury deposed and excommunicated from the Church of England for scandalous disobedience. Bury was also fined £500. The pamphlet was burnt in the Schools' Courtyard, which of course meant increased circulation for its two reprints.[44]

The affair of *The Naked Gospel* prompted John Locke to publish (anonymously, for Locke was always careful) his last book, *The Reasonableness of Christianity*.[45] Bury's ideas of disrobing the faith of its unnecessary beliefs were entirely to Locke's liking. Locke put forward the idea here, too, that Christianity had got lost in a maze of 'wrong notions and invented rites' in the early centuries AD, and at that time only the 'rational and thinking part of mankind' found the 'one supreme invisible God', but was compelled to keep these beliefs secret from the priests, 'those wary guardians of their own creeds and profitable inventions'. Reason had never gained the authority to speak to the multitude. The gospel of Jesus was of one invisible God. Since that time, belief in One God has become common across the world. Locke continues, 'For even to the light that the Messiah brought into the world with him, we must ascribe the owning and profession of one God which the Mahometan religion hath derived and borrowed from it.'[46] In other words, Islamic monotheism grew from the Christian gospel; the teaching of both is of the one and the same God. Locke, who never referred to the Trinity in any of his writings, was saying here that Islam is in effect a cousin to our own belief system and culture, and its view of the divine is similar to that of Christianity. There need be no opposition. We all believe approximately the same thing. We are all on the same side.

Locke's positive attitude to Islam raises an interesting idea. Since the philosopher's ideas played a large part in the formulation of the American Constitution, could it be argued that there is an Islamic dimension to that significant document? Perhaps a case can be made for the notion that the United States of America is, at heart, if not an Islamic state, a state with an Islamic dimension to it.

In the decade 1690–1700 the Trinitarian beliefs of the Church of England were under constant attack and came close to vanishing. Neither archbishop of Canterbury, Tillotson or Tenison, had any love for them. But orthodox Trinitarians provided a strong reaction. Charles Leslie, a combative theological traditionalist and a more subtle opponent than Stillingfleet, first made the Unitarian Epistle Dedicatory public, by publishing it in full in 1708. He attacked its proponents without respite. He could not tolerate their rationalism and rejection of theological mysteries. In *The Socinian Controversy Discuss'd*, he declared that Muslims held 'exactly the Socinian tenets' – indeed that Muhammad 'was not half so scandalous, nor so heterodox as Ebion and Theodotian [Jewish Christians from late antiquity, who held Unitarian views], and that stream of hereticks . . . Mahomet is more Christian than these, and an express Unitarian, but these are not so well known in the world now as Mahomet is . . . And as Mahomet improved Arianism, so the Socinians have exceeded even the Alcoran, in their contempt for Christ, as I have showed, bringing him lower, and making him more a mere man than the Alcoran does.'[47]

Leslie was proclaiming that Unitarians were actually further from Christianity than Muslims. In a later book he repeated the claim: the Unitarians were 'much more Mahometans than Christians'.[48] None could seriously deny that the Unitarians viewed Jesus in a manner close to that of Muslims, but to Leslie the Unitarians were the more wicked, less on the grounds that they had ceased to see Jesus as a person of the Trinity than because they came from his own culture. The issue was one of cultural treachery. As in the case of Robert Sherley, the question of their allegiance to East or West hovered in the background, although the Unitarians in their disdain for florid showiness would never have garbed themselves in oriental fantasy like Shah Abbas's emissary. Even though they were the legatees of over a thousand years of European Trinitarian culture, they had concluded by disavowing the Trinity. Islam, by contrast, appeared to Leslie as a kind of early Christian heresy (the view of the Syrian annalists of the time) and as such its theological standpoint was not shocking. And it was a long way away.

In their determination to challenge anti-rational Trinitarianism and the strange justifications found for it both in the Athanasian Creed and in the ramblings of Pseudo-Dionysius the Areopagite, the Unitarians had introduced Lockean rationality into religion. Faith needed to be released from scholasticism and its futile formulae, just as astronomy and mechanics had been liberated by Galileo and Newton. The deists went one step further and removed virtually all faith, and certainly all enthusiasm, from religion. Edward Herbert, Lord Herbert of Cherbury (1583–1648), had laid the foundations of deism with his essay on comparative religion, *De Religione Gentilium* (published posthumously, and abroad, in 1663).[49] He identified the characteristics common, as he conjectured, to all religions: belief in and worship of God, aspiring to virtue and piety, and belief in a 'future state'. When Herbert's objective categorisation of religions encountered the ideas of Descartes and Newton, and when the implications of the scientific revolution were even partially understood, the rational unenthusiastic faith of deism was born. Here was a break: for the Unitarians, besides believing in the gospels, were spiritual optimists, seeking to draw out the good in humankind, a quality which was expressed in their later quest for law reform and in their involvement in the campaign for the abolition of slavery. By contrast, the eyes of the deists were fixed on the chill vault of existential pessimism.

To the deists the world had already grown old; it was a late-flowering bloom, autumnal, perhaps enjoyable, definitely unimprovable, and its creator was not an active and concerned being, involved perpetually and permanently with his creation, but a kind of divine absentee who had wound up the machinery of nature and then left it to run untended, declining to take further interest in the plight of the universe: a *deus absconditus*. Deism is the philosophical faith of managing the end-game, not a relationship with a loving God. Deists were strengthened in their beliefs by surveying the damage done by religious wars. Moreover they distanced themselves from the multiplicity of quarrelling sects, driven not by Christ-like men of faith but by harsh controversialists. They sought to live by the light of nature alone. Virtue was performed not in order to avoid punishment in the hereafter, but because it was a civilised thing to do, leading to a higher and better society. Worship was unnecessary, as was the self-chastisement which appeared to accompany faith. Divine providence could not be squared with logic or scientific fact, and in human terms was irreconcilable with natural disasters such as the great Lisbon earthquake of 1755.

Deism was popular among several classes. On the one hand it was a gentlemanly, even aristocratic faith – Henry St John, Viscount Bolingbroke, wrote voluminous deistical texts – but the beliefs also found favour with dissenters and Catholics who had rejected their systems of faith. These men, mostly forgotten names today and none of them outstanding, included John Toland, Anthony Collins, Charles Blount, Matthew Tindal and Thomas Chubb. Lady Mary Wortley Montagu wrote memorably of deism and its significance within Islam.

Toland, an Irishman with a pugnacious wit whose best-known book *Christianity Not Mysterious* was burnt by the public hangman in Dublin in 1697, attempted to apply a critical and comparative method to the gospel story, although he had hardly the materials or the temperament to do so. Born a Derry Catholic, he lived the wild and rackety life of a man driven entirely by dissent. He declared that Christianity could not be 'mysterious' (that is, it could not have unintelligible dogmas) because thereby offence would be done to reason; and, as John Locke had declared, 'He that takes away reason to make room for revelation puts out the light of both; and does much what the same as if he would persuade a man to put out his eyes, the better to receive the remote light of an invisible star by a telescope.' Toland's book may have been a sly attempt to show the falsity of religion, beyond the level of belief in some sort of supreme being and having a will to do good, since mystery was and is so much part of the popular taste in religion. If the mysterious and magical is stripped away from religion, not much remains beyond ethical teaching and a cultural heritage. The book went through many editions. His later works showed a desire to create a unity between the monotheistic faiths; he held no prejudices against Islam. His last book was the blueprint for a religion which took bits from all faiths; the sort of believing-in-everything-and-nothing ideal which the anguished, open-minded devout yearn for in our own times (a handy source-book for *Thought for the Day!*).

Toland's most audacious work was – if it is by him – the *Letter from an Arabian Physician* of 1706, allegedly addressed to a professor of the

University of Halle, in Saxony. This was a response to the typical European criticisms of Muhammad and Islam: that the faith was spread by force of arms, that Muhammad had had too many wives to have been a serious religious leader and that the sensualities offered in Paradise were repellent to religion.

The response is clear and well argued. Muhammad only took up arms to recover Mecca, and if Alexander the Great, Caesar, William the Conqueror and 'Lewis le Grand' may be accounted great men, why not Muhammad? The Emperor Constantine abolished paganism by force, and Christian behaviour on St Bartholomew's Eve showed that Christianity is not a pacific religion. Moreover, 'Christians do nothing but persecute, wherever the Clergy's Power prevails over that of the magistrate.'[50] On relations with the female sex, the author quotes many examples from the Old Testament of multiple marriage: for instance, David, and Solomon. On the issue of a sensual paradise, Toland pointed out that the resurrection will be of the body, and that there was nothing base in eating and drinking and propagating our kind. (The author even quotes public health statistics to back up his claim.) As for sex in Paradise, its embarrassed denial was based on a prudishness about sex, which in reality was a normal, healthy appetite; moreover without sex humanity dies out. Adam and Eve did it in the Garden of Eden. Toland continues by quoting the opinions of the Flemish mystic Antoinette Bourignon (1616–80), who held that 'there will be an eternal propagation of mankind in heaven. . . . her very learned and pious apologist believes' that the blessed Angels are continually multiplying their kind, and will do so for ever and ever.'[51] (Perhaps it is instructive to recall that the ideas of Antoinette Bourignon took hold with some strength among the Calvinist clergy of Scotland; indeed, a form of words was introduced at their installation demanding their abjuration of the doctrines of the Flemish prophetess.)

The alleged Arabian physician continues, 'Tis true, both of them differ from us as to the manner of Propagation, for they imagine it done by a pure act of divine love, without any mixture of Sexes; which is mere fancy, and of which we can have no manner of idea: whereas we think it will be by a Junction of the Sexes, which is agreeable to the order and constitution of things, and of which every man may have a very clear and distinct Idea.'

A clear and distinct idea: this is the key phrase, which shows the author to have been a follower of John Locke. A central test for the validity of notions within the *Essay* is that they be 'clear and distinct'.

The traditionally devout execrated Toland for his impiety. But he gained a wide popularity both at home and abroad. When Lady Mary Wortley Montagu was staying in Belgrade with a cultured Turkish effendi in 1717, she was asked 'among other things, How Mr Toland *did?*' Toland tapped a nerve, among Muslims as well as Christians, stimulating those for whom the old sectarian narrownesses were too bigoted and small. His fertile, mercurial mind was moving towards vistas of a globalised faith, where a sacred text would be seen as an allegory, and where virtue would be practised for its own good.[52]

A theme common to both Socinians and deists is one that might be called a genealogy of monotheism: that Christianity had come about in order to refine ancient paganism, and Islam had developed to clean Christianity of its corruptions. (A more radical seam of thought among the deists led them to anticipate scientific atheism.) One can see the process occurring in the early eighteenth century; it is even hinted at in Bury's *Naked Gospel*. Toland and Thomas Chubb remained faithful to some sort of belief in a higher power. The title of Toland's *Christianity Not Mysterious* echoed Locke's *The Reasonableness of Christianity*. Chubb, writing a few years later, puzzled over 'whether the Mahometan revelation be of a divine original or not; there seems to be a plausible pretence [i.e. claim], arising from the then circumstances of things, for stamping a divine character on it.' Elsewhere he wrote, 'As to the want of miracles, with respect to the Mahometan revelation, it does not appear, to me, to be a negative proof that such a revelation is not divine.'[53] The deist author dismissed the popular Christian view, that religion by its very nature was filled with miracles and wonders. To the calm, unzealous deists a true God was a rational and universal God, not a conjurer who won over the masses with clever tricks.

Anthony Collins and to some extent Lord Bolingbroke were on the edge of total free-thinking disbelief. Henry St John, Viscount Bolingbroke, the Jacobite secretary of state who fled to France, and who was the most venturesome of the deists, combined the notion of the genealogy of monotheism with an attack on the notion of the Trinity. He declared, 'The doctrine of the Trinity gives the Mahometans as much reason to say, that the revelation which Mahomet published was necessary to establish the unity of the Supreme Being, in opposition to the polytheism which Christianity had introduced, as Christians have to insist, that the revelation which Christ published a few centuries before, was necessary to establish the unity of the Godhead against the pagan polytheism.'[54] Here, as in Chubb, the monotheistic faiths were given a lineage; but Lord Bolingbroke's trenchant and dismissive writing elsewhere about religion makes one wonder whether he did not at heart wish to see an end to all faiths. He viewed the established Church as necessary in the interest of the state and for the safety of public morals. He did not consider its doctrines to be true, or necessary for the safety of his own morals.

The theological attitude which tended to see Islam as a rational alternative to Trinitarian Christianity led to the publication of a fiercely polemical work by Dr Humphrey Prideaux, an Oxford orientalist who, disliking the free and open discussion of university life, abandoned Christ Church and its lax and indulgent ways, forsaking the impiety of scholarship in order to rasp out anathemata from the pulpit to a docile congregation as dean of Norwich. His 1697 work, *The True Nature of Imposture Fully Display'd in the Life of Mahomet,* had no need to hide itself from the censors. A pungent and polemical compilation of the oriental translations and researches of others, it was without merit as original work and it showed characteristics in common with late-medieval demonisations of Islam. Within a few decades its errors had been pointed out. Prideaux had been a pupil of Richard Busby at Westminster School, a man with high standards and an Arabist, but there is no evidence of the persistence of Busby's standards in the pupil's work.

Prideaux was an energetic upholder of traditional Christianity. The preface to *The True Nature* makes clear that his assault on Islam was really a part of his attack on 'impious' deism. By 1697 it was already clear that the deists were showing sympathy for Islam and its prophet, and Prideaux attacks their faith relentlessly in this preface. Like Leslie, he was outraged at the attacks on the Trinity (especially that of Charles Blount). His anger was equally addressed at the advances made by 'natural' (that is, non-miraculous) religion and he spat venom at the Epicurean deists, who, he affirmed, 'do leave no room for any argument but that of the whip and the lash, to convince them of those impious absurdities, and therefore deserve not by any other method to be dealt with. Besides, if you will know the true reason which induceth the atheist to deny the being of a God, and the Epicurean deist his government over us; it is, That they may give themselves up, without fear of future judgment, to all those bestial enjoyments of lust and sensuality which their corrupt hearts carry them after; and therefore it not being the reason of the man, but the brutal appetite of the beast that makes them such, they deserve no otherwise to be treated by us; and for this reason, as I write not to them, so I desire to be understood to have nothing to do with them.'[55] Prideaux was clearly someone who was not going to allow scholarly objectivity to mar a marmoreal morality, although it is noticeable that his moral stance was itself one of Epicurean hedonism, since he measured moral actions not for their intrinsic goodness, but merely for the amount of pleasure that they afforded the doer in the hereafter.

He also upheld the viewpoint that Muhammad's message was a craftily constructed fraud, whereas a more reasonable viewpoint is to see the Prophet's often desperate sincerity. The imposture of Islam was the most persistent view of the faith held throughout the seventeenth and early eighteenth century. Among other more moderate writers (for Prideaux loathed Islam, and had no conception of objectivity towards it) it looks as though the words 'imposture' and 'impostor' were used as safety words, employed to keep away those who were sniffing out heresy, while the writer might be indicating that the faith had more to it than fakery and fraud. The Dutch scholar Adriaan Reland's 1705 study of Islamic theology proclaims the 'imposture' of the faith, but the author's own careful clear-headedness goes a long way to countering such a viewpoint; indeed the book was attacked by theologians for being too objective and insufficiently polemical.[56]

But within Islam itself, how deistical was belief at this time? Did Muslims themselves hold a philosophical faith in a clockwork universe, presided over by an absentee deity, or were they filled with the perfervid enthusiasm of apocalyptic fundamentalism? Lady Mary Wortley Montagu, who had noted the hunger for news of Toland, was among the most articulate and observant of English deists. As she travelled in the Ottoman Empire, she caught echoes of conflicts at home and was shrewd enough to perceive similarities between Islam and the sects of Christianity, as understood by the people, and between the essence of Islam and the essence of Christianity, as understood by the 'philosophers'. Lady Mary has been praised for the impact of her *Turkish Letters* on the English literary scene but less attention has been paid to her views on Islam. And in the 1980s and 1990s her reputation received a bizarre 'literary' critical drubbing which was entirely at variance with her achievement.

In 1716 Lady Mary's husband, Edward Wortley Montagu, had been appointed ambassador to Constantinople and Lady Mary travelled out that winter, arriving in Ottoman Belgrade in February 1717. The ambassador's host was an educated effendi, Achmet [Ahmet] Bey, the same who had enquired after Toland. He instructed Lady Mary in the institutions, culture and religion of the empire. On the matter of religion, he revealed to her that educated and enlightened Turks believed not in literal, word-for-word faith but in calm deism. The point of introducing superstition and revelation into religion, he assured her ladyship, was to win over the ignorant people. Ahmet Bey's views showed some similarities to those of the Mutazilites of 900 years earlier, whose views hovered between belief and unbelief. The Koran, he said, contained only the purest morality, delivered in the very best language. Lady Mary was pleased to encounter such rational views, which conformed to her own sensible and non-fundamentalist ideas.[57]

She reached Adrianople (Edirne) in April, and gave her impressions of the Albanians (known as Arnavuts): 'These people, living between Christians and Mahometans, and not being skilled in controversy, declare, that they are utterly unable to judge which religion is best; but to be certain of not entirely rejecting the truth, they very prudently follow both. They go to the mosques on Fridays, and to the church on Sunday, saying for their excuse, that at the day of judgment they are sure of protection from the true prophet; but which that is, they are not able to determine in this world.'[58]

Religion in Albania and Serbia appeared in general to be either a matter of tribal-type spats or a kind of multifaith insurance policy. A wise individual kept quiet if confronted by anything indicating a contradiction. For the few educated souls, belief constituted the pacific universality of deism, which might appear as the essential moderator between all faiths but which was apt to prove to be a mediator on the point of disappearing altogether.

Lady Mary also understood the variety of schools of interpretation within Islam, which made up variety within the faith. She realised that Islam was many, and not one: that there were Islams, rather than Islam: 'Mahometanism is divided into as many Sects as Christianity, and the first institution as much neglected and obscur'd by interpretations. I cannot here forbear refflecting on the natural Inclination of Mankind to make Mysterys and Noveltys. The Zeidi, Kadari, Jabari, etc. [these are schools of Koranic interpretation] put me in mind of the Catholic, Lutheran, Calvinist etc., and are equally zealous against one Another. But the most prevailing Opinion, if you search into the Secret of the Effendis, is plain

Deism, but this is kept from the people, who are amused with a thousand different notions, according to the different interest of their preachers.'[59]

Lady Mary's observations contain neither scornful Christian triumphalism nor an attempt to exalt Islam beyond its proper limits; just an informed and sceptical comparative view of the faiths. It was reasonable and sensible to seek out parallels between Christianity and Islam, especially where they coincided when considered in an atmosphere of calm philosophical reflection. Those with understanding could remove superstition and mysteries from religion, and so the truths of the universe would become clear.

Lady Mary was also a pioneer of smallpox inoculation, a practice she observed in Adrianople while on the way to the ambassadorial posting. She had her son inoculated in February 1718. It seems that excellent medical attention was provided at the Embassy; indeed something approaching modern medical practice was provided by the embassy doctor, Maitland, and the surgeon Dr Emanuel Timoni. Lady Mary was to become a fervent supporter of inoculation on her return to England.[60]

❖❖❖

In the world of scholarship, away from the drowsy universities, a fine English translation of the Koran came out in 1734, the work of George Sale, who was working for the Society for the Promotion of Christian Knowledge. Sale was no wide-eyed admirer of Islam and its prophet, but he did point out that, with respect to the polytheism and superstition of pre-Islamic Arabia, Muhammed 'followed the example of the most famous legislators, who instituted not such laws as were absolutely the best in themselves, but the best their people were capable of receiving'. Sale also noted his 'wise conduct and great prudence', and his charity – that, according to one Arab historian, there was seldom any money in the house because he had given it all away. Nevertheless, Sale still held the notion that 'Mohammed pretended to be a prophet sent by God', the orthodox view of the time.[61] Sale's translation was much admired and his Christian faith came to be suspect. Gibbon, besides calling him 'our honest and learned translator', described him as 'half a Musulman', probably an ironical aside on the part of the historian, originating in the exactness of Sale's scholarship which almost invited belief. Following his distinguished translation Sale was in effect suspended from his religious duties within the SPCK. The brilliant and original Preliminary Discourse which introduces his version, praised as 'learned and rational' by Gibbon, looked at Islam with the same seriousness and scholarship as were habitually granted by men of learning to the politics and society of ancient Greece and Rome.

Sale looked at Islam in the manner of a modern scholar; the deists felt drawn to Islam for its rational anti-Trinitarian stance and its lack of miracles. Political philosophers admired Islam for its lack of a priesthood. In France, the life of Muhammad came in some circles to be seen as an ideal for the Enlightenment. *Comte* Henri de Boulainvilliers carried this sentiment to an extreme in his 1730 *Vie de Mahomed*, in which the Islamic prophet, who was compared to 'a Hero of the most unbounded courage',[62] was viewed as a grand figure upon the stage of history, filled with a disinterested genius akin to that of the finest of Republican Rome. Islam, the Count believed, was 'the system of a religion stript of all controversy, and which proposing no mystery to offer violence to reason, confined the imagination of men to be satisfied with a plain invariable worship, notwithstanding the fiery passions and blind zeal that so often transported them beyond themselves'.[63] To Boulainvilliers, Muhammad's faith 'seems to have been the result of long and deep meditation upon the nature of things, upon the state and condition of the world at that time, and upon the reconcilement of the objects of religion with reason, which must always try the things presented to the understanding'.[64] Gibbon acknowledged that Boulainvilliers 'shews a strong understanding, through a cloud of ignorance, and prejudice', though he classed the cold Prideaux in the same circle as the enthusiast Boulainvilliers with the comment that 'the adverse wish of finding an impostor or an hero, has too often corrupted the learning of the doctor and the ingenuity of the count'.[65]

Gibbon himself, and a number of historians of his date, admired Abulfeda, or Ismail ibn Muhammad Abu l-Fida, Prince of Hama (1273–1331). He was a distinguished and largely accurate geographer and historian, and his works had been receiving translations into Latin from 1650. In 1723 his text on the life of Muhammad was printed at Oxford (by John Gagnier) and later, in 1754, his *Annales Muslemici* were translated by J.J. Reiske and printed in Leipzig. Gibbon wrote of 'Abulfeda, whose testimony I esteem the most convenient and creditable'.[66]

Voltaire, another deist, had a more complex attitude to Islam and Muhammad than that of Boulainvilliers. He declined to express anything like his ardour; indeed, he was in many ways quite negative (but interestingly so) about Islam's Prophet, whom he saw not as the impostor of common Christian parlance, but rather as an opportunist and certainly less of an impostor than most Christians. His tragedy *Mahomet*, given its première in 1741, is usually considered to be his best play. Although the full title of the play is *Mahomet, ou le fanatisme* (although this subtitle does not appear in a 1742 edition), the play is not about fanaticism in the modern sense. There is no devout praying, tiresome preaching or wearisome self-mortification. Such qualities were added by Voltaire's English translators (especially the Revd James Miller, whose 1745 English edition adds passages of entirely spurious religious fanaticism not found in the original, such as an expostulation to the Koran as an instrument of prophetic chicanery). Voltaire's text concerns politics, ideology and personal ambition within a believing environment. It seems that British audiences, backward at understanding politics and ideology, were only content when such a drama was presented as a righteous condemnation of religious fraud.[67]

Voltaire's dramatic work has certain internal problems. On the one hand the structure of the play is stagey and somewhat static. But it is written in vivid and fast-moving language, alert to the deep currents of human action.

The plot is entirely Voltaire's own, being unconnected to the factual events of Muhammad's life, which were well enough known by 1740. Mahomet as conceived by Voltaire is an almost entirely imaginary creation, far removed from Muhammad the Prophet. The play pits Mahomet's family against that of 'Zopire' (= Zubayr, who in reality was one of the Prophet's earliest converts). Zopire, believing Mahomet had caused a death in his family, has killed Mahomet's (unnamed) son; Zopire's long-lost children, Palmire, a slave girl, and Seide (Zaid), whom we meet as a hostage, have been brought up secretly by Mahomet, in ignorance of the fact that they are brother and sister. They are in love, but Mahomet has designs on Palmire. The Prophet's cause is making headway throughout Arabia. He arrives in Mecca, allegedly to negotiate but really with the twin intentions of persuading Seide to murder Zopire, and then of killing Seide in order to claim Palmire. Seide, devoted to the Prophet's cause, agrees to carry out the murder, believing it to be an act of religious duty and the way to Palmire's heart. As soon as he has wiped the blood from his knife he realises he has slain his own father and attempts to turn the army against Mahomet. But his moment of understanding is brief, for he has been poisoned. Mahomet declares the consequent death of Seide to be a sign of his own divine mission. At the moment that Arabia hails him as its prophetic leader, Palmire stabs herself.

Voltaire himself summed up the essence of the plot thus: 'It concerns a young man born virtuous, who, seduced by fanaticism, murders an old man who loves him, a young man who, thinking to serve God, unknowingly becomes a parricide; it concerns an impostor who orders this murder, and who promises the murderer an [act of] incest for reward.'[68] Combative Christians liked it. Pope Benedict XIV, to whom it was dedicated, read this *'bellissima tragedia'* *'con sommo piacere'* (with the greatest pleasure).[69] Perceptive critics were less sure. Lord Chesterfield, who saw a performance in Brussels, declared in a letter that he 'soon perceived he [Voltaire] had Jesus Christ in view, under the character of Mahomet'. His lordship complained of the 'foppery, errors and impertinence of authors'.[70]

One agreeable if lesser-known English champion of Arab history and literature was James Harris (1709–80). He was the grandson of the 2nd Earl Shaftesbury, with whose education John Locke had been charged. A sociable man, who nevertheless lived a retiring life in the shadow of Salisbury Cathedral, he was the constant correspondent of Henry Fielding. His main claim to fame is his book *Hermes*, which looked towards the possibility of a universal grammar. In his posthumous *Philological Inquiries* (1781) he dedicated three chapters to Middle Eastern matters, written in a spirit of open-mindedness and generosity. His text displays none of the arrogance and superiority which one finds in English writings of a later date or in the tepid conventional pieties of Samuel Johnson. Harris admired Pococke's work and used it and Abu l-Fida as his main sources. He also put in a word of praise for Ibn Tufayl's *Hayy ibn Yaqzan* ('that elegant fiction concerning the self-taught philosopher').[71] In Harris's own copy of the 1671 bilingual Arabic–Latin text he has penned the note, *'Liber lectu vere dignus'* – a book truly worth reading.

To men and women with lucid and flexible minds, Islam fitted into the non-miraculous disillusioned spiritual landscape of the eighteenth century, which stood in contrast to the religious wars and witch-burnings of the earlier era, when Europe had allowed itself to be driven by zealous faith, with deadly consequences. A perception of the dire effects of zealotry underlay Edward Gibbon's scepticism towards religion. His coolness towards enthusiasm can be explained by recollection of the acts of the devout.

Gibbon's attitude to Islam and its prophet was complex. As towards Christianity, he was sceptical and irreligious; but generous too, and happy to acknowledge greatness of spirit. He praised the civic qualities that the Arabian Prophet encouraged, noting that, despite summoning up a warlike spirit within his people, he imposed restraints upon them, and that his belief system was the 'rational creed of the unity and perfections of God'.[72] 'The Mahometans have uniformly withstood the temptation of reducing the object of their faith and devotion to the level with the senses and imagination of man. "I believe in one God, and in Mahomet the apostle of God," is the simple and invariable profession of Islam. The intellectual image of the Deity has never been degraded by any visible idol; the honours of the prophet have never transgressed the measure of human virtue; and his living precepts have restrained the gratitude of his disciples within the bounds of reason and religion.'[73]

On Muhammad's legacy, if Gibbon doubted the universal, he favoured the particular, for the Prophet 'breathed among the faithful a spirit of charity and friendship, recommended the practice of the social virtues, and checked, by his laws, the thirst for revenge and the oppression of widows and orphans'. There was an irony, a local political irony, with regard to the surge of enthusiasm which propelled the tribes out of Arabia.

Had the impulse been less powerful, Arabia, free at home, and formidable abroad, might have flourished under a succession of her native monarchs. Her sovereignty was lost by the extent and rapidity of conquest. The colonies of the nation were scattered over the east and the west, and their blood was mingled with the blood of their converts and captives. After the reign of three caliphs, the throne was transported from Medina to the valley of Damascus and the banks of the Tigris; the holy cities were violated by impious war; Arabia was ruled by the rod of a subject, perhaps of a stranger; and the Bedoweens of the desert, awakening from their dream of dominion, resumed their old and solitary independence.[74]

Gibbon had read the Koran in Sale's translation and he viewed it as 'a glorious testimony to the unity of God. The prophet of Mecca rejected the worship of idols and men, of stars and planets, on the rational principle that whatever rise must set, that whatever is born must die, that whatever is corruptible must decay and perish. In the Author of the universe, his rational enthusiasm confessed and adored an infinite and eternal being, without form or place, without issue or similitude, present to our most secret thoughts, existing by the necessity of his own nature, and deriving from himself all moral and intellectual perfection.' This passage shows that Gibbon did indeed understand religion, despite scepticism towards sacrificial cults, private fetishes, and theology from which no meaning could be extracted.[75]

The historian also thought about Islam at a greater depth than he is usually given credit for. The popular view, that he used it merely as a stick with which to berate Christianity and Christian practice, is unsustainable – although he did this too. He looked seriously at the structure of the faith on its own terms, noting that the fact that it had no priestly caste had allowed it to stay virtually unchanged from its origins. (By contrast, 'If the Christian apostles, St Peter or St Paul, could return to the Vatican, they might possibly enquire the name of the Deity who is worshipped with such mysterious rites in that magnificent temple.'[76]) The bonds created by Islam activated civic virtue.

But to individuals there were dangers: he noted 'how the conscience may slumber in a mixed and middle state between self-illusion and voluntary fraud'.[77] Perhaps Gibbon was here alluding to the point that Islam may lead its adherents not to try any harder; to believe that since they have been granted the final and fullest revelation, they are superior and even unassailable, thereby suffering from a belief similar to that which brought the crusaders down, which was their unquestioning conviction that they were right, that God was on their side, and that those who opposed them were a discordant alliance of babbling godless barbarians: the shadow-side of themselves.

The historian confronted prejudices against Islam on several fronts. He pointed out that 'notwithstanding a vulgar prejudice, the gates of heaven will be open to both sexes'.[78] And, in a less excitable manner than Antoinette Bourignon or John Toland, he is unembarrassed by the idea of sex in paradise: the presence of the dark-eyed houris, which has brought ridicule from Christian theologians and has lured imaginative writers to speculate on a rich and turbid mix of the physical and the spiritual. Gibbon makes the issue make sense. A central Christian belief, then and now, has been the Resurrection of the Body. The term is spoken every time the Apostles' Creed is recited: not the resurrection of the soul, but the resurrection of the body. This was an old Christian belief, very important to St Paul. The idea was also part of Islamic belief. Gibbon makes the point that the resurrection of the body would be incomplete without the resurrection of sexual organs and sexual function. Christians might prefer to anticipate some kind of eunuchoid resurrection, but that is merely a result of the prudery and the general denial of sexual function which has characterised Christianity. Gibbon understood that

Islam comprehended that the resurrection of the body would be entire; and that, as a result, a body instinct with desire would need to be satisfied. Hence the houris. He suggests that the reason that male desires alone were addressed, and that the yearnings of the female sex were left unacknowledged, was so that male jealousy would not be provoked. This is clearly a weak argument. But Gibbon's general acknowledgement of Islam's attempt to come to terms with the resurrection of the body, in contrast to the more usual avoidance of the issue, is clear.[79]

Gibbon treated Islamic history seriously, as part of ordinary historical experience. He is neither especially adulatory or especially disparaging. Arabia never stole his wits away. In his work he sensed the dynamics of the rise and fall of its dynasties with the same rational application as those of the other powers with whom he treats. There is neither condescension nor contempt, and in this he was ahead of a large number of more recent European historical writers and miscellaneous travellers whose works reflect embedded colonialist attitudes. Gibbon's study breathes the air of an equality of spirit amongst the peoples he writes of. This was thanks partly to Simon Ockley's work, partly to Sale, partly the researches incorporated in d'Herbelot's magnificent *Bibliothèque orientale* (1697), and even on occasion to enthusiasts like the *comte* de Boulainvilliers. Discernable above all in the background is Edward Pococke's *Specimen Historiae Arabum*, the vital standard of scholarship and non-partisanship. 'Consult, peruse and study the *Specimen* . . . !' he mock-ordered his readers, as if setting them homework. Gibbon's respect for the humane, intelligent and non-triumphalist Pococke is strong, and frequently expressed, in *The History of the Decline and Fall.*

The impact of Islamic literature on European letters was more ambiguous than the legacy of 'Arabickness' on scholarship. Only in Germany was the force and subtlety of Eastern literature fully recognised, in the works of August von Platen and Eduard Mörike, and the greatest of all, in Goethe's *West-Östlicher Divan*, poems whose lucidity, calm and rational passion seem to signal a great inner liberation for that most liberated of poets: a foreshadowing of some kind of international literature. Goethe had been introduced to Islamic literature by von Hammer-Purgstall, the historian of the Ottoman Empire, and the effect had been an astonishing upsurge of creative power, leading to the writing of some of the greatest poems in any language. For those who say that translated poetry is mere empty versification, the example of von Hammer-Purgstall's translations, and the effect they had on Goethe, must remain a puzzle.

For the most part, though, the East became trivialised following the publication in France in 1704 of *The Arabian Nights*, which fastened into European imagination the phantasmagorical apparatus of sultans and jinns, thieves and magicians, sultriness and splendour with which the Orient became, to all except the discerning, imaginatively coterminous, to the detriment of its reason, realism, power and passion. In Britain the Arabian Nights infatuation reached a climax with Thomas Moore's *Lallah Rookh* (1817, largely unread today, though popular in its day, and providing the text for Schumann's *Das Paradies und die Peri*); earlier it had been put to savagely subversive use by William Beckford, who combined oriental fantasy and Gothic horror to create *Vathek* (1774), exciting at the time but hard to get to grips with today (and barely worth the effort). It remains a mystery why the second-rate of Oriental literature should have had an impact so much greater than the first-rate. One can only be grateful that Goethe knew the difference.

One Englishman who minimised the fantastic and lurid in his English Augustan versions of oriental poetry was the great scholar Sir William Jones (1746–94), who was compelled to become a lawyer since scholarship and verse did not pay bills. He briefly thought of standing for parliament but, being too liberal even for the constituency of Oxford University, withdrew before the vote. He spent the last ten years of his life as a judge in Calcutta but literature remained his chief passion. (He knew thirteen languages perfectly and had a reasonable fluency in twenty-eight others.) As a public servant he was devoid of the self-regarding superiority and facetious whimsical arrogance which are often characteristics of imperial proconsuls. His liberalism led him to express vocal support for the American Revolution. He also showed an instinctive sympathy with animals and loathed blood sports.[80]

His translations include work from Arabic, Persian, Turkish and Hindi. Goethe wrote (in the notes on the *West-Östlicher Divan*) of Sir William: 'The qualities of this man are world renowned, so that all I can do is acknowledge in general terms that I have long sought to make use of his work.'[81] Jones also wrote scholarly pastiches of oriental poetry, of a type which could easily be imagined to be trite or tiresome but which in his hands are successful as poems. He was the first to make prose versions from the Arabic of the Seven Odes which probably date from pre-Islamic Arabia. (They were known as the *Muallakat*, perhaps meaning 'suspended poems', because they were said to have been suspended from a public – possibly sacred – building as an inspiration and a challenge.) His publication brought into focus the centrality of poetry for the Arab peoples; and it also started the controversy on the authentic date of the Seven Odes, believed by some not to be pre-Islamic.

Sir William Jones's *Poems Consisting Chiefly of Translations from the Asiatick Languages* (1772) provided an opening on the East for the literate public. The verses that he created consisted of indirect translations from the Eastern languages – reworkings, in the gliding, glassy style of Pope, of oriental originals. Typically for a man of Jones's liberal temperament, his versions in no way created, or pandered to, European stereotypes of the East. Jones was keen to open up, rather than to close off, his readers' knowledge of Eastern things and opportunities for emotional exploration. The venture is rooted in the East – an East East, not a West East. It is possible to say that the Popeian language tames the content, domesticates and anglicises it, captures it in a net and turns it loose into a pen on a lawn artfully laid out by Capability Brown; but that is to ignore the inescapably Eastern aspects of the content of the verses.

From his volume one may select a few lines from 'Solima: an Arabian Eclogue', an ode in praise of an Arabian princess who had built a caravanserai with pleasant gardens for the refreshment of travellers and pilgrims, an act of munificence not uncommon in Asia. What is so brilliantly surprising here is that it is an Arabian ode to a woman, and as such it deals not with warfare, honour, horses, raiding parties, harsh justice, blood in the sand or destruction (all those things beloved of a later generation of British Arabists – the kind of people who clustered around the myth of T.E. Lawrence – whom one may describe as the 'British Beduin' and who saw the Middle East as a kind of extended old-style public school), but with charity and feminine generosity. This passage is most closely based on the Arab original:

> When, chilled with fear the trembling pilgrim roves
> Though pathless deserts and through tangled groves,
> Where mantling darkness spreads her dragon wing,
> And birds of death their fatal dirges sing,
> While vapours pale a dreadful glimmering cast,
> And thrilling horror howls in every blast;
> She cheers his gloom with streams of bursting light,
> By day a sun, a beaming moon by night,
> Darts through the quivering shade her heavenly ray
> And spread with rising flowers his solitary way.[82]

But to a greater extent the weakness of Islam gave rise to a literature where 'turcquerie' was no more than a cultural embellishment. Mozart's *Die Entführung aus dem Serail* is perhaps the best known example, where, although the Pasha (a speaking part) is brave and self-disciplined and high-minded, an ideal Enlightenment philosopher-ruler, the wily bass Osmin is crafty, cunning and cruel – but comic. The quartet of Europeans are those with whom an audience can most readily identify, since they display the characteristics of recognisable society, even (or especially) when they are being scheming and snobbish. Mozart was also a man with the beliefs of his time and central to his attitude to life was deistical Freemasonry. In his penultimate opera we can hear how the Trinity of Father, Son and Holy Ghost, occasionally having emerged alternatively as the Neoplatonic trinity of The One, Mind and Soul, came to rest in the three flattened notes of the key-signature of the overture to, and main tonality of, *The Magic Flute*. Here the former incomprehensibles have become comprehensible.

From the late eighteenth century, Islam and the Islamic nations drew the attention of Europe for their potential for commerce, colonies and warfare. The situation was very different from that of 100 years earlier when (in 1683) Kara Mustafa had been defeated on the hills of Kahlenberg, just outside Vienna. That overblown attempt to recreate the days of the conquering sultans had proved to be delusory. Europe showed that it could deal effectively with an invading force. Since then, Ottoman Turkey had grown weak. There was a tendency among its population to believe that the empire could not be improved upon, since it was sanctioned by God. But the Janissaries demonstrated violent opposition, the army was a shadow, the political situation was set in stone, its legal system was threadbare and people of all communities were degraded by poverty and ignorance. Nevertheless its geographical position and its possibilities for colonialism led the European powers to focus interest on it. The character of Baron de Tott is an example. Writing in 1784, he memorably observed the empire's crumbling defensive fieldworks and the despotism of the political system.[83] At the same time the baron's real intention in being in the eastern Mediterranean was to spy out the land for the French king and to check on the provinces for their suitability as future French colonies.

Yet even de Tott, and others of the same date, did not foresee the manner in which the empire's weakness would draw the interest of the great powers throughout the following century, and that it would become a willing receptacle for their jealousies and diplomatic anxieties, thereby accelerating any internal tendencies to somnolence and passivity. Colonialism would have to wait a century.

The passivity could hardly stand in greater contrast to the intellectual excitement created by half-belief at two critical junctures of Islamic civilisation: during the period of translations, when the caliphs were Mutazilite, and during the intellectual upsurge of Islamic Spain. Both these periods were brief, the first closed down by religious orthodoxy, and the second by political reaction, but both were sufficiently intense to create texts which altered the condition of Europe. The Ottoman Empire, never interested in intellectual speculation, did however initially teach Europe religious toleration: Ottoman Salonika had received Andalusian Jews after their expulsion by Ferdinand and Isabella, and it was in Transylvania, under Ottoman suzerainty, that the Edict of Torda, Europe's first law of religious toleration, was proclaimed in 1568. After the shock of the burning of Servetus in Geneva, humane religious reformers looked to Ottoman Constantinople as an example of the possibility of shared difference. It did not last and the Ottoman state became a byword for oppression, the worst of which fell upon the minorities. Its punishments were peculiarly cruel. Nothing of interest to the mind was produced. But when the army could no longer satisfactorily defend its frontiers, its unique geography fell to the gaze of the powers, who, to fend off collapse, fed it with diplomatic steroids for a century.

CHAPTER NINE

Ottoman Fortunes: Military Debacle, Diplomatic Rescue

The failure of the Turks to take Vienna in 1683 was one episode in a developing and drawn-out conflict between Habsburg Austria and Ottoman Turkey. Already at St Gothard in 1664 the Turks had experienced defeat at the hands of the Austrians, a defeat in the field which broke the spell of Ottoman invincibility as much as Lepanto had ended the Turks' naval supremacy.[1] When in 1669 the Ottomans went on to make a surprising gain over France and Austria in a naval encounter at Crete and win the island, their success was in large part due less to their own prowess than to the Europeans' foolish tactics. The Turks intervened in Podolia in 1672 when the Cossacks rose in revolt against Poland, thereby legitimising the principle of intervention in the affairs of another power that was to become so troublesome to the Ottoman Empire in its declining years.[2] In this region (today Ukraine), a complex situation arose between the Ottomans, Poles and Russians. The Ottomans were left as victors in 1676, in control of Podolia, through whose leading city of Kamaniets William Harborne had entered Turkey. Moreover the Polish leader John Sobieski (later king) had been defeated, despite his victory over the Turks at Khotyn (or Chocim) three years earlier.[3]

At this time the Ottoman sultans barely functioned at all; power was left in the hands of the grand viziers, and the empire was fortunate to have a dynasty of able Albanians, the Köprülüs, who transmitted the subtle arts of statecraft from one to another, and whose loss was much felt when the position was passed to a Köprülü son-in-law, the aggressive, warlike first minister Kara Mustafa.

His advent signalled a forward policy, though he first met with with defeat across the Danube. In 1683 an opportunity arose: the Hungarians under Count Emmerich Tekeli (Imre Thököli) rose in revolt against their Habsburg overlords, who had instigated a reign of terror against them, and Kara Mustafa advanced to Vienna. The Austrians were outnumbered. But the Ottomans delayed fatally, allowing the Austrians to call upon the aid of John Sobieski and his valiant Polish cavalry. The alliance between Austrians and Poles worked with a near-miraculous ease and the Ottoman invaders were soundly beaten at Kahlenberg, a range of hills overlooking Vienna. Kara Mustafa was recalled and beheaded. In the years following, the Austrians pressed home their victory.[4]

At the same time the Venetians, under their dour but capable commander Francesco Morosini, fought the Turks in the land which is Greece today. In the course of one of the campaigns, the Turks fired on the Parthenon, used by the Venetians as a powder magazine, damaging it irreparably and coming close to destroying it. Venetian rule supplanted Ottoman, but to the Greek people themselves the new rulers were as oppressive and mean-spirited as the old. There was nothing between them. Oppression was the same, whether Christian or Muslim.[5] Ottoman reverses continued for the rest of the century, only relieved for the Turks by a defeat of the Poles and the repulse of a Russian army in the Crimea. Further catastrophic defeats attended the Ottomans in the 1690s, culminating in a disaster on the River Theiss in 1697. A peace conference was called at Karlowitz (Sremski Karlovci today, in Serbia) and the subsequent treaty recognised for the first time that all the European powers had a stake in the future of the Ottoman Empire.[6] Imperial Turkey was divested of large areas of territory. The militarised empire of the Ottomans was no longer a fearsome conquering lion, raging deep into central Europe; it was quietly caged at Karlowitz and subsequent treaties of Passarowitz, Kutchuk-Kainardji, Adrianople and Berlin confirmed its domestication.

Despite the presence of the Köprülüs, the empire continued to decline; the systemic faults were too great. These were rooted in the presence of two elements: the Janissaries, an armed corps similar (if only in their capacity to make trouble) to the *streltsy* in Russia, which Peter the Great gunned down in 1698; and the dominance of the religious authorities, the *ulema*. It should be stressed that at a certain early point in the empire, the Janissaries and the *ulema* were forces for power and for coherence. They gave the empire a sense of certainty and direction. But governmental instruments which work at one stage are apt to fail later; revolutionary structures of inspiration to the people can to a later generation seem empty, impedimental and reactionary. So too with the Ottoman system of immuring the imperial successor in a cage: it may have prevented rivalry and faction, but it led to mental collapse and regnal incompetence for the caged sultan-to-be. Nevertheless it should be noted that the Köprülüs acted with tolerance to the non-Muslims of the Empire, giving it a cohesion and unity that might have been absent under an intolerant, bigoted warrior.

In 1696 Peter the Great seized the fortress of Azov from Turkey at his second attempt. He was forced to disgorge it fifteen years later but its capture was indicative of the southward movement of the Russian Empire and the dynamic momentum of the struggle with Ottoman Turkey. Despite the tsar's capture of the fort, the lasting impression of his experience vis-à-vis the Ottoman Turks is of a great failure. In 1711 the Turks scored a remarkable victory over the Russians at the River Prut, today the border between Romania and Moldova. Here the Russian army came close to complete destruction. Legend has it that the day was saved by the resourceful action of the tsar's wife Catherine, with him on the campaign. She is said to have raised all the money she could, taking off her jewellery, and to have bribed the grand vizier to open negotiations. The alternative was unconditional surrender. Peter the Great limped away from the engagement, wary for ever afterwards of engaging with the Ottoman Empire. He lost Azov and his entire fleet, and had come close to seeing his whole project wrecked.[7] At this time the Turks saw improvements to their position; they reconquered the Peloponnese ('the Morea') and Albania, besides regaining Azov. An agreement was reached with the Russians on dividing up former Persian territory. But in the heartland of Europe, there were only losses, with the Austrians commanded by the resourceful and unconquerable Prince Eugène of Savoy, who had first shown his mettle at the siege of Vienna.

Shifts were occurring in Europe at the time. Despite Russia's defeat on the Prut, she was replacing Austria as the Ottomans' most powerful opponent. This was important for two reasons: first, Russia was Orthodox, like the Greeks, the Slavs and the Bulgarians under Ottoman control. And secondly there existed in Russia a strong anti-Turkish sentiment, if only because to the Russians the Turks were reminiscent of the Tatars who had held their land and people in subjection from the fourteenth to the sixteenth centuries.

In 1715 the Ottoman Empire renewed conflict with the Venetian Republic. Corinth was besieged and captured by the Ottomans (giving us

Byron's poem *The Siege of Corinth*, but not Rossini's opera of the same name) and the Peloponnese was invaded. The Greeks showed no inclination to come to the aid of their Christian Venetian overlords, who had treated them like serfs. Only Corfu remained Venetian. In response Austria restarted the Turkish war, and in Hungary – today Serbia – at Peterwardein Eugène of Savoy again defeated the Turks, but it was a costly victory. In Belgrade in the following year the same commander scored his most stunning victory, against an immense Ottoman army whose leader had committed the fatal mistake of hesitating before battle.[8] Belgrade passed to the Austrians, though the Turks were to recapture it twenty-two years later.

The Treaty of Passarowitz (Pozarevac) of 1718 saw substantial Austrian gains, losses for Venice and disquiet for Turkey. The last remaining fear in Europe of the Turkish armies evaporated and any notion of a westward military threat posed by the Turks was at an end. In a real sense they had lost their nerve. The large slice of east-central Europe known as Hungary was now free from the Turks; but the Habsburg emperor, like the Venetian doge, was viewed with equivocation or hostility, since Imperial Austrian rule was scarcely less tyrannical than Ottoman.[9] Peace reigned in the region until 1730. In the east, Turkey attempted to take advantage of a revolution in Persia, in which an Afghan dynasty briefly seized power, to capture the whole of what is now known as the South Caucasus (Transcaucasia) and did nominally achieve control of much of the region; but local militias (including some made up of Armenians, organised by the *meliks*, or local Armenian feudal lords, who were especially effective in Halidsor, southern Armenia) prevented the Turks from formally gaining possession of their treaty gains. Peter the Great, threatened by the possibility of an Ottoman–Afghan alliance, invaded northern Persia in 1722 and seized Derbent on the Caspian Sea. Briefly the Turks gained a kind of ineffectual control of Yerevan and Tbilisi; but the gains were annulled by Nadir Shah when he came to power in Persia in 1736.[10]

Ottoman Turkey was in a profoundly enfeebled state in the 1730s and the rise of Nadir Shah meant treaty gains for Persia. Russia renewed its attack on the Ottoman Empire under the Empress Anne, and the resourceful Marshal Münnich seized the Crimean fortresses of Ochakov and Perekop. In Europe the Ottomans were granted a limited success; despite Ottoman political decrepitude, the Austrians at this time were even more incompetent, and two empty-headed boastful generals managed to lose Belgrade, with the result that much of Serbia and Bosnia returned to Ottoman control. The Russians had been victorious in 1738–9, but their victories were empty with the failure of the foolish Austrians. All the conquests of Anne and Münnich in the Crimea and in Moldavia had to be disgorged. Ottoman Turkey ended the year 1739 in a mood of unexpected triumph. Peace again broke out and the region stayed thus until 1762. In that year the Empress Catherine assumed the Russian throne and a new complex system of alliances began to appear. Russia sought gains at the expense of both Turkey and Poland. Prussia, under Frederick the Great, formerly anti-Russian, now entered into treaty relations with her. The Austria of Maria-Theresa joined the plot against Poland and Turkey. Catherine's Russia went on to impose the first partition of Poland and fostered revolts in the Crimea, Greece, Montenegro and Georgia.[11]

There was an interesting and unusual unspoken alliance between Britain and Russia in 1770, at the time of Russia's first victory (in a sea battle) over the Ottomans. This was the first showing of Catherine the Great's Oriental Project, which could be summed up simply as destroying the Ottoman Empire and reconstituting the empire of Byzantium. Emissaries were sent to all parts of Greece; a rising was prepared under the supreme command of Alexis Orlov, brother of her then lover. But the actual command of the fleet was in the hands of Admiral John Elphinston, accompanied by a number of other British officers. A rising took place in the Morea. Although it failed and many Greek insurgents were killed, the fleet defeated the Ottomans at Chios (then known as Scio) and Admiral Elphinston blockaded the surviving ships in the harbour of Cheshme, on the Anatolian mainland. Lieutenant Dugdale piloted a fireship against them, which sent the entire surviving Turkish fleet up in flames. Subsequently the Ottomans were able to salvage a kind of victory, which left the situation a score draw.[12]

Diplomacy was never straightforward in the region and this was certainly so from 1780. The triangle of policy as it existed between Britain, the Ottoman Empire and Russia was frequently reconfiguring itself in accordance with the perceived significance of ideas which floated into dominance: the attitude to France, the understanding of Islam, imperial security, perception of the nature of Russia.

Charles James Fox viewed Russia as an ally, or at least a potential ally, against France.[13] She was undeveloped and, with reasonable leadership, could become an ideal partner for Britain. But there was a problem:

Catherine the Great was indifferent to her. England failed to capture her interest. Britain lagged as a trading partner. At the same time Catherine drove forward a policy of conquest of the Ottoman Empire, distasteful to Pitt.

Nudged by Catherine's impetuous southern policy, the powers of Europe began to explore ideas concerning the disposal of the territories of the Ottoman Empire. Even after the great losses of the last 150 years, it was still overextended and internally seriously weak. Following the sea battle of 1770, further Russian victories occurred in 1774. On this occasion, by the terms of the Treaty of Kutchuk-Kainardji ('little spring'), a village in Romania today, Russia won certain ill-defined rights to intervene on behalf of the Orthodox Christian population of the Ottoman Empire and to 'make representation' on their behalf.[14] Russia could also oversee the building of churches throughout Turkey and allow Russian pilgrims to travel to the Holy Land. The scheme was an extension of the extra-territoriality agreed between Suleyman the Magnificent and Francis I in 1535; there was nothing demeaning about it to either side. However, conditions were different 250 years on, and the legal position of the Ottoman Empire vis-à-vis its own citizens contained a flaw with the potential for great harm.

On the one hand, the empire was an autonomous self-ruling entity, with a ruler who could govern his provinces through governors, as happened in other empires. Most of the sultans, with the exception of Mahmud II, the 'reforming sultan', were weak and ineffectual, perhaps assisted by powerful grand viziers, but leaving provincial administration to distant pashas, of whom little was required beyond the return of sufficient tax revenue and the supply of recruits for the army. On the other hand, they could be dismissed by the sultan; he had the final veto. The final executive sultan of the Ottoman Empire, however, Abdul Hamid II, who ruled from 1876 to 1909, chose to be rigidly centralist. His authority overmastered the protection which the outside powers might think they could offer to the non-Muslim communities. Such communities were citizens of his empire, not theirs. So the protection granted to the minorities by outside powers turned out to be illusory; and it left the Christian populations themselves worse off than if the outside powers had offered no 'protection' in the first place.

In 1783 Count Potemkin annexed the Crimea for Russia. None of the other powers was consulted in advance and none objected subsequently; indeed Fox, Britain's prime minister at the time, fully approved of the action. In 1787 the Empress Catherine herself, in the company of Emperor Joseph II, travelled down the Dnieper to the Crimea in a theatrical victory celebration of Arabian Nights-type fantasy and splendour.[15] She was acclaimed as the new Cleopatra: her progress inevitably recalls Shakespeare's magnificent scene, 'The barge she sat in, like a burnished throne / Burned on the water.' Diplomatic relations with Austria were honed with delicacy, while those with the old allies Britain and Prussia grew tarnished. The powers most eager to see Ottoman Turkey's decline were the two seated in the imperial barge. The same year they made a plan to crush it and to re-establish the predominance of Orthodox Christianity at Constantinople. Byzantine echoes were found in the Greek names, quite non-Russian, which Catherine granted to the new cities in the Crimea, names which resonated like the bells from an ancient Orthodox steeple, indicating her ambitions: Odessa, Simferopol, Eupatoria, Sevastopol, Mariupol. Her second grandson had been named Constantine and was always dressed in Greek fashion.

But the plot did not unroll according to plan. The Austrian emperor Joseph II was enlightened, well-meaning and the friend and patron of Mozart. In 1788 he declared war on Turkey, for little apparent reason. At the time Russia could not form part of any intended pincer movement, since she was occupied with Sweden. Joseph led the field – one can hear the trumpets and drums of *Non più andrai* – and was catastrophically defeated near Lugosch, where he had rushed to the support of one of his generals, Wartensleben. At the head of 80,000 men the emperor panicked and in the subsequent mêlée the Austrian infantry mistook their own retreating artillery for the invading Turks and formed themselves into squares. In the carnage 10,000 Austrians were killed by their own soldiers. Joseph II never took to the field again, entrusting the command to Marshal Laudohn (i.e. Loudon, of Scots descent) and the Prince of Coburg. Thereby the Austrians regained some initiative, cooperating effectively with the Russian force of Alexander Suvorov. Joseph II died in 1790 and his successor, though pursuing the Turkish war, disentangled himself from alliance with Russia.[16]

The war continued to be fiercely fought between the northern and southern empires. But as Habsburg Austria was demonstrating incompetence, in the same year, 1788, the Russian general Suvorov, a 'wizened little veteran who ate bread with the soldiers, [and] startled them at dawn by his cock crows',[17] captured the fort of Ochakov from a force of 5,000 Ottoman Janissaries. The international community did not stir itself to offer even a listless complaint. In December 1790 the Russians, under Suvorov, seized the fortress of Izmail on the Danube in a brutal but effective engagement, savagely fought. The orders received by Suvorov had read, 'You will capture Izmail, whatever the cost,'[18] and the battle was given brilliant colouring in its verse description by Byron. The loss of Izmail – the Turks called it *Ordukalesi*, army fortress – marked the first stage of the end of Ottoman power along the Danube.

William Pitt, partly in response to matters unconnected to Russia or Turkey, alone expressed opposition to Russia's predominance. Catherine's ambition was overreaching itself. He determined to reverse the southward expansion of Russia and to ally himself to Ottoman Turkey. His aim bore some resemblance to English policy of 200 years earlier, when the Elizabethan court, fearful of Spain, ignored the distinction between Muslim and Christian in the interest of state policy. Pitt's action was conducted in the new politics of spheres of influence and the concept of the 'balance of power', passionately believed in in some quarters but dismissed as an 'incomprehensible nothing' by Richard Cobden, and certainly a concept which has been out of favour in the post-1991, unipolar world. The British prime minister, seeing international politics as a bloody, multi-clawed struggle to ascend the heap, perceived that Ottoman Turkey had a place in his considerations. Queen Elizabeth I had been somewhat of the same mind.

Pitt endeavoured to make Russia disgorge Ochakov and return it to Turkey, despite the diplomatic slumber which had accompanied its accession by Russia. His aim was to maintain the position of the Ottoman Empire. 'Anything tending to render the power of that [Ottoman] Empire in Europe unstable and precarious' must 'be highly detrimental to our interests,' he said.[19] The context was that of a defensive alliance with Prussia; but the principle was undoubtedly a general one as far as the prime minister was concerned. He declared his ambition to be to 'restore the tranquillity of Europe on a secure and lasting foundation'.[20] To that end he planned to send the British fleet to the Black Sea to keep the Russian navy out, though it is hard to see how the presence of a British naval force in the Black Sea could do anything but stir up European war. In a fine parliamentary debate on 29 March 1791, his great opponent Fox was heard to exclaim that 'it was new to a British House of Commons to hear the greatness of Russia represented as an object of dread'.[21] Edmund Burke, from Pitt's own side, also proposed that 'the considering the Turkish empire as any part of the balance of power in Europe was new,' adding, 'I very much dislike this anti-crusade.' His position was that of an anti-war conservative.[22] To the trenchant and convincing anti-war arguments of Fox and Burke and their associates, Pitt and the government had few real answers.

Pitt attempted to stand his ground, and returned to the subject later, when he reminded the House of Commons that it was Montesquieu 'who best understood the subject, [and who] expressly declared that the Turkish empire, although it undoubtedly contained in it many symptoms of decay, must last much longer than was generally imagined, because when an attack of an alarming nature should be made upon it, the European maritime powers would feel it to be their interest to come instantly to its aid, and rescue it from danger.'[23] This remark was given substance by the length of the empire's precarious survival for a further 126 years.

The government's position was also bolstered by an element of sheer Russophobia. This was articulated by Lord Belgrave (later the 1st Marquis of Westminster) in another later debate. He saw Russian intentions in the manner in which Disraeli was to view the northern power some eighty years later, and indeed in the manner of Tories of the Suez Group in their perception of Soviet Russia in the mid-1950s. The advance of Russia, he floridly declared, would be alarming to every maritime power. 'As soon as the Russians should have passed the Dardanelles, they would to a certainty be joined by the faithless Greeks; and where their victories would afterwards end, God alone could tell. They might fall upon Lower Egypt, and seizing upon Alexandria, restore the commerce of that once mighty city . . . which would give to Russia the entire supremacy of the Mediterranean, and render her a formidable rival to England, as a commercial and a maritime power.'[24] Although Pitt had won the original debate by 228 votes to 135, no squadron of British naval vessels was dispatched to the Black Sea. The prime minister realised that although he had won the vote he had lost the argument. The country was against him. His government would fall if he persisted. It would be a further sixty years before British public opinion could be cajoled into a mood of sending serious military assistance to Ottoman Turkey.

In the meantime, unhampered by Pitt's bellicose exuberance, Russia and Turkey went on to sign a treaty at Jassy (modern Iasi, Romania) in 1792, allegedly 'of perpetual peace', which gave Russia the border of the Dneister and secured Ochakov for her.[25]

With the advent of Napoleon, the Treaty of Campo Formio (of 1797) abolished the Venetian Republic, ending Venetian rule over the Ionian Islands (Corfu and its neighbours) and relaunching them as the Septinsular Republic, under a French (and later British) protectorate. The new title fitted well with the natural Greek allegiance to republicanism rather than monarchy. But Napoleon's ambitions were focused further east and of much greater substance.[26]

In 1798 he arrived in Egypt. Now Islam came face-to-face with modernity. Not since the later Crusades of the thirteenth century, with their casts of aggressively devout Christian visionaries bringing fire, sword and mayhem to Damietta and Alexandria, had Egypt been confronted by such a force from western Europe. However, the Corsican soldier brought rationality rather than religion. He would respect Islam. Nevertheless it was an inauspicious moment for the Islamic world and Britain forced him out with acerbic efficiency. The Ottoman Empire was crouched in weakness, showing the faults that Baron de Tott had memorably enumerated in his book published in 1785. In most ways it was still medieval, yet believed itself to be uniquely touched and guided by God. But fortifications had been abandoned half-finished and an atmosphere of relaxed ineptitude prevailed. Conservatism had ossified into fossilisation. The outlook for such an empire, lacking all internal dynamism, was not good.

Napoleon's stay in Egypt was brief, before he was ousted, first by Nelson at Aboukir Bay and then at Acre by a British army. Whether he was there for the light of science and humanity, or for the grandeur of empire, is a subject which will be endlessly discussed. But while he was there, with his scholars and philosophers, he showed a path to modernism for Egypt. The *Description de l'Egypte* is a monument of rationality and good sense, a cool and lucid guide to millennia of history.[27]

Persia's effective antagonism to Turkey had long vanished and Isfahan was now a prey to weakness. Persia had recently been overrun by a brutal Afghan eunuch called Agha Mohammed, who had sacked Tbilisi in 1795, an event which led to Russia being invited into Georgia (an invitation disputed by Georgian nationalists), bringing about a higher profile for the Russian presence in the Caucasus and north-west Persia; and the Indian Muslims were becoming drawn into the circle of Britain, and would end up subjects of the British Crown. Having driven off Napoleon, in 1801 Britain intervened to reimpose Ottoman rule on Egypt. The British alliance with Ottoman Turkey glinted in that act. However, it should be seen more as an action against France and against republicanism than as support for Ottoman Islam.

❖❖❖

The Islamic world in the early nineteenth century is perhaps best seen as changing in three distinct ways. In the first place, various nationalities, mostly Christian, were in the process of decolonising themselves from the Islamic empires and edging towards a position of nation-states. The principalities of Moldavia and Wallachia (later to become the major part of Romania), Serbia, Greece, Bulgaria and, in the early twentieth century, Albania undertook a long process of decolonisation and their independence or semi-independence often came after being pitched into the control of another imperial power. Their freedom was experienced in the emergence of states which could give voice to the interests of their members, and which saw the ousting of imperial military bureaucratic satrapies ruled by oppressive officials who ground down the villagers for their own enrichment. In the Caucasus, Georgia, in order to escape outbreaks of uncharacteristic Persian violence, had been compelled to seek the protection of Russia, which meant ending its monarchy. Armenia became, as the 'Armenian district' (1828–40), also part of Russia. Here nationalities exchanged one imperial hegemony for another, before achieving independence in the following century.[28]

In the second place, the European powers, in part jealous of one another, and in part driven by their own desire for greater imperial control, sought to gain ascendancy and 'spheres of influence' within the weakened Islamic world. France secured its authority in the Maghrib and got a foot in the door in Lebanon; Britain made its presence known in the Persian Gulf and after a struggle which lasted longer than the defeat of Napoleon gained the upper hand over France in Egypt. Italy came in late on the act, seizing Libya in 1911. The powers made long-winded and high-sounding justifications for their involvement, but in each case the motive was virtually the same: greed for concessions, markets and raw materials, the extension of a sphere of strategic and commercial influence and the creation of a series of secure military bases.

At the same time changes were taking place within the Islamic world itself usually very slowly. The reforming sultan Mahmud II destroyed the Janissaries and centralised the administration; but this led to a loss of local priorities in the provinces and many non-Muslim peoples were forced to endure double taxation, first by their traditional landlords, and second by the new central authorities. The same sultan reformed the army but it failed against the powerful and well-deployed Egyptian invasion of Syria and Anatolia. In the years following the documents of Ottoman reform, the *Hatti-Sherif of Gulhane* ('noble rescript', of 1839) and the *Hatti Humayun,* were not entirely extracted by the powers to make the Ottoman Empire welcome in the society of nations – there were genuine internal Ottoman aspirations towards reform – but for the most part they lacked credibility and brought no results outside the capital and large cities such as Smyrna (Izmir); so the charge of window-dressing to please the ambassadors cannot fully be rebutted.[29]

As for faith: there was little movement amid the half-believed statist Islam of the Ottoman capital. The succession of nineteeth-century sultans differed only in their varying degrees of worldliness. The last sultan of any substance, Abdul Hamid II, showed no evidence, beyond public duty, of believing any of the tenets of the Islamic faith of which he was leader, although he held securely on to the absolutism that his position granted him.

There was a stir in the depths of the Arabian peninsula. The year 1741 had seen the first preaching of Muhammad ibn Abdul Wahhab in Arabia. In 1804 his followers, the puritanical Wahhabis, had gained control of the Islamic holy places and ousted the easy-going Ottomans who been guardians of the sacred areas hitherto. A lax regime of flexibility and non-fanaticism was expelled to make way for strict belief in the harsh Hanbalist version of Islam, which gave a central position to devout literalism and punishment. The new regime was also an act of rebellion against the Ottoman sultan, who requested Muhammad Ali to end the revolt. In 1812 Ibrahim, the son of Muhammad Ali, captured Medina and then Jeddah on behalf of the Ottomans. The Saudi state appeared destroyed by 1818. Briefly Arabia returned to a less extreme version of the faith. But then Wahhabism regrouped in the interior, in Riyadh in 1846, under Faisal al-Saud. Gradually over the following decades the Wahhabis, in the form of the Saud family, extended their power. The favour shown to hard Islam by Ottoman Sultan Abdul Hamid II in 1876–1908, was a further help to them.[30]

The attitude of Europeans to the Wahhabi takeover in Arabia has always been puzzling. Observers have described it in terms of the return of Islam to its authentic roots. Islam has been perceived and described as becoming fully itself by being hard and unflinching and attuned to desert life. The desert has been seen as the cradle of uncompromising monotheism, a view which is at odds with the reality of the pleasure-loving polytheism of pre-Islamic Mecca. The edge of mercilessness and uncompromisingness was always attractive to a certain kind of westerner. Westerners thrilled at the sharpened blade of tempered steel and loved the idea of blood draining cleanly into the desert sand.

But was there anything in Islam itself that demanded that the faith become uncompromising and austere? Islam had been Islam when it was the scholarly, Mutazilite faith of the Abbasid court of al-Mamun, which had translated Aristotle and enforced doubt and scepticism. Islam had been equally itself when Lady Mary Wortley Montagu had discussed a disbelieving deistical theology with her Turkish host in Belgrade. The faith had, and has, been equally authentic when it had been allied to art and mysticism in Persia. It was to a great extent a western male military fantasy that it was solely its authentic self when it was harsh, uncompromising, desert-driven, blood-edged, knowledge-free and lacking in the fine arts. The fantasy was driven by ignoring the parts of the Koran that talk of compromise, tolerance and peace, giving focus instead only to warlike texts. It is as though Christianity were to be described as inauthentic except for its appearance as an austere mortificatory practice among solitary hermits in the Egyptian desert; or Judaism incomplete except among those entirely observant of the minutest details of the 613 precepts of the Torah. Lord Cromer's dictum was that 'Islam cannot be reformed, that is to say, reformed Islam is Islam no longer; it is something else; we cannot as yet tell what it will eventually be.'[31] This surely is an unhistorical fantasy, ignoring both the Mutazilite Abbasids who had sponsored the translation of Aristotle, and the Sufistic brotherhoods of popular Islam practised in Anatolia, Iran and the Indian subcontinent.[32]

The political topic most visibly carried on within the Ottoman Empire during the first third of the nineteenth century was the decolonisation of eastern Europe. Of this the most memorable part was the struggle for the independence of Greece.[33] Here the European powers were seriously involved; but the assistance they rendered to Greece was not offered for devout, religious or crusading reasons. The adventurers, and occasionally governments, were not motivated by the fact that the Greeks were a Christian people (as the historians of Turkey, S.J. and E.K. Shaw, have declared). Rather, the independence of Greece represented freedom and liberation; and help for a free Greece could be seen as a homage to the creation and development by the Greeks of those prime ideas which had led and were leading Europe itself away from clerical and imperial absolutism and towards democratic freedoms and rights. The Hellenic ideal was indissoluble from freedom, even if the reality of modern Greece was much more problematic. The Ancient Greeks themselves had been as capable of being tyrannical and fond of dictatorship as any people; but at the heart of the legacy almost imperceptibly conveyed from the ancient world lay a jewel of freedom, openness and fine civilisation, encompassed in a magnificent language and superb art. The divine fresh air with which Prometheus celebrates his own mental freedom, experienced in spite of near-death struggles with the oppressive deities of official terror, was heard just twenty years before Greece gained its freedom, in the prisoners' chorus in Act I of Beethoven's *Fidelio*. If freedom is in part a romantic idea (though it is also serious and requires many practical measures), the liberation of Greece was the climax to a series of events in which romanticism played a large part. The involvement of Byron and Shelley, both atheists, shows how little religion, or religious sentiment, counted. Byron himself, with his dedication to freedom, first of Italy and then of Greece, showed sympathy for Islam and Islamic peoples, expressed both in his admiration for Ali Pasha of Jannina, and in his ironic and many-layered anger at the treatment by the Russians of the Turks at Izmail, brilliantly described in Cantos VI–VIII of *Don Juan*. This sympathy is left out of most accounts of the poet and of his attitude towards Greek independence. In the great poem, Byron's affection for Leila, the Turkish orphan saved from the carnage at Izmail, 'homeless, houseless, helpless', is vividly and unforgettably portrayed.[34]

But freedom was dangerous. The Duke of Wellington was strongly opposed to the liberation of Greece and spoke against it. He would have preferred that the country remained unfree, with the people still held down by Ottoman despotism. Wellington would have ordered the prisoners back into their gloomy dungeon. He notoriously described the battle of Navarino, by which Greece gained the freedom lost to Sultan Bayazid, as an 'untoward event'. Against the idealistic clamour of the Philhellenes he brusquely declared that Turkey was 'our ancient ally'. (The reference appears to have been to the semi-alliance between Queen Elizabeth I and the sultan.) Wellington was not driven by a personal admiration for tyranny, but rather by a fear of the dissolution of the notion of property – the 'changes in possession', as he put it – that occurred when a nation was liberated from an empire. To the Iron Duke, property ownership was paramount. He may well have feared for his own landholdings in Ireland, should Greek methods of self-determination be emulated by the Irish. Freedom to His Grace was a morally relative term. Property came first. And religion had no place at all.[35]

The British, often thought of as stolid, phlegmatic and pragmatic, displayed a mercurially romantic changeability on the issues of freedom of nations and support for, or rage against, harsh or cruel regimes. The nature of the world and of the empires was such in the nineteenth century that support for one 'suffering nation' subjugated beneath a controlling empire's 'dastardly heel' could well be interpreted as support for the neighbouring empire's equally harsh regime of suppression and intolerance. Most British people throughout the century opposed the authoritarianism and autocracy of the Russian Empire above all; their widespread but not total Russophobia was encapsulated by Queen Victoria. The sentiment created strong bonds between the monarch and her people. The freedom of Poland became a central issue in many liberal and less-than-liberal circles of British society. Russia was seen as the prime oppressor, and since Russia was almost always an enemy of Ottoman Turkey, the champions of Polish liberty, fluent in that country's defence, resisted talk about the oppressive and sometimes brutal nature of the Ottoman Empire, focusing instead on the crimes of Russia. Only towards the end of the century, when Turkey clearly outran Russia in the despotism stakes, was there some shift in opinions. In most circles talk was allowed of Ottoman weakness only, not of Ottoman misgovernment.

Despite the apparent somnolence of political life in the Ottoman Empire at this time, events in the eastern Mediterranean were driven by a dynamic new force following the ousting of Napoleon. In Egypt, Britain had effectively driven the French out and reinstalled the authority of the Ottoman Empire. Yet Britain was not fully convinced of the merits of Ottoman rule – nor indeed were the Ottomans themselves – and shifted its support instead to the local (but alien) authority of the Mamluk Beys, the nearest the British could find to an upper class. These were a privileged Turkish-speaking relic from the pre-Ottoman days. Britain, backing a hobbled nag for class reasons, was to look to them to bolster its authority in its years of running Egypt.

France, though expelled, left a legacy of political energy in Egypt. Napoleon might have been driven out but his spirit remained. France's occupation indicated that, given a careful and intelligent stimulation, life and modernity and modernisation could be discovered within Islamic society, and that the Western image of 'Oriental' torpor was a misplaced fantasy. One man of those who had fought with the Ottoman armies against the French was an Albanian tobacco merchant called Mehemet Ali. (His name is more usually Arabised to Muhammad Ali.)[36] Napoleon had temporarily destroyed the corrupt and venal politics of the Mamluks, who had been supported by the British agent Major Missett.[37] The Turkish-speaking Mamluks had held on to their power because they were granted it by licence from Constantinople. The Ottoman rulers in the capital declared that the Mamluks could do what they liked with the peasantry – no level of extortion and corruption was off limits – so long as they paid an annual tribute to the Turkish Empire.

Muhammad Ali, rather than returning to Albania, stayed on in Egypt, showing a capacity for politics and intrigue that led him to gain the governorship of Egypt in 1805, and to assume total authority six years later. As he embarked on the modernisation of the country, he decided to switch sides and work with his former French foes. Revolutionary France was a modern and likeable power, he believed. But the consequent growth of French power in Egypt was seen by Britain as merely an attack on its essential world interests, that is, its global imperial reach. Britain habitually berated the other powers, especially France and Russia, for destabilising world affairs, while seeing its own gunboat diplomacy as pure and righteous. There is an element here of the dreamworld paranoia of aiming at, but not quite achieving, world domination. Britain occupied Alexandria in March 1807 and considered seizing the Nile delta. Displaying a lack of political capacity, Britain continued to ally itself politically with the exploitative Mamluks, imperious remnants who stood in contrast to the progressive modernism of Muhammad Ali. (The British continued to believe they shared a style with the Mamluks, whereas Muhammad Ali was only a self-elevated tradesman.) But the class was too feeble to be shored up. By October of that year Lord Castlereagh found his vapid policy of snobbish folly in shreds.[38]

Working with his former French adversaries, Muhammad Ali built up an army and a navy, and moved towards setting up a modern economy. He also established a printing press. He had agreed to the request of the Ottoman sultan to take action against the Wahhabi state set up by the Saud family in Arabia. The Sudan was conquered too, and (through his son Ibrahim) military assistance was given to the Ottomans against the Hellenic insurgents in the Greek War of Independence. But Ibrahim was dissatisfied with the reward offered by the Turkish sultan and set out on a campaign of broad conquest throughout Syria and into Anatolia. As his forces conquered towns and cities, it seemed as though Egypt might finally smash the Ottoman Empire. In 1831–2 he captured all of Syria, reaching Adana, routing the sultan at Konya and leaving him without an army. Further advances took Ibrahim's army to Kutahya, in western Anatolia, about 100 miles from Constantinople. The prostrate Ottoman sultan begged Britain for help but was met with a refusal. Devoid of allies he turned to Russia, 'a drowning man clinging to a serpent' as it was said at the time, and the tsar craftily gained (in the Treaty of Unkiar Skelesi) a kind of protectorate over Turkey.[39] This was not as absurd and devoid of substance as some commentators have made it out to be, focusing on the outward aspect of the situation – that Russia and Turkey were 'hereditary foes'. Hereditary foes can often make good allies, as the Second World War was to show. The notion of 'hereditary foes' is almost always misplaced. An element shared by Russia and Ottoman Turkey in 1833 was that they were both absolute empires and disliked any sort of populism, least of all the kind of liberating national self-determination seen in Greece. Neither was keen that their population should advance in knowledge and prosperity. They hated the early buds of freedom and took steps to freeze them back into a dark winter.

His back strengthened by the Russian alliance, Sultan Mahmud II thought he now had a chance against Egypt. He burned for revenge for Ibrahim's victory in Syria and resolved to send a large expeditionary force to crush his fellow-Muslim's pretensions. Egyptian rule was not popular in Syria, being oppressive and harsh. But the second Ottoman army was no more successful than the earlier one, and in the summer of 1839 it was comprehensively routed at Nisibis, the site of a Persian disaster against the Romans in 350, an engagement in which a diversion of the Tigris had brought quicksands which had slowly but remorselessly dragged a contingent of elephants to their doom. The collapse of the Ottoman army at the same location some fifteen centuries later led to the defection of the entire Ottoman navy to Egypt. Was it motivated by treachery or by some aspect of devout faith? The admiral was said to have believed that Constantinople had been sold to the Russians and was now an infidel city. At the same moment Sultan Mahmud died. 'In three weeks Turkey lost her army, her sultan, and her navy,' noted a diplomat.[40] The Ottoman state seemed to be disappearing with the slow, gravitational inevitability of the Persian elephants inexorably sucked into the mud of Mesopotamia.

The powers of Europe however held different ideas concerning the future of Ottoman lands: Britain supported a weak Ottoman Empire, while France endorsed the notion of a strong dynasty in Egypt. Britain seems not to have realised that, while it might be possible to impose one's will on a state prepared to demonstrate tame compliance, extreme weakness breeds disorderly, violent and chaotic administration, which may lead to further difficulties for the assumed puppet-mastery of the superior power. Muhammad Ali was offered a hereditary governorship in Egypt if his troops would quit Syria. He refused. A British fleet, representing the combined intent of Austria, Russia and Britain (but not France), appeared off the Palestine coast in 1841. It bombarded the forts of Acre and Beirut, then threatened Alexandria. Muhammad Ali capitulated; he quit Syria and restored the Ottoman navy, which received a new Kapudan Pasha (admiral of the fleet) in the form of a British infidel, Captain B.W. Walker (no relation to this author). The Englishman's appointment disproves one of the axioms that one is taught about Muslim statecraft – that no infidel may lead a Muslim force. The admiral was known first as Walker Bey, and later as Yaver (meaning aide-de-camp) Pasha, a somewhat slighting title for one who had rescued the entire Ottoman navy.[41] The title of Hereditary Pasha of the Ottoman Navy devolved upon Walker's descendants. It is possible that the Ottomans showed a tolerance of British infidels above their other allies, and likely that they trusted Britain more than any other power. Perhaps they saw Britain as an effectively Muslim power, for there was an identifiably Islamic dimension to the reigns of both William IV and Queen Victoria.

A crisis had been averted but the condition of the Ottoman Empire grew more perilous. Russian pressure continued and the tsar tried to enforce his authority in upholding the religious rights of the Orthodox community. He was driven by the southward spirit too, empire against empire, that had animated Catherine the Great.

Further north, an altogether stranger confrontation had occurred in the Black Sea, which might have have brought Britain and Russia into conflict had not Palmerston acted with restraint.

The Greek War of Independence had gathered many disparate men around its cause; it was a great expression of dissent, represented by several nationalities. One of those individuals who served with distinction, being wounded at the battle of Amphissa (Salona), off the island of Euboea, was David Urquhart, an able but eccentric Scotsman.

Born in Braelangwell, Cromarty, in 1805, he had been encouraged to travel east by Jeremy Bentham. In 1828–9 he fought the Ottoman navy on the side of the Greeks, and in May 1830 worked on mapping out the frontier of the new Greek state. At this time he turned, by a strange alchemy, from being a dedicated promoter of Hellenic freedom to an upholder of the entrenched conservatism of the Ottoman Empire. Having been at one with the drop-outs and dissidents who made up the supporters of the Greek War of Independence, he now became part of the establishment, but in a manner which was to combust into extremism and eccentricity. Initially things went well. His reports reached King William IV, who noted their clarity and lucidity. In November 1831 he was employed as a diplomat under Stratford Canning in Constantinople, acting as the ambassador's confidential agent. His sincere support for the Ottoman Empire seemed driven by a kind of mystical sense of union with the sultan's empire. After a brief return to England, Urquhart was sent east again by the king and the prime minister, as in effect a commercial traveller, carrying 'samples of British manufacture'; perhaps as a spy. He arrived back in the Ottoman capital in December 1833.[42]

In the following summer he toured the territory of the northern Black Sea, newly Russian following the Treaty of Adrianople (1829), although not actually specified as such. The condition of the Circassians along this coastline, south-west of present-day Chechnya, seems to have deepened his dramatic inner sense of his destiny among the peoples of the East, though at this stage he expressed less an attachment to Turkey than a powerful detestation of Russia, sacred in its intensity. Russia became for him truly a satanic power, an embodiment of profound evil. A personal dimension was observable: his words concerning Russia were only in part an articulation of the day-by-day course of events; they seemed to relate more to a powerful and symbolic interior world.

On the northern shores of the Black Sea he found the Circassian inhabitants rejecting the terms of the Treaty of Adrianople, refusing to become part of the Russian Empire. Urquhart encouraged them. He had landed at Anapa and here the Circassians, with their Scots leader, issued a declaration of independence. The man from Braelangwell designed a flag for them. Palmerston hesitated to offer support for his visionary diplomat, but then suggested to him the post of consul general in Constantinople. Urquhart turned down the offer, believing that the heart of the fierce struggle between Turkey and Russia, a struggle he saw as between the powers of light and darkness, lay in London. London was the powerhouse of political machinations and the centre of the plot. It was there that the fate of the unwieldy empires was decided, however much local people may have believed that they controlled their own affairs. Urquhart was back in London in early 1835. He plunged himself into agitation and publicity, producing vivid and plot-filled articles for his publication *The Portfolio*.[43]

Urquhart, despite believing in the importance of agitation in London, left for the east for the third time in 1836, as first secretary of the British embassy in Constantinople. This was a disastrous appointment. Urquhart seems to have let fantasy take over. He ignored the British embassy and went native with a vengeance. Adopting oriental dress, he lived as a Turk in a cottage near the embassy, sitting crouched on carpets, abandoning the use of furniture as a European inauthenticity, smoking a hookah. He became popularly known as Daoud Bey. There was no question of his carrying out embassy business. The bidding of his political masters went unheeded. He himself would formulate policy.[44]

The most notable piece of policy that he took charge of occurred in November 1836. In that month he and a colleague attemped to provoke a serious crisis between Britain and Russia. They hired a schooner, the *Vixen*, from the firm of George Bell of Constantinople, loaded her with salt and dispatched her across the Black Sea to the port of Sudjuk-kale, which after 1829 had been Russian-held territory. Urquhart's ostensible purpose was to trade with the Circassians, but his real intention was to get the vessel impounded by the Russians, and to create a diplomatic incident between Britain and Russia which with any luck would lead to war.

The Russians predictably impounded the *Vixen*. British chauvinists – jingoes, though not yet known as such – demanded that the fleet should be ordered into the Black Sea and stridently called for an attack upon Russia. (So far the plan had gone according to Urquhart's prediction.) But Palmerston was not roused and refused to play along. He declared that the port was *de facto* and *de jure* Russian. The affair ended quietly, with the *Vixen* being returned to Constantinople.[45]

Palmerston was justifiably fractious that the action had been undertaken by a government employee. The prime minister did not expect British diplomats to mutate into mystical, warmongering drop-outs. The obsessive tedium of the alternative diplomat's continuing campaign against the prime minister (whom he sought later to impeach as a paid Russian agent) confirmed his view of him. Urquhart was recalled and sacked. His royal patron William IV died soon after.

In a sense, Urquhart had been acting in a variation of the Byronic spirit. If Greece could have her freedom from Ottoman Turkey, why should Circassia be left subject to the alien empire of Russia? Why should the Circassians, or the Chechens, not be free? There was indeed a serious issue here, as later events have proven. A more circumspect spirit might have found a way of offering practical and intelligent support to the Circassians, by advising them on building up their culture and identity so that they could put forward an unequivocal demand to be heard as a nation. But Urquhart's extremism and his manic self-belief meant that his naval adventure amounted to no more than a mad farce. Certainly, in 1827, the battle of Navarino had been instrumental in liberating Greece. But an alliance between the disparate players of Britain, Russia and France had been assembled. Urquhart had done nothing to help forge a comparable alliance. His sole basis was his own mad act of publicity. He hoped his provocation would lead to war. At the heart of the liberation project of Byron and his colleagues, half-hidden amidst buoyant and bold spirits, there lay a calm calculation. Urquhart had no capacity for manifesting any such spirit. Also unlike Byron, he had no sense of humour and could never see any absurdity in his actions. He took himself dreadfully seriously and so is ultimately a bore. Byron's intimation of fallible mortality was absent from Urquhart. It is probably fair to say that whereas Byron's lightness of touch and humorous good nature aided the Greeks immensely, Urquhart's scowling paranoia and elemental hatred of Russia were no help for the Circassians.

He remained committed to views which were a curious mixture of commercial acumen, over-the-horizon vision and political extremism: a kind of gimlet-eyed travelling salesman. The propaganda campaign in favour of the Circassians and against Russia continued across Britain. Speaking in Glasgow in 1838 at a dinner given by the commercial community of that city, he described the flag he had designed for the Circassians and recalled the colour that he had chosen: 'Green, the colour that robes their mountains, and that indicates the faith of Mecca, was that which I chose. On it I placed a bundle of arrows, their peculiar arms, and a crown of stars, that in the nightly bivouac they might associate their independence with the works of their Creator, and the glories of the heavens. This language, speaking through the eye to the heart, was understood; a cry of union arose on the Euxine, and spread to the Caspian: a new nation was called into existence. If a new world was not called into life, a new people was created to change the destinies of the old. That people are the doorkeepers of Asia, and the champions of Europe.' In words which vaguely echoed the rhetoric of Pitt, Urquhart spoke of destiny; he seemed to be identifying himself with those men and women of faith (who have been either Christians or Muslims) who have contended that they were incapable of being wrong, and that their thoughts and aspirations amounted to an articulation of the voice of God, or Destiny, or a similar necessitarian figure. The world of *Greenmantle* seems not too distant.[46]

The Edinburgh barrister Joseph Hume, extraordinarily known as a Radical, replied to Urquhart and toasted Sultan Mahmud, 'the commercial ally of Great Britain', referring in passing to the 'disastrous result of Navarino'. The liberation of Greece appears to have rankled among Scottish business-Radicals, even though more than ten years had passed. The freedom of Greece had had an inhibiting effect on their Turkish trade. The freeing of nations was of lesser significance than their commercial profits. This was certainly a curious Radicalism.

Urquhart may have been extreme, but he was not alone. Sir John MacNeill, a member of a British military mission to Persia of 1834, wrote, also in 1838, of the threat of Russia to Turkish trade: 'By every movement she [Russia] threatens to interrupt the only line of communication by which British manufactures to the value of £1½ million are yearly carried through Turkey into Persia. She has already advanced to within nine miles of this road, and to about ninety from Trebizond, the port from which it leads. . . . She is our rival in the market of Persia . . . she has to put a stop to the transit trade through Georgia, because it interfered with her exclusive commerce on the Caspian.'[47]

Such proponents did not have the argument to themselves. Voices from the mercantile world opposed support for Turkey. Business by itself was not a sufficient ground for granting or denying support to the eastern empire. A counterblast was sounded by the Radical textile maker Richard Cobden. His pamphlet *Russia: by a Manchester Manufacturer*, also of 1838, was dismissive of Ottoman Turkey. Russia, in Cobden's opinion, was 'immeasurably superior in laws and institutions'. Persia, too, was preferable to Turkey, having made 'some advances in science'. What had Turkey to offer but decay, resulting from the 'fierce, unmitigated military despotism' of the government there?[48] English Radicals showed a greater consistency than their Scottish counterparts. Cobden and his fellow Radical John Bright were almost the only British political figures to oppose the Crimean War. In almost all their speeches of 1853–4 they relentlessly attacked the position of Palmerston. Here was the true voice of Radicalism, looking at political structures, war and human rights.

By now the issue of religion was almost invisible. The High Church party would reclaim it over Bulgaria in 1876–7; but that most Europeans were Christians, and most western Asians were Muslims, were issues which the materialism of the times had quietly covered. Almost no one thought in religious categories about world affairs. Those who supported Ottoman Turkey were driven by commerce and strategy, which had been serious issues in the sixteenth century, and which had now returned as dominant matters. Those who opposed Turkey did so, as the example of Cobden showed, on account of its military despotism, not its predominant faith. (Edmund Burke was probably the last Briton to oppose a pro-Ottoman policy out of dislike for Islam. He would not have felt comfortable in Queen Victoria's Britain.) Neither imperialists nor radicals were concerned either way by the fact that Turkey or Persia was Islamic. The issue hardly rated.

The Crimean War was immensely popular in Britain. Even before the country actually joined the conflict, the crowds were seething for war with Russia. Charles Greville noted in his diary, 'The House of Commons as well as the country are so excessively warlike that they are ready to give any number of men and any amount of money, and seem only afraid that the government may not ask enough. . . . It is disgusting to hear everybody and to see all writers vying with each other in laudation of Stratford Canning, who has been the principal cause of the war.'[49] Cobden and Bright continued to be almost the only public figures showing principled opposition to the war. Cobden declared that it was a war in which Britain had a despot for an enemy, a despot for an ally and a despot for a client.[50] More typical were the sentiments of Charles Kingsley, Anglican clergyman and proponent of muscular public-school Christianity, whose personal background was of an established slave-owning family in the West Indies. Kingsley rallied British troops fighting alongside the Turks, boosting their pride with the reassurance for them to 'be sure that you are doing God's work'.[51] His support for the Turks was quite dissimilar to the Anglican High Church support for the Christian nationalities under Ottoman rule that was to become common some twenty years later. It was also diametrically opposed to the atheistic support given by Byron and Shelley to the liberty-seeking Greeks of the 1820s. For Kingsley, despite his clerical status, the Christian religion had been assumed into the heaven of imperial power and political triumphalism. Victorian imperialism was the new religion and therefore British policy was right and 'Christian', even though the ally was Muslim and the foe Christian. 'Doing God's work' did not mean engaging in a crusading battle against the infidel, since the British soldiers in the Crimea were on the same side as the 'infidel'. It meant, to those of the Kingsley mentality, fighting wholeheartedly in support of the British Empire, which was to them the embodiment of Christianity and all public virtue. 'We have proved we have hearts in a cause, we are noble still,' echoed Tennyson in *Maud*, expressing the mysterious inner theory of British imperial qualities, finding a voice to match the bold facts of world-encompassing imperial might, ignoring specific details of regional conflict and any issue that might concern any specific religion, focusing only on the bravery and virtue of fighting for the British Empire of Queen Victoria.

After the Crimean War, the Ottoman Empire became a member of the European state system known as the Concert of Europe. The war's end found it still in control of its diverse territories, a patient granted a reprieve. It was granted a loan initially of some £3 million (offered at 6 per cent) by Britain, underwritten by the British government. Further loans brought the sum to £191 million, with the rates often at 12 or 13 per cent, since Ottoman Turkey was considered high-risk. Ninety per cent of this cash was squandered by the recipients on frivolities and prestige projects.[52] Diplomatic efforts led to the neutralisation of the Black Sea. No warships (even Turkish or Russian) were allowed there. Some commentators argued that, because the loans had been issued from London with British government support, Ottoman Turkey had in effect become a British protectorate.

The post-Crimean system broke down after fourteen years. Russia denounced the Black Sea clauses in 1871. Ottoman Turkey showed no willingness or capacity to reform; no real equality was granted to non-Muslims, outside a few communities in towns and cities of the west where Europeans resided. Ottoman society had become ossified, and the recent attempts to show that there was life in its society ignore relations between the Turkish-speakers and the other nationalities and the legal disabilities endured by the non-Muslim communities. In the countryside things continued as they always had. The Christians were kept firmly in their place; as infidels, any proper recourse to the law was blocked to them. Britain's enthusiasm for its alliance with Ottoman Turkey, which stretched back to the younger Pitt, and could be traced to Elizabeth I, showed signs of cooling. Could an alliance against Russia really be justified when the object of the alliance was such a despotism? Moreover the Turkish empire was apt to default on the payment on the loans and suspended payment altogether in 1875; the Ottoman state, after reckless spending on palaces and other luxuries for its sultans, in effect declared itself bankrupt.[53] Enthusiasm for Ottoman things diminished in Britain (especially since the payment of high-interest dividends had been suspended) and was soon largely the preserve of military men, committed imperialists, and the Queen herself.

Within the Ottoman Empire itself the aspirations of the non-Turkish communities changed. With the example of the freedom of Greece, some of them began to seek their own national freedoms. Serbia had gained a measure of freedom in 1804 but the Ottomans continued to hold some authority. Freedom had not yet been achieved. The Slavic-speaking nations of the Balkans began to look to the Russia of Alexander II, whose language was that of qualified liberation. The Russian Empire might be seeking warmer waters than the frozen north for the deployment of its navy, but the movement south coincided with the yearning of Ottoman Slav peoples for the end of tyranny from Constantinople and for a new, less discriminatory type of political arrangement.[54]

There was a crisis in the Ottoman Empire in the years following 1875. The peasantry of Bosnia-Herzegovina rose in revolt; foreign consuls were murdered by the mob in Salonika. The Austro-Hungarian minister of foreign affairs, Count Andrassy, proposed in a note a system of fair government for the provinces. Britain opposed this measure initially and, even when it accepted it, refused to try to persuade the Ottomans to implement it. The crisis continued with a series of demonstrations (not armed risings) in Bulgaria in April 1876, brutally put down. Thirty-seven villages in the region of Batak were destroyed and their inhabitants put to the sword. Ghastly deeds were perpetrated. The general massacre had been conducted by Ottoman irregulars or *bashibozuks*. Unfortunately for the Turks, a representative of a British newspaper, the *Daily News* (forerunner of the *News Chronicle*) found his way to the region and vividly described the aftermath of the massacre.[55]

In London Disraeli treated the entire matter with a dangerous frivolity in the House of Commons but was ultimately forced by the power of popular demand to send a commissioner to make a proper enquiry. Walter Baring was sent from the British embassy, and his report, issued in September 1876, was fair and unsparing. Baring's report persuaded

Gladstone to step into the controversy, which he did with the publication of his pamphlet on the Bulgarian atrocities. This pamphlet, measured, detailed and well argued (although only the rhetorical froth is ever quoted from it), summed up the British shock at the conduct of their Ottoman ally and puzzled over the nature of future alliances. Despite the favour expressed for eighty years by the British towards the Turkish empire (sentiments that had developed from Pitt to Wellington and on through Palmerston, in which the Ottomans were seen as protectors against the imperial rival Russia, which was allegedly ready to pounce on the plains of India), the sense that something was now very wrong within the Ottoman polity was strong. It was not for the most part an anti-Islamic movement, since the British people had been supportive of the Ottoman Empire over the Crimea, and earlier – although now extreme Islamophobic clerics joined in. It was a revulsion against methods of extreme brutality, a hostility towards a spate of official killing which for the first time had been delivered to the tables of the British people by the popular press. The pressure of the European powers, manifested at the Constantinople Conference of December 1876, pushed the Turks into proclaiming a constitution, liberal and enlightened. This instrument was abandoned within months, when it was sensed that the foreigners' backs were turned.[56]

Russia, sensing the pointlessness of waiting for genuine Ottoman reform and for the end of state-sponsored killings, determined to intervene, which she did in April 1877 with a declaration of war on Turkey. Britain nearly entered the war on the side of Turkey, to the support of which Disraeli and Queen Victoria were firmly committed. Neither of them sensed the new mood of revulsion against massacre and of committed moral energy shown by the *Daily News* reports. The Queen despised Eastern Christians – Russians, Greeks and Bulgarians – and perhaps actually detested them. (The campaign on behalf on the murdered Bulgarians was, she wrote, 'mawkish sentimentality for people who hardly deserve the name of real Christians'.[57]) Disraeli had held a lifelong admiration for Turkish ways, ever since his journey to Constantinople and the Levant in 1831–2. Eager supporters of Turkey were given important diplomatic postings. Sir Henry Elliott, Britain's ambassador in Constantinople in 1876, wrote in ringing tones of the folly of supporting nations opposed to Turkey. Sir Henry Layard followed him as ambassador; he strenuously made the case for the interests of imperial Turkey to be seen as almost indistinguishable with those of imperial

Britain.[58] (Queen Victoria was to complain of the near-treasonableness of those who resented support for the Ottoman Empire, and in 1877 she threatened to abdicate unless the British government became more firmly associated with the war aims of Ottoman Turkey.) The might of the British Empire was poised for action alongside Turkey. A number of the full-page cartoons in *Punch* of the time show John Bull offering an array of treacly commitments in support of the Ottoman Empire, often shown as pathetic, ramshackle, run down, pitiable, despite the horror and pitilessness of its governmental methods.

Britain did not come to the eastern empire's assistance. A kind of gloom enfolded Disraeli's utterances of late 1877, as he saw failure succeed failure in Turkey's war with Russia. The reform schemes had all failed. The system was finished. All the old safeguards had proved illusory. Disraeli grew weary and ill, his spirits only lifted by the inability of the Russians to take Plevna.[59] When it fell, a section of the British body politic seemed to be overtaken by a kind of madness. Lord Derby, never sold on the Turkish project and loathed by Queen Victoria, resigned. Gladstone's windows were broken by 'patriotic' thugs. The British fleet was ordered to Constantinople but many wondered what it could do; it could no more fight the Russian army than a whale could a bear. An Anglo-Russian war looked inevitable. In England the army reserves were called up. The appointment of Lord Salisbury as foreign secretary brought a measure of stability.

The earnest anti-Ottoman advocacy of Gladstone haunted Disraeli. Gladstone did not and could not feel the contempt for Eastern Christians that was shared by Queen Victoria and her post-1874 prime minister. Gladstone's High Church Anglican beliefs meant that he held a serious regard for Eastern Christians, unlike his sovereign or his rival. To him the Anglican Church to which he belonged was a divine institution to be preserved from political changes, not a narrowly configured organ of state. It possessed, as Archbishop Laud had envisaged, worldwide significance. Eastern Christians were as much witnesses to the Christian tradition as those of the West. The Eastern churches, and their members, were brothers in Christ to the High Church Tractarians. This viewpoint was absurd to Disraeli and the Queen, to whom virtue existed within and through the British Empire, which gained its moral force from the established Anglican Church. To the supporters of Unionist conservatism (but not to Disraeli himself, a man too practical and worldly to admit such an arcane concept) the British Empire was coterminous with good;

the British Empire was the Will of God in action. But nevertheless, their utterances show that they entertained occasional doubts about their superficial morality.

To many of the populations of eastern Europe at the time, this was a time of decolonisation and the freedom of their nations. Bulgaria was on the way to liberty; Greece cast off further shreds of the gloomy Ottoman mantle. The Habsburg Empire also felt a chill wind in the Balkans. Throughout the region the cornices crumbled from empires like masonry from tottering, unrestored, queasily vulgar palaces, and oppressive imperial bureaucracies were levelled as authority fell into the popular hands of the local inhabitants.

Ottoman Turkey lost catastrophically in the war of 1877–8. Large areas of eastern Europe were regained by their native inhabitants, and the grieving Ottoman Turkish villagers who had taken advantage of the land laws of empire were made bereft of their lands and livelihood, and forced out. They were genuine victims. In the east an Armenian commander had liberated the region of Kars from Ottoman rule; this action seemed to set the scene for a modernising future in the region. The Ottoman campaigns around Mount Ararat had been disfigured by murderous attacks on defenceless Armenian villagers by *bashibozuks,* who had been allowed in to commit slaughter and atrocity against the villagers in an attempt to instil fear in the population.[60]

At the subsequent international conference, the Congress of Berlin (July 1878), at which Bismarck presided, Disraeli broadly supported the claims of the Ottoman Empire against the policy of the Russian tsar (which had within it elements of genuine liberation) and with great charm manifested a hard strategic conservatism characteristic of large areas (but not all) of the British upper classes. In all his actions he was firmly supported by Queen Victoria, a woman who had little devotion towards liberty, least of all for Eastern Christians. Britain undertook certain responsibilities for Ottoman Turkey's north-eastern provinces, known as Turkish Armenia, and a descriptive book was written of the area with the title *Our New Protectorate.*[61] But the complexity of international relations and a lack of political will meant that Britain did not put into practice its undertakings for the region for a period much longer than a year.

The Treaty of Berlin saved Ottoman Turkey for more than a generation; but the frozen politics of the country and the restless sometimes murderous paranoia of its ruler, from 1876 the absolutist

Abdul Hamid II, meant that it was held in a kind of suspended animation. The politics of the empire under Abdul Hamid had something in common with one of the impressive mechanical toys presented to the sultan in the sixteenth century, but with the mechanism jammed. Attempts to loosen the immobile mechanism were made by Islamic reformers, especially by the revolutionary thinkers Jamal al-Din Afghani and Muhammad Abduh.[62] These two, in their different ways, sought to show that Islamic polity need not mean total political immobility; that social and other advances were possible under Islam; and that staid, unchanging, deeply conservative Islamic ways would lead only to a takeover by the agile and energetic capitalists of Europe. They sought to find renewal within Islam so that it could defend itself. Their Islam was more deistical than deeply believed and they have been heavily criticised for that. But since Islam itself can be interpreted as near to deism, the charge (advanced frequently by the late Professor Kedourie) of religious unbelief is foolish; the more so, since it is doubtful that the Sultan's own beliefs themselves went beyond a kind of nebulous deism.

Attention switched to Egypt, Britain's semi-colony, and to the dynasty founded by Muhammad Ali, which continued to rule it. Egypt was a most important country for Britain, holding a key position on the way to India; unquestionably so since Disraeli had in 1875 bought for Britain not far under half of all the shares in the Suez Canal. The Middle East's position as a stepping stone to India meant that Britain was concerned with the entire region and keen to create political compliance. By the same token, after Britain left India in 1947, Egypt and the wider Middle East lost their significance. Britain and France were compelled to cooperate in Egypt for most of the nineteenth century, echoing their alliance in the Crimea. But by the 1870s Egypt's ruler Ismail had led the country into a disastrous debt, even though he had created a forward-looking country ('We are now part of Europe.'). The politics of the country were further held back by the remnants of the Turko-Circassian aristocracy and a rebellion was hatched by the native-born Arab Colonel Urabi (often written 'Arabi'). All powers, French, British, Ottoman, in their different ways saw the revolt of the native colonel as a threat.

In May 1882 Britain and France sent a joint squadron as a show of force. Rioting broke out in Alexandria. Several hundred were killed or injured. The British Liberal cabinet, except for the radical Unitarian John Bright, swung behind the idea of overthrowing Urabi, preferably by means of the Ottoman army. Nothing happened, so the colonel was issued an ultimatum to dismantle the fortification he was building in Alexandria. This was rejected and British forces bombarded the ancient city, leaving it in flames.[63] England was gripped by a mood of high jingo imperialism and an expeditionary force led by Sir Garnet Wolseley sailed up the Nile and defeated Urabi at the battle of Tel el-Kebir. The British occupied Egypt, dissolved the Egyptian army, dispatched Urabi to Ceylon (Sri Lanka) and had no idea what to do next. Eventually a clever compromise was reached: British troops would remain in occupation but Egypt remained, on paper at least, an autonomous viceroyalty of the Ottoman Empire. Britain controlled all aspects of the government, and it was the subtlest of imperialists, Lord Milner, who devised the designation 'The Veiled Protectorate'. Sir Evelyn Baring, sent to sort out the country's finances, was the most imposing – some would call him obstinate, self-righteous and insufferably superior – pro-consul; as Lord Cromer, his term of office lasted from 1883 to 1907.

Most members of the Egyptian intelligentsia hated the occupation, and none more so than Yaqub (James) Senua, who, under the nom de plume of Abu Naddara, 'the Man in Blue Shades', relentlessly attacked the occupation, writing tirelessly in favour of the regaining by the Egyptian people, all the Egyptian people, of their land. What was interesting about Senua was that he was Jewish, a point which shows that it was perfectly possible for religious or racial origin to matter little in the context of serious discussion of the high political topics of the day. It was only later, with the emergence of Zionism, that atavistic ideas such as religion and race origin started to matter.[64]

The pace for liberation in Egypt increased markedly as a result of an incident that occurred in 1905–6. In a village called Dinshawai, near Tanta on the Nile delta, pigeons were raised by the community for food. A party of British officers went pigeon-shooting for sport and the villagers protested, with little result. Their food was lost for the sake of the officers' sport. When the 'sportsmen' returned the following year, the villagers were armed with staves and defended their livelihood as best they could; but four of their number were killed, which led them to take up stones too. The tribunal that was set up took punitive retribution on the villagers: a number were hanged or flogged, merely for defending their livelihood. The events, which arose from crass imperial arrogance and subsequent misunderstandings, were not seen that way by Lord Cromer and others like him. To them they represented xenophobic fanaticism fanned by nationalists, which was everywhere prevalent. (In the era of Bush and Blair they would be called 'terrorists'.) But to the native literate political class of Egypt, a class always hated by occupiers and imperialists, it was a further point of fierce alienation. Perhaps the best comment on the incident came from George Bernard Shaw in his preface to *John Bull's Other Island:* 'Try to imagine the feelings of an English village if a party of Chinese officers suddenly appeared and began shooting the ducks, the geese, the hens, and the turkeys, and carried them off, asserting that they were wild birds, as everybody in China knew, and that the pretended indignation of the farmers was a cloak for hatred of the Chinese, and perhaps for a plot to overthrow the religion of Confucius and establish the Church of England in its place.'[65]

In Ottoman Anatolia, the politics of the time murmured with dissatisfaction. Although certain ill-defined undertakings had been made to the Armenians in the Treaty of Berlin, and despite the victory of the Russian-Armenian commander at Kars, nothing was done for them, and no power pushed Turkey to reform the administration in the empire's Armenian provinces. Britain had dispatched some special consuls to Anatolia who, with limited powers, represented a kind of impartial authority not seen before in those vast and ill-governed lands. Britain was curiously ambivalent. It was Turkey's most important ally, yet at the same time a section of its people spoke strongly in favour of the Armenians, expressing serious criticism of the Ottoman administration. It soon became apparent that any public criticism was powerless against the pro-sultan might of the establishment. Nothing was done in the region; the weak consular presence was withdrawn and the situation grew worse, despite undertakings. In the provinces Armenians were denied legal protection – there was no redress for injuries done to them – and no justice was administered for the brutality, theft or rape suffered by them at the hand of local non-Armenian ruffians. The rule of law did not exist for them, even though theoretically the protection of the law had spread to all communities by the Treaty of Paris (1856).[66] Against the violence of the government and its hangers-on they were left powerless.

Armenia was at the time a land divided between two empires, those of Turkey and Russia; and throughout the Russian Empire violent methods were being learnt for the unseating of the autocracy. The Armenians had few complaints with Russian rule (until 1903); their enemy was the systematic oppression foisted on them by the Turks. The background was acknowledged to be dire: the British ambassador commented on a series of reports on Ottoman Armenian provinces in early 1884, 'These documents repeat the same tale of wrong, misery, corrupt and incapable administration.'[67] Ottoman oppression was making life intolerable and revolutionary ideas were reaching them from across the imperialist-made frontier, in Russian Armenia. Attempts to establish newspapers and set up schools were made impossible by the authorities. Political societies emerged, at first quiet and orderly (though secret, since all political activity was against the law) and later showing an edge of terror. There were a few demonstrations, and slogans declaring 'liberty or death'.

An uprising took place in 1894 in the Sasun region, eastern Turkey today, against local feudal landlords and the system of double taxation. It was savagely suppressed and an impartial enquiry concluded that extermination had been the intention. It was the prelude to a widespread campaign of official Ottoman killings throughout Turkish Armenia, in which probably 200,000 died. A large demonstration took place in Constantinople in September 1895, followed by the seizure of a bank by a group of desperadoes in August 1896.[68] In each case the Sultan used the opportunity, as oppressive governments tend to make use of terroristic acts, to increase the scope of his own arbitrary authority and to broaden the state degradation or murder of the oppressed people. The linguist and traveller Arminius Vambery, an observer largely sympathetic to the Sultan, and his frequent guest, felt compelled to describe Abdul Hamid's rule as 'a *régime* of terrorism'.[69] One can note similar symbioses of terror with terror in a number of parts of the world today.

In two fine speeches, in Chester in August 1895 and in Liverpool in September 1896, the aged Gladstone spoke powerfully about the events. The most interesting question he asked was, What should be the scope and limits of the power of one state to intervene in the internal affairs of another, especially if the state which was keen on intervention was bound by treaties to other, third-party, states? This is an issue which has continued to haunt politicians. Gladstone came to no firm conclusion, beyond outlining the idea that, despite his belief in a united 'Concert of Europe', freedom to act alone was sometimes right. If the consensus was wrong, one had to break from it.[70]

The European powers sought to compel the Sultan to abdicate in 1896; there was discussion about the idea; but France demurred, since it feared that it would lose the income that it had gained from the Ottoman tobacco concession (*Régie des tabacs*). Britain, in the person of Lord Salisbury, voiced a doubt about the whole direction of British policy towards the Ottoman Empire since 1791: had Great Britain 'backed the wrong horse', he mused in 1897.[71] This was in truth an interesting line of self-questioning. Suppose, we can imagine with hindsight, Britain had supported Russia against Turkey, instead of instinctively always jumping to the support of the Ottomans, and had rather allowed the Ottoman Empire to wither like some Central Asian khanate, while giving support to the liberation of Greece and Bulgaria. Armenia would have been able to come fully into the orbit of a no-longer-threatening Russia. At the same time Britain would have helped re-energise the empire's Muslim parts (Kurdistan, the ethnically Turkish part, and the Arab world). All this would have upheld the people, rather than the ruler. Salisbury seems almost to have been recognising the folly of the concern of the 'great powers' for Ottoman Turkey: that all their interest, especially the unflinching support offered by Britain, had infantilised the empire and helped lead it backwards to greater political passivity and to outbreaks of brutality and massacre. The world might have become a safer and more just place if all parties had denied it preferential treatment and left it to wither or grow strong on its own.

Despite the diplomatic isolation experienced by the Ottoman Empire, it achieved a surprising military victory over the Greeks in 1897 in a war which followed a revolt in Crete. Part of the Turkish success can be traced to the presence of German officers (under von der Goltz Pasha) since 1882. But the diplomatic success lay on balance with the Greeks, and Crete was, step by step, freed from Ottoman control.[72]

Germany grew to be the ally of choice to the Ottoman Empire. It asked no questions and expected no standards. Its imperial ambitions lay to the east and in 1898 the Kaiser made a preening theatrical tour of the Ottoman Empire, dressed in a white uniform. In the same decade the first two sections of the projected Berlin–Baghdad railway were completed.

The Turks themselves grew embarrassed by their reactionary, immobile sultan, who was opposed to all reform; a British intelligence man spoke of his 'warped ideas and insane prejudices'. A cell of Ottoman exiles established itself in Paris. It became a scene of quarrels and disputes, but eventually the disagreements were smoothed over by Armenian revolutionaries and all parties launched an Ottoman revolution, which burst upon the streets of the capital in July 1908. Constitutional revolutions were the great idea of the time; Russia had seen its first revolution in 1905 and the more complex Iranian constitutional revolution had taken place in the same year. In Ottoman Constantinople (not quite yet known as Istanbul) *hürriyet* (freedom) was proclaimed, and for six months there was a genuine freedom and a burgeoning sense of equality and renewal. Old taboos were dispensed with and the new rulers demonstrated a cheerful irreligiosity. No one bothered henceforth about mosques and churches and Friday prayers. Religion was seen as a divisive legacy of the old regime, out of place in the new unified Ottoman realm. There was a genuine coming-together of peoples. It is very hard to claim that the regime, that of the Young Turks, otherwise known as the Committee of Union and Progress, was reactionary, racist and statist from the start. Yet as soon as the revolution was secure, its leader, Enver Bey (later Pasha), travelled to Berlin to study military tactics and the German language.[73] His keenness on the Kaiser's Germany was troubling.

Britain, a key player, did not view the constitutional regime with favour. No British representative was in the Ottoman capital when the revolution was declared, and on 31 July 1908 the new ambassador was given firm instructions by the foreign secretary, Sir Edward Grey, to keep a distance from the regime. The reason was simple, and supremely selfish. Any kind of constitution in Egypt or India would threaten British rule, where legitimacy was derived not from the consent of the people but from the threat of military force. 'If, when there is a Turkish constitution in good working order and things are going well in Turkey, we are engaged in suppressing by force and shooting a rising in Egypt of people who demand a constitution too, the position will be very awkward,' Grey declared. So there had to be no involvement with constitutional developments in Turkey. Britain did not want a democratic world to emerge from a constitutional Ottoman Empire. It preferred the barked orders of empire to the consent of democracy. The field was left further open for German diplomacy and military missions.[74]

Flaws in the Ottoman constitutional movement began to appear after about six months. The politics remained secretive; the 'Committee' ran the democracy and remained in Salonika, even though the hub of political activity was Constantinople. There was a counter-revolution in April 1909, a massacre of Armenians in Adana, and a move away from multicultural liberalism towards monoethnic statism. This was an anomaly in a multiethnic society. The Committee steadily lost popularity; there was a split and a new liberal party, the Ahrar, appeared in November 1911. It went on to win a by-election in Constantinople. The Committee of Union and Progress decided to halt the political advance of its opponents and procured its own success in a massively corrupt general election of April 1912. A group calling themselves the Saviour Officers took to the hills and persuaded the Committee to relinquish power in July 1912. The democratic dissidents took power in the 'father-and-son' government of Ahmed Muhtar and his son. Foreign minister was the Armenian Gabriel Noradungian, an appointment which showed how far the new government had distanced itself from the Committee's newly oppressive narrow and chauvinistic politics.[75]

Events were inauspicious, and conspired to create a wretched outcome that echoed the bleak right-wing judgement of the British Turkophile Aubrey Herbert three years earlier: 'Whoever is in office in Turkey, it is the soldier who is in power.'[76] The Italians had swept in and seized Libya in 1911, and the empire was sorely threatened in eastern Europe; the last remnant of Ottoman territory there was under heavy pressure, since the hitherto quarrelling Balkan states had united to throw the Turks out. It seemed that the Ottoman government was on the verge of surrendering Adrianople. In January 1913 leading revolutionary Enver Pasha stormed his way back to power, seized authority from the Saviour Officers' regime with the barrel of a gun and imposed a fierce dictatorship.[77] Ottoman Turkey was now a closed and controlled security state.

The same year a large German military mission arrived. Germany had been growing closer to Turkey ever since von der Goltz Pasha had arrived earlier with a small military mission (which had borne fruit in the defeat of the Greeks in Thessaly in 1897), and since the negotiation of a loan from the Deutsche Bank in 1888. The Germans never complained to the Turks about the Armenians and human rights, so they were welcome. Now, Liman von Sanders arrived with forty-two officers. The battle-lines for world war were drawn.[78]

The times were secular. No one paid much interest to the declaration of the Sheikh ul-Islam, when he proclaimed a *jihad* in 1914; he was just a useful instrument of the Committee (which was made up of atheists). His pronouncements would be heeded by few beyond backward villagers, less responsive to political directives from Committee activists. A declaration from the highest sheikh was moreover questionable, when the Ottoman Empire was in alliance with the empires of Germany and Austria. Outside the Ottoman Empire the declaration fell flat. Within the Quraysh, the Prophet's tribe noted in pre-Islamic times for secularism, the leading family was the Hashemites, and their leader, Husain, held the hereditary position of Grand Sharif of Mecca. He had returned from Constantinople to Arabia, where, with imprecisely expressed British help, a revolt was raised against distant Committee-run Turkey. The situation was darkened by a background of secret negotiation between Britain and France on the future colonial status of much of the Arab world. Despite the success of the revolt, the dreams of Arab independence turned to dust at the Paris Peace Conference, and the Hashemites – inclined to modernity – were within a decade ousted from the Hejaz by the Saud family, spiritual heirs of Ahmed ibn Hanbal, who had pronounced firmly against knowledge and discussion. In this way the strong Arab aspiration not to be colonised was stifled, and the reputation for enquiry, found in Abbasid Baghdad and Islamic Andalusia, was given little chance to re-emerge. The region and its people deserved better.[79]

Notes

ABBREVIATIONS:

DNB   *Dictionary of National Biography*, London/Oxford, 1881–1996
EB 11   *Encyclopedia Britannica*, 11th edn, 1912
EI 1   *Encyclopedia of Islam*, Leiden, 1st edn
EI 2   *Encyclopedia of Islam*, Leiden, 2nd edn
ODNB *The Oxford Dictionary of National Biography*, Oxford, 2004
PPTS The Palestine Pilgrims' Text Society
Schaff–Herzog *The New Schaff–Herzog Encyclopedia of Religious Knowledge*,
     Grand Rapids, Baker, 1966

INTRODUCTION

1. John Hales, *Tract Concerning Schism and Schismaticks*, ?London, 1716, p. 181; first printing, 1642.

CHAPTER ONE. SOPHRONIUS AND OMAR

1. H. Wace and P. Schaff (eds), *A Select Library of the Nicene and Post-Nicene Fathers*, Oxford, Parker & Co., 1891, vol. 2, pp. 21 (Socrates), 258–9 (Sozomen).
2. Desiderius Erasmus, *Pilgrimages . . .* , Westminster, J.B. Nicols, 1849, pp. 21–2.
3. Charles Diehl, *History of the Byzantine Empire*, New York, AMS Press, 1969, p. 41.
4. A.A. Vasiliev, *History of the Byzantine Empire*, Madison, University of Wisconsin Press, 1984, p. 195.
5. C.A. Trypanis (ed.), *The Penguin Book of Greek Verse*, Harmondsworth, Penguin Books, 1971, p. 422.
6. Koran, 30: 1.
7. Edward Gibbon, *The History of the Decline and Fall of the Roman Empire*, complete edition, ed. David Womersley, Harmondsworth, Penguin Books, 1995, vol. 3, p. 237 [ch. 51].
8. Richard Bell, *The Origins of Islam in its Christian Environment*, London, Macmillan, 1926, p. 45.
9. Ibid.
10. Ibid., pp. 43–4.
11. Maxime Rodinson, *Mohammed*, Harmondsworth, Penguin Books, 1971, p. 97.

12. Bell, *Origins of Islam*, p. 71.

13. Ibid., pp. 73, 83.

14. Peter Brown, *The Rise of Western Christendom*, Oxford, Blackwell, 1998, p. 180.

15. Philip K. Hitti, *History of the Arabs*, London, Macmillan, 1968, p. 166.

16. Bernard Lewis and P.M. Holt (eds), *Historians of the Middle East*, London, Oxford University Press, 1962, p. 247.

17. Hitti, *History of the Arabs*, p. 152.

18. Ibid., pp. 130 ff.

19. Charles Dowsett, *Sayat'-Nova* Louvain, Peeters, 1997, p. 36.

20. Aram Ter-Ghewondyan, *The Arab Emirates in Bagratid Armenia*, tr. Nina G. Garsoïan, Lisbon, Livraria Bertrand, 1975, p. 20.

21. [Thomas Hyde?], '*Historical and Critical Reflections . . .*', in *Four Treatises concerning the . . . Mahometans*, London, 1712, p. 170.

22. Koran, 17: 1.

23. *EI* 1, 'al-Kuds'.

24. Gibbon, *The Decline and Fall*, vol. 3, p. 237.

25. Andrew Palmer (ed. and trs.), *The Seventh Century in the West-Syrian Chronicles*, Liverpool, Liverpool University Press, 1993, p. 231.

26. Ibid., p. 131; Brown, *Western Christendom*, pp. 187–91.

27. Palmer, *Seventh Century*, p. 50.

28. J.S. Assemani, *Bibliotheca Orientalis*, Rome, 1719–28, vol. 3, pt i, p. 131; T.W. Arnold, *The Preaching of Islam*, London, Darf, 1986, p. 82.

29. R.W. Thomson (tr.), James Howard-Johnston and Tim Greenwood (eds), *The Armenian History attributed to Sebeos*, Liverpool, Liverpool University Press, 1999, vol. 1, pp. xxii, xxv, 95.

30. R.W. Southern, *Western Views of Islam in the Middle Ages*, Cambridge, Mass., Harvard University Press, 1962, pp. 16–18.

31. Walter Besant and E.H. Palmer, *The History of Jerusalem*, London, Richard Bentley, 1889 edn, pp. 76 ff.

32. Theophanes: *The Chronicle of Theophanes Confessor, 284–813* [*Chronographia*], tr. Cyril Mango and Roger Scott, Oxford, Clarendon Press, 1997, p. 471.

33. Ibid., p. 433.

34. Ibid., p. 471.

35. Ibid., p. 443.

36. Ibid., p. 471.

37. *EI* 1, 'al-Kuds'.

38. Gibbon, *The Decline and Fall*, vol. 3, p. 269.

39. C.R. Conder, *The City of Jerusalem*, London, John Murray, 1909, p. 239; Guy Le Strange, *Palestine under the Moslems*, London, A.P. Watt, 1890, p. 143; Palmer, *Seventh Century*, p. 162.

40. Theophanes, *Chronicle*, p. 471.

41. [Arculfus], *The Pilgrimage of Arculfus in the Holy Land*, tr. J.R. Macpherson, London, PPTS, 1889, pp. 5–6, 4.

42. Gustav von Grunebaum, *Medieval Islam*, Chicago, University of Chicago Press, 1969, p. 287.

43. R.A. Nicholson, *A Literary History of the Arabs*, Cambridge, Cambridge University Press, 1907, pp. 196–7.
44. Gibbon, *The Decline and Fall*, vol. 3, p. 227.
45. Nicholson, *Literary History*, p. 194
46. Albert Hourani, *Europe and the Middle East*, London, Macmillan, 1980, pp. 8–9; Brown, *Western Christendom*, pp. 189–90; *Butler's Lives of the Saints*, London, Burns and Oates, 1956, vol. 1, pp. 689–91.
47. Sir Harry Charles Luke, *Mosul and its Minorities*, London, Martin Hopkinson, 1925, p. 75; Peter Brown, *Western Christendom*, p. 193; Frits Holm, *My Nestorian Adventure in China*, London, Hutchinson, 1924, pp. 159–84; F.L. Cross (ed.), *The Oxford Dictionary of the Christian Church*, 1961, 'Sigan-fu Stone'.
48. Henri Pirenne, *Medieval Cities*, Princeton, Princeton University Press, 1925, p. 27; Peter Brown, *Society and the Holy in Late Antiquity*, London, Faber and Faber, 1982, pp. 63–79.
49. Sir Reader Bullard, *Britain and the Middle East*, London, Hutchinson, 1952, p. 13.
50. Besant and Palmer, *Jerusalem*, p. 124; Conder, *Jerusalem*, p. 250; Steven Runciman, 'Charlemagne and Palestine', *English Historical Review*, 200/50 (October 1935), 606–19.
51. [Bernard], *The Itinerary of Bernard the Wise*, tr. J.H. Bernard, London, PPTS, 1893, p. 7.
52. Ibid., p. 11.
53. Elinor A. Moore, *The Ancient Churches of Old Jerusalem*, Beirut, Khayats, 1961, p. 19.
54. Southern, *Western Views*, p. 21; Arnold, *Preaching*, p. 137; see also Brown, *Western Christendom*, pp. 193–4.
55. *Cambridge Medieval History*, vol. 7, 1932, p. 637.
56. *The Legacy of Islam*, ed. T.W. Arnold and A. Guillaume, Oxford, Clarendon Press, 1931, p. 337.
57. *Cambridge History of Iran*, vol. 4, 1975, pp. 144–5.
58. Omar Khayyam, *Rubaiyyat*, tr. Edward Fitzgerald, 1st edn, stanza 32; also Conder, *Jerusalem*, p. 268.
59. Mukkadasi, *Description of Syria (including Palestine)*, tr. G. Le Strange, London, PPTS, 1886, p. 37.
60. Conder, *Jerusalem*, p. 259.
61. Le Strange, *Palestine under the Moslems*, p. 204.
62. Nasir-i Khusraw, *Diary of a Journey through Syria and Palestine [1147]*, tr. G. Le Strange, London, PPTS, 1888, p. 60; Le Strange, *Palestine under the Moslems*, p. 205.
63. Conder, *Jerusalem*, p. 264.
64. [Arculfus], *Pilgrimage*, pp. 3–4; Besant and Palmer, *Jerusalem*, pp. 139–40
65. *Cambridge Medieval History*, vol. 4, pt i, 1966, p. 737.

CHAPTER TWO. THE ASPERITY OF RELIGIOUS WAR

1. Ernest Barker, *The Crusades*, London, Oxford University Press, 1939, p. 23.
2. William of Tyre, *A History of Deeds Done beyond the Sea*, tr. E.A. Babcock and A.C. Krey, New York, Columbia University Press, 1943, vol. 1, p. 372.
3. [F.P.G.] Guizot, *Collection des mémoires . . .* , Paris, Brière, 1825, 'Raoul de Caen', pp. 241–2.
4. Ibid., 1824, 'Albert d'Aix', p. 350.
5. David Hume, *History of England*, Edinburgh, Peter Hill etc., 1818, vol. 1, ch. 5, p. 292.
6. Gibbon, *The Decline and Fall*, vol. 3, pp. 649, 727, 583, 624, 610.
7. William Robertson, *Works*, London, Whitmore and Fenn, 1824, vol. 3, p. 31.
8. John Lawrence [Johann Lorenz] Mosheim, *An Ecclesiastical History*, London, T. Cadell, 1768, vol. 2, pp. 237–9.
9. Charles Mills, *The History of the Crusades*, London, Longman, 1822; Besant and Palmer, *Jerusalem*.
10. Wm Shakespeare, *1 Henry IV*, I. i. 18–27.
11. Geoffrey Barraclough, 'Deus le Volt?', *New York Review of Books*, 21 May 1970, 12–17.
12. Samuel Johnson, *Notes on Shakespeare's Henry IV, Pt i, Act I, Scene i*, quoted in Mills, *Crusades*, vol. 2, p. 337n.; Francis Bacon, *Works*, 1803, vol. 3. 'War with Spain', p. 505, quoted in Mills, *Crusades*, vol. 2, p. 338n.
13. Brown, *Western Christendom*, p. 182.
14. Edward William Lane, *Arabian Society in the Middle Ages*, London, Chatto and Windus, 1883, pp. 120–1; also James Harris, *Philological Inquiries*, in *Works*, Oxford, 1841, p. 489, quoting Abulfeda.
15. *EI* 1, 'Dar al-Harb', 'Dar al-Islam', 'Dar al-Sulh'.
16. *EI* 2, 'Crusades' (by Claude Cahen).
17. Hitti, *History of the Arabs*, p. 635; Steven Runciman, *A History of the Crusades*, Harmondsworth, Penguin Books, 1965, vol. 1, p. 279.
18. Guizot, *Collection*, 1825, 'Foulcher de Chartres', p. 76.
19. Barker, *Crusades*, p. 8.
20. *Cambridge Medieval History*, vol. 4, pt i, 1966, p. 212.
21. *Cambridge Medieval History*, vol. 5, 1926, p. 79.
22. William Tronzo, *Cultures of his Kingdom: Roger II and Cappella Palatina in Palermo*, Oxford, Princeton University Press, 1997.
23. Gibbon, *The Decline and Fall*, vol. 3, p. 566.
24. *EB* 11, 'Crusades'.
25. Besant and Palmer, *Jerusalem*, p. 135.
26. Ibid., pp. 146–7.
27. Gibbon, *The Decline and Fall*, vol. 3, p. 655 [ch. 60].

28. *Cambridge Medieval History*, vol. 5, 1926, pp. 66–82.

29. *The Legacy of Islam*, ed. J. Schacht and C.E. Bosworth, 2nd edn, Oxford, Clarendon Press, 1974, pp. 92–3.

30. W.M. Watt, *The Influence of Islam on Medieval Europe*, Edinburgh, Edinburgh University Press, 1972, p. 83; *The Song of Roland*, tr. Glyn Burgess, London, Penguin Books, 1990, pp. 9–10.

31. Besant and Palmer, *Jerusalem*, p. 146.

32. Frank Barlow, *William Rufus*, London, Methuen, 1983, p. 362.

33. Gibbon, *The Decline and Fall*, vol. 3, p. 558.

34. Anna Comnena, *The Alexiad*, tr. E.R.A. Sewter, Harmondsworth, Penguin Books, 1969, p. 309.

35. Besant and Palmer, *Jerusalem*, p. 156.

36. Runciman, *Crusades*, vol. 1, p. 117.

37. *Cambridge Medieval History*, vol. 5, 1926, p. 271.

38. William of Malmesbury, *Chronicle*, tr. J. A. Giles, London, Bohn, 1847, pp. 338–9.

39. Besant and Palmer, *Jerusalem*, p. 167; Gibbon, *The Decline and Fall*, vol. 3, p. 570, quoting Albert of Aix.

40. Besant and Palmer, *Jerusalem*, pp. 153–4.

41. Anna Comnena, *The Alexiad*, p. 370.

42. Besant and Palmer, *Jerusalem*, pp. 139–40; [Arculfus], *Pilgrimage*, pp. 3–4.

43. Besant and Palmer, *Jerusalem*, pp. 252–3; *EB* 11, 'Tripoli' (by D.G. Hogarth); Ibn al-Qalanisi (ed. and tr. H.A.R. Gibb), *The Damascus Chronicle . . .* , London, Luzac, 1932, p. 89; J.F. Michaud, *Histoire des Croisades*, Paris, Ponthieu, 1825, vol. 2, p. 54; René Grousset, *Histoire des Croisades*, Paris, Plon, 1934, vol. 1, p. 358.

44. Lewis and Holt, *Historians*, p. 255.

45. Barker, *Crusades*, p. 51; Runciman, *Crusades*, vol. 2, pp. 281–3.

46. Jacques de Vitry, *The History of Jerusalem, AD 1180*, tr. Aubrey Stewart, London, PPTS, 1896, p. 64; Barker, *Crusades*, pp. 48–9.

47. Gibbon, *The Decline and Fall*, vol. 3, p. 653.

48. Martin Scott, *Medieval Europe*, London, Longman, 1964, p. 150.

49. Dorothy M. Stenton, *English Society in the Early Middle Ages*, Harmondsworth, Penguin Books, 1951, pp. 194–5.

50. Philip K. Hitti, *Syria: A Short History*, London, Macmillan, 1959, p. 194; Edward G. Browne, *Arabian Medicine*, Cambridge, Cambridge University Press, 1921, pp. 69–70.

51. Barker, *Crusades*, p. 73n.

52. *Cambridge Medieval History*, vol. 6, 1929, p. 17.

53. Eric Christiansen, *The Northern Crusades*, London, Penguin Books, 1997, pp. 175, 176.

54. Runciman, *Crusades*, vol. 3, pp. 139–44; Besant and Palmer, *Jerusalem*, pp. 500–3.

55. Runciman, *Crusades*, vol. 3, pp. 151–69.

56. Ernst H. Kantorowicz, *Frederick the Second 1194–1250*, London, Constable, 1931, pp. 186–7.

57. Kantorowicz, *Frederick II*, pp. 130–1.

58. Runciman, *Crusades*, vol. 3, pp. 188–9; Kantorowicz, *Frederick II*, pp. 197–201.

59. Gibbon, *The Decline and Fall*, vol. 3, p. 648.

60. Runciman, *Crusades*, vol. 3, pp. 187, 209; Kantorowicz, *Frederick II*, pp. 186–7.

61. Jean de Joinville, *Saint Louis*, tr. James Hutton, London, Sampson Low, 1868, p. 10; Barker, *Crusades*, p. 78; *Cambridge Medieval History*, vol. 6, 1929, p. 347.

62. Gregorius Abulpharagius, *Historia Compendiosa Dynastiarum*, tr. Edward Pococke, Oxford, 1663, p. 323.

63. Gibbon, *The Decline and Fall*, vol. 3, pp. 651–2.

64. Conder, *Jerusalem*, p. 322.

65. Aziz Suryal Atiya, *The Crusade in the Later Middle Ages*, London, Methuen, 1938, p. 133.

66. Ibid., pp. 354–67; Runciman, *Crusades*, vol. 3, pp. 445–7.

67. Atiya, *Later Middle Ages*, pp. 437–8.

68. Sir John Froissart, *Chronicles*, tr. T. Johnes, London, Bohn, 1855, vol. 2, pp. 601-2, 622-8.

69. Atiya, *Later Middle Ages*, p. 445.

70. M. Bellaguet (ed), *Chronique du religieux de St-Denys*, Paris, Crapelet, 1840, vol. 2, p. 511.

71. Edwin Pears, *The Destruction of the Greek Empire*, London, Longman, 1903, pp. 165 ff.; J. von Hammer-Purgstall, *Histoire de l'Empire ottoman*, tr. J.-J. Hellert, Paris, Bellizard, 1835–41, vol. 2, pp. 120 ff.

72. Christopher Tyerman, *England and the Crusades*, London and Chicago, University of Chicago Press, 1988, p. 352; Paul S. Crowson, *Tudor Foreign Policy*, London, A. & C. Black, 1973, p. 69.

73. Atiya, *Later Middle Ages*, p. 468.

74. R.H. Bainton, *The Travail of Religious Liberty*, London, Lutterworth Press, 1953, p. 39.

CHAPTER THREE. EUROPE'S LOSS AND RECOVERY OF KNOWLEDGE.

1. See *The Oxford Companion to Philosophy*, Oxford, Oxford University Press, 1995, 'Aristotle'; J.L. Ackrill, *Aristotle the Philosopher*, Oxford, Clarendon Press, 1981; Aristotle, *The Metaphysics*, ed. and tr. Hugh Lawson-Tancred, London, Penguin Books, 1998 (especially the Introduction).

2. Gertrude Himmelfarb, *Darwin and the Darwinian Revolution*, London, Chatto and Windus, 1959, p. 141.

3. Anthony Kenny, *A Brief History of Western Philosophy*, Oxford, Blackwell, 1998, pp. 96–8; Gordon Leff, *Medieval Thought*, Harmondsworth, Penguin Books, 1958, pp. 15–16.

4. Ibid., pp. 110–12; Boethius, *The Consolation of Philosophy*, tr. V.E. Watts, Harmondsworth, Penguin Books, 1969.

5. Brown, *Western Christendom*, p. 122; Agathias, *The Histories*, tr. J.A. Frendo, Berlin, Walter de Gruyter, 1975, p. 65.

6. *The Legacy of Persia*, ed. A.J. Arberry, Oxford, Clarendon Press, 1968, pp. 336–7.

7. Gibbon, *The Decline and Fall*, vol. 2, p. 615; George Rawlinson, *The Seventh Great Oriental Monarchy*, London, Longman, 1876, pp. 448–9.

8. *Cambridge History of Iran*, vol. 3, pt ii, 1983, p. 754; Browne, *Arabian Medicine*, p. 20.

9. *EI* 2, 'Gondeshapur'.

10. Majid Fakhry, *A History of Islamic Thought*, New York, Columbia University Press, 1970, p. 18.

11. Thomas Warton, *The History of English Poetry*, London, Thomas Tegg, 1840, vol. 1, p. clxxvii.

12. Hitti, *History of the Arabs*, p. 310; Philip K. Hitti, *Makers of Arab History*, London, Macmillan, 1969, p. 91.

13. *Legacy of Persia*, p. 295.

14. *Legacy of Islam*, 2nd edn, p. 427.

15. *Cambridge History of Islam*, vol. 2, 1970, p. 505.

16. Hitti, *History of the Arabs*, p. 375; George Sarton, *Introduction to the History of Science*, Baltimore, Carnegie Institution, 1927, vol. 1, p. 558.

17. Leff, *Medieval Thought*, pp. 145–6; Hitti, *Makers of Arab History*, pp. 184–201.

18. Leff, *Medieval Thought*, pp. 146–8; Arthur Hyman and James J. Walsh, *Philosophy in the Middle Ages*, Indianapolis, Hackett, 1977, pp. 211–32.

19. Leff, *Medieval Thought*, pp. 148–55; Hyman and Walsh, *Middle Ages*, pp. 233–62.

20. Hitti, *History of the Arabs*, p. 372.

21. Donald Campbell, *Arabian Medicine and its Influence on the Middle Ages*, 2 vols, London, Kegan Paul, 1926, vol. 1, p. 80; Browne, *Arabian Medicine*, pp. 61–2.

22. Frederick Copleston SJ, *A History of Philosophy*, vol. 2, London, Burns and Oates, 1959, p. 191.

23. Fakhry, *Islamic Thought*, p. 179.

24. Browne, *Arabian Medicine*, pp. 44–52.

25. *Cambridge History of Islam*, vol. 2, 1970, p. 755.

26. Leff, *Medieval Thought*, pp. 156–62; Hyman and Walsh, *Middle Ages*, pp. 283–325; Hitti, *Makers of Arab History*, pp. 219–37; *Cambridge Medieval History*, vol. 6, 1929, pp. 713–15.

27. Leff, *Medieval Thought*, p. 157.

28. Leff, *Medieval Thought*, pp. 158–62; Fakhry, *Islamic Thought*, pp. 320–5.

29. *EI* 1, 'al-Mu'tazila'.

30. H.A.R. Gibb, *Arabic Literature*, Oxford, Clarendon Press, 1963, p. 68.

31. Hitti, *Makers of Arab History*, p. 90.

32. William of Malmesbury, *Chronicle*, p. 173.

33. Ibid.

34. Lynn Thorndike, *A History of Magic and Experimental Science*, London, Macmillan, 1923, vol. 1, p. 705.

35. Ibid., p. 176.

36. *Legacy of Islam*, 1st edn, p. 28; Browne, *Arabian Medicine*, p. 35; Campbell, *Arabian Medicine*, pp. 141–2.

37. Charles Homer Haskins, *Studies in the History of Medieval Science*, Cambridge, Mass., Harvard University Press, 1927, pp. 20–42, esp. p. 34; A.C. Crombie, *Augustine to Galileo*, Harmondsworth, Penguin Books, 1969, vol. 1, p. 66; C. and D. Singer, 'The Jewish Factor in Medieval Thought', in *The Legacy of Israel*, Oxford, Clarendon Press, 1928, p. 208.

38. James Hastings (ed.), *Encyclopedia of Religion and Ethics*, Edinburgh, T. and T. Clark, 1908, 'Adelard'.

39. Haskins, *Medieval Science*, p. 189; Charles Homer Haskins, 'England and Sicily in the Twelfth Century', *English Historical Review*, 26 (1911), 438–43; *ODNB*, 'Brown, Thomas'.

40. *Legacy of Islam*, 2nd edn, p. 16; James Kritzeck, *Peter the Venerable and Islam*, Princeton, Princeton University Press, 1964, p. 21.

41. Lynn Thorndike, *Michael Scot*, London, Nelson, 1965, pp. 22–3; Haskins, *Medieval Science*, pp. 272–98.

42. Warton, *English Poetry*, vol. 2, p. 206.

43. Thorndike, *Michael Scot*, p. 28.

44. *DNB*, 'Michael Scot'; S.T. Coleridge, *The Collected Works*, Princeton, Routledge/Princeton University Press, vol. 14, pt i, 1990, 'Table Talk', entry for 16 February 1833.

45. Haskins, *Medieval Science*, p. 127; *DNB*, 'Daniel [of] Morley'.

46. On Siger, see Leff, *Medieval Thought*, pp. 228–30; Ernest Renan, *Averroès et l'Averroïsme*, Paris, Michel Lévy, 1861, pp. 271–3; *Encyclopedia of Philosophy*, ed. Paul Edwards, 8 vols, New York, Macmillan, 1967, vol. 7, 'Siger'.

47. Gordon Leff, *Paris and Oxford Universities in the 13th and 14th Centuries*, 2 vols, New York, John Wiley, 1968, vol. 2, p. 200; Leff, *Medieval Thought*, p. 172.

48. Leff, *Medieval Thought*, p. 229.

49. Crombie, *Augustine to Galileo*, vol. 1, p. 103; Thorndike, *History of Magic*, vol. 2, pp. 874-913; Renan, *Averroès*, pp. 326–8.

50. *Cambridge Medieval History*, vol. 8, 1936, pp. 626 ff.; *Encyclopedia of Philosophy*, vol. 5, 'Marsilius of Padua'.

51. J.W. Allen, *A History of Political Thought in the Sixteenth Century*, London, Methuen, 1964, p. 5.

52. Paul Oskar Kristeller, *Eight Philosophers of the Italian Renaissance*, London, Chatto and Windus, 1965, pp. 72-90; *Encyclopedia of Philosophy*, vol. 5, 'Pomponazzi'; Renan, *Averroès*, pp. 354–60.

53. Richard Morison, *An Exhortation to styrre all Englyshe men to the defence of their countreye*, London, 1539, sig. D4v.

54. Dante, *The Divine Comedy*, Paradiso, Bk 10, 133–8.

55. Miguel Asin Palacios, *Islam and the Divine Comedy*, tr. Harold Sunderland, London, John Murray, 1926, p. 5.

56. Dante, *Divine Comedy*, Inferno, Bk 12, 46 ff.

57. *Cambridge History of Islam*, vol. 2, 1970, p. 879; *Legacy of Islam*, 2nd edn, pp. 94, 344–5.

58. Asin Palacios, *Islam and the Divine Comedy*, p. 55.

59. Ibid., p. 58.

60. René Descartes, *Discourse on Method*, tr. A. Wollaston, Harmondsworth, Penguin Books, 1960, p. 49.

61. C. and D. Singer, 'The Jewish Factor', p. 274.

62. Samuel Chew, *The Crescent and the Rose*, New York, Oxford University Press, 1937, pp. 389—97.

63. *DNB*, 'John Tillotson'.

64. William of Malmesbury, *Chronicle*, p. 208.

65. Warton, *English Poetry*, vol. 1, p. xci.

66. Ibid., p. ii.

67. Ibid., vol. 2, p. 217.

68. Ibid., vol. 1, pp. 56–7.

69. Watt, *The Influence of Islam*, p. 27.

70. William Langland, *Piers the Ploughman*, tr. J.F. Goodridge, Harmondsworth, Penguin Books, 1959, pp. 233, 235.

71. Chew, *Crescent and Rose*, p. 391.

72. Wm Shakespeare, *Hamlet*, III. ii. 15.

73. Wm Shakespeare, *King Lear*, III. iv. 148.

74. [Charles I], Εικων βασιλικη: *The Portraicture of his Sacred Majestie in his Solitudes and Sufferings*, [London, William Royston], 1648 [i.e. 1649], [Madan 1, iii], p. 68.

75. Dorothy Vaughan, *Europe and the Turk*, Liverpool, Liverpool University Press, 1954, pp. 191–2; Chew, *Crescent and Rose*, p. 102n.

76. Wm Shakespeare, *1 Henry IV*, V. iii. 46.

77. Chew, *Crescent and Rose*, p. 102n.

78. Jean Bodin, *Colloquium of the Seven about the Secrets of the Sublime*, tr. M.L.D. Kuntz, London, Princeton University Press, 1975, p. 225.

79. Ibid., p. 219.

80. Ibid., p. 232.

CHAPTER FOUR. 'ALMOST CONTINUAL WARRES'

1. Sir Percy Sykes, *A History of Persia*, 3rd edn, London, Macmillan, 1958, vol. 2, p. 84.

2. Matthew Paris, quoted in Sykes, *Persia*, vol. 2, p. 87.

3. V. Minorsky, 'The Middle East in Western Politics in the 13th, 15th and 17th Centuries', *Journal of the Royal Central Asian Society*, 27/4 (October 1940), 433.

4. Ibid., p. 434.

5. Sykes, *Persia*, vol. 2, p. 113.

6. Richard Knolles, *The Generall Historie of the Turkes*, London, Adam Islip, 1610, p. 219.

7. Ibid., pp. 220–1.

8. Henry Ellis, *Original Letters*, 3rd series, vol. 1, London, Richard Bentley, 1846, pp. 54-8; *Cambridge History of Iran*, vol. 6, 1986, p. 375.

9. Minorsky, 'The Middle East', p. 448.

10. Sykes, *Persia*, vol. 2, p. 142.

11. Ibid., p. 159.

12. *Cambridge History of Islam*, vol. 1, 1970, p. 398.

13. John-Thomas [Giovanni Tommaso] Minadoi, *The History of the Warres betweene the Turkes and the Persians*, tr. A. Hartwell, London, John Wolfe, 1595 (repr. Tehran 1976), p. 1.

14. A.G. Busbequius, *The Four Epistles*, tr. Nahum Tate [?], London, J. Taylor, 1694, pp. 171–2. The first Latin edition was Paris, 1589, as Gislenius.

15. George Abbot, *A Briefe Description of the Whole World*, London, 1599, sig. B4r; Chew, *Crescent and Rose*, p. 250.

16. Wm Shakespeare, *The Merchant of Venice*, II. i. 25 ff.

17. John Milton, *Paradise Lost*, bk 10, 431–6.

18. Sykes, *Persia*, vol. 2, p. 160.

19. Ibid., p. 162.

20. Sir Charles Eliot ['Odysseus'], *Turkey in Europe*, London, Frank Cass, 1965, p. 93.

21. *Cambridge History of Iran*, 1986, vol. 6, p. 382.

22. Sykes, *Persia*, vol. 2, p. 166.

23. Ibid., p. 168.

CHAPTER FIVE. 'THE MAGNIFICENCE OF THE QUEEN HIS MISTRESS'

1. Richard Hakluyt, *The Principal Navigations Voyages . . . of the English Nation*, Glasgow, James MacLehose, vol. 5, 1904, p. 243.

2. Roger B. Merriman, *Suleiman the Magnificent 1520–1566*, New York, Cooper Square, 1966, pp. 126–44.

3. Quoted in Southern, *Western Views*, pp. 79–80.

4. Vaughan, *Europe and the Turk*, p. 135.

5. Ibid., p. 272.

6. Allen, *History of Political Thought*, p. 5.

7. G.R. Elton, *Reformation Europe, 1517–1559*, London, Collins/Fontana, 1969, pp. 108–9.

8. Michael Servetus, *De Trinitatis Erroribus*, [Hagenau], 1531, bk i, §59, tr. Earl Morse Wilbur, *The Two Treatises of Servetus on the Trinity*, Cambridge, Mass., Harvard University Press, 1932, pp. 66–7. On Servetus, see Earl Morse Wilbur, *A History of Unitarianism: Socinianism and its Antecedents*, Cambridge, Mass., Harvard University Press, 1945, chs 5 and 9–14; R.H. Bainton, *Hunted Heretic:*

The Life and Death of Michael Servetus, Boston, Beacon Press, 1953; John F. Fulton, *Michael Servetus, Humanist and Martyr*, New York, Herbert Reichner, 1953; *EB* 11, 'Servetus'.

9. Martinus Bellius (i.e. Sebastian Castellio, or Chateillon), *De haereticis, an sint persequendi*, Magdeburg (i.e. Basle), 1554, p. 137.

10. Koran, 2: 257.

11. [Anon; ? by B. Lamy], *Four treatises concerning the Doctrine . . . of the Mahometans*, London, 1712, pp. 214-24; see also G.H. Williams, *The Radical Reformation*, London, Weidenfeld and Nicolson, 1962, pp. 809–10; G.W. Lessing, *Sämtliche Schriften*, Leipzig, 1897, vol. 12, pp. 220 ff.

12. On the origins of Socinianism, see Wilbur, *History of Unitarianism*, on Transylvania under John Sigismund, see E.M. Wilbur, *A History of Unitarianism in Transylvania, England and America*, Boston, Beacon Press, 1952, pp. 3–56.

13. Wilbur, *History of Unitarianism in Transylvania*, pp. 37–58.

14. Faustus Socinus, *Opera*, vol. 2; Bibliotheca Fratrum Polonorum, vol. 2; Irenopolis [i.e. Amsterdam], 'Irenaeus Philalethius', post 1656, pp. 535b–536a.

15. Hakluyt, *Principal Navigations*, vol. 5, pp. 168–9; M. Epstein, *The Early History of the Levant Company*, London, Routledge, 1908, p. 9; Alfred C. Wood, *A History of the Levant Company*, London, Oxford University Press, 1935, p. 8; S.A. Skilliter, *William Harborne and the Trade with Turkey, 1578–1582*, Oxford, Oxford University Press (for the British Academy), 1977, pp. 34–48.

16. Conyers Read, *Mr Secretary Walsingham and the Policy of Queen Elizabeth*, 3 vols, Oxford, Clarendon Press, 1967, vol. 3, p. 373.

17. Epstein, *Early History*, pp. 245–51; Skilliter, *William Harborne*, pp. 28–30.

18. Read, *Walsingham*, vol. 3, p. 374.

19. Hakluyt, *Principal Navigations*, vol. 5, pp. 169, 175.

20. Edward S. Creasy, *History of the Ottoman Turks*, London, Richard Bentley, 1877, p. 228; von Hammer-Purgstall, *Histoire de l'empire ottoman*, vol. 7, p. 252 n.

21. Crowson, *Tudor Foreign Policy*, p. 176.

22. Vaughan, *Europe and the Turk*, p. 162.

23. Knolles, *Generall Historie*, 1610 edn, p. 880.

24. *Cambridge History of Iran*, vol. 6, 1986, p. 384.

25. W.E.D. Allen, *Problems of Turkish Power in the Sixteenth Century*, London, Central Asian Research Centre, 1963, p. 29.

26. Vaughan, *Europe and the Turk*, p. 163.

27. J. M. Neale, *A History of the Holy Eastern Church* , London, Joseph Masters, 1847, vol. 2, pp. 356–455; also Hugh Trevor-Roper, 'The Church of England and the Greek Church . . . ', in *From Counter-Reformation to Glorious Revolution*, London, Pimlico, 1993, pp. 83–111; Thomas Smith, *An Account of the Greek Church*, London, Miles Flesher/Richard Davis, 1680, pp. 239–91; Eliot, *Turkey in Europe*, pp. 247, 249.

28. Hakluyt, *Principal Navigations*, vol. 5, p. 247.

29. Ibid., p. 251.

30. Great Britain, *Calendar of State Papers (Venetian)*, vol. 8 (1581–1591), London, 1897, nos. 130, 332.

31. Hakluyt, *Principal Navigations*, vol. 5, p. 251.

32. Ibid., p. 257.

33. Ibid., p. 255; H.G. Rawlinson, 'The Embassy of William Harborne to Constantinople', *Transactions of the Royal Historical Society*, 4th series, vol. v (1922), p. 8.

34. Vaughan, *Europe and the Turk*, p. 170.

35. Wood, *Levant Company*, p. 13.

36. Read, *Walsingham*, vol. 3, p. 330.

37. E.S. de Beer, 'The Dictionary of National Biography', section 'Edward Barton', *Bulletin of the Institute of Historical Research*, 19 (1942–3), 158–9.

38. *New Cambridge Modern History*, vol. 3, 1968, pp. 368, 369–70; also *ODNB*, 'Barton'.

39. *CSP Venetian*, 8, no. 651.

40. Ibid., no. 673 (28 May 1588).

41. Ibid., no. 729 (3 Sept 1588).

42. Ibid., no. 943, despatch of 26 June 1590.

43. Paul Wittek, 'The Turkish Documents in Hakluyt's "Voyages"', *Bulletin of the Institute of Historical Research*, 19/57 (1942–3), 122.

44. Chew, *Crescent and Rose*, p. 163.

45. J.T. Bent, *Early Voyages and Travels in the Levant*, London, Hakluyt Society, 1893, p. 68.

46. Chew, *Crescent and Rose*, p. 169.

47. Michael Strachan, *Sir Thomas Roe: A Life*, Wilton, Michael Russell, 1989, p. 145.

48. Sir Thomas Sherley, *Discours of the Turkes . . .* , ed. E. Denison Ross, London, Camden Miscellany, vol. XVI, 1936 [original MS dates from 1607], p. 10.

49. Strachan, *Sir Thomas Roe*, pp. 145–6.

CHAPTER SIX. SHAH ABBAS AND THE SHERLEY BROTHERS

1. *Legacy of Persia*, p. 343.

2. Sykes, *Persia*, vol. 2, p. 168.

3. Ibid., p. 201.

4. Sykes, *Persia*, vol. 2, p. 173.

5. *DNB*, 'Sir Thomas Shirley the Elder'.

6. Chew, *Crescent and Rose*, pp. 174–5.

7. Ibid., pp. 177–9.

8. E. Denison Ross (ed.), *Sir Anthony Sherley and his Persian Adventure*, London, Routledge, 1933, p. 5.

9. Chew, *Crescent and Rose*, pp. 240–1.

10. Ross, *Sir Anthony Sherley*, p. 12; Chew, *Crescent and Rose*, pp. 241–2.

11. Ross, *Sir Anthony Sherley*, p. 13; Sir Anthony Sherley, *Sir Antony Sherley His Relation of his Travels Into Persia*, London, N. Butter etc., 1613, pp. 4 ff.; Chew, *Crescent and Rose*, p. 271.

12. Ross, *Sir Anthony Sherley*, p. 186; Chew, *Crescent and Rose*, pp. 244–5.

13. Ross, *Sir Anthony Sherley*, pp. 15, 193–4; E.P. Shirley, *The Sherley Brothers*, Chiswick, Roxburghe Club, 1848, p. 18; Chew, *Crescent and Rose*, p. 249.

14. Ross, *Sir Anthony Sherley*, pp. 153–4.

15. Ibid., p. 155.

16. Ibid., pp. 155–6.

17. Ibid., p. 17; Sherley, *Relation*, pp. 80 ff.

18. Shirley, *Sherley Brothers*, p. 19; Chew, *Crescent and Rose*, p. 258.

19. Samuel Purchas, *Hakluytus Posthumus or Purchas his Pilgrimes*, 20 vols, Glasgow, James MacLehose, 1905–7, vol. 10, p. 376; Ross, *Sir Anthony Sherley*, pp. 20–1; Chew, *Crescent and Rose*, p. 324.

20. Ross, *Sir Anthony Sherley*, p. 22.

21. Ibid., p. 36.

22. Ibid., p. 37.

23. Ibid., p. 40; Chew, *Crescent and Rose*, pp. 266, 271.

24. Chew, *Crescent and Rose*, p. 272.

25. Ross, *Sir Anthony Sherley*, p. 47.

26. Chew, *Crescent and Rose*, p. 274.

27. Wm Shakespeare, *Twelfth Night*, II. v. 197; Chew, *Crescent and Rose*, pp. 274–7.

28. Chew, *Crescent and Rose*, p. 282.

29. Ibid., pp. 287–97.

30. Ibid., p. 299.

31. Ibid., pp. 301, 302.

32. Ibid., p. 303.

33. Shirley, *Sherley Brothers*, p. 61.

34. Ibid., p. 62.

35. Thomas Middleton, *Works*, ed. A.H. Bullen, London, John Nimmo, 1885, vol. 8, pp. 303 ff.

36. Chew, *Crescent and Rose*, p. 305; *CSP Venetian*, 9, nos 330 and 341.

37. Chew, *Crescent and Rose*, p. 306.

38. Shirley, *Sherley Brothers*, p. 64; Chew, *Crescent and Rose*, p. 308.

39. Ibid., p. 309.

40. Ibid.

41. Ibid., p. 311.

42. Shirley, *Sherley Brothers*, p. 79.

43. Chew, *Crescent and Rose*, p. 312.

44. Ibid., p. 313.

45. Ibid., pp. 313–14.

46. Ibid., p. 320.

47. Ibid., p. 324.

48. Ibid, p. 325.

49. Shirley, *Sherley Brothers*, p. 94.

50. Chew, *Crescent and Rose*, pp. 327–8; Sir John Finett, *Finetti Philoxenis*, 1656, pp. 145, 172 ff (quoted in Chew, ibid.).

51. Chew, *Crescent and Rose*, p. 328.

52. Great Britain, *Calender of State Papers (Domestic)*, ed. J. Bruce, London, Longman, 1858: 1625, 1626, p. 309; 1625–6, p. 345; 1627–8, pp. 98 f.

53. Chew, *Crescent and Rose*, pp. 332–3.

54. Ibid., p. 334.

55. Thomas Herbert, *Relation of some yeares travaile*, London, Stansby and Bloome, 1634, p. 203; Chew, *Crescent and Rose*, p. 335.

CHAPTER SEVEN. STUART LEARNING AND THE IMPROVEMENT OF HUMAN REASON

1. George Abbot, *Briefe Description*, sig. B4r.
2. P.M. Holt, 'Arabic Historians in Sixteenth- and Seventeenth-Century England', in *Studies in the History of the Near East*, London, Frank Cass, 1973,pp. 37–42; *DNB*, 'Sir Thomas Adams'; A.J. Arberry, *Oriental Essays*, London, Allen & Unwin, 1960, pp. 12–13.
3. *Legacy of Islam*, 1st edn, p. ix; Schaff–Herzog, 'Aram'.
4. *DNB*, 'Lancelot Andrewes', quoting Thomas Fuller; Alistair Hamilton, *William Bedwell the Arabist 1563–1632*, Leiden, E.J. Brill, 1985, *passim*.
5. See Hugh Trevor-Roper, 'The Church of England', esp. pp. 88–91; Hamilton, *William Bedwell*, p. 79.
6. Trevor-Roper, 'The Church of England', p. 99; Eliot, *Turkey in Europe*, p. 249.
7. Leonard Twells, *The Lives of Dr. Edward Pocock, the Celebrated Orientalist . . .*, London, Rivington, vol. 1, 1816, pp. 4–5; *DNB*, 'Matthias Pasor'; G.J. Toomer, *Eastern Wisedome and Learning*,

Oxford, Clarendon Press, 1996, pp. 98–101.
8. Chew, *Crescent and Rose*, p. 397.
9. *DNB*, 'Edward Pococke'; Twells, *Pocock*, pp. 10-13; Toomer, *Eastern Wisedome*, pp. 116–38.
10. Twells, *Pocock*, pp. 14–28.
11. Ibid., p. 30.
12. Ibid., p. 15.
13. Toomer, *Eastern Wisedome*, p. 119.
14. Ibid., pp. 106, 108; H.R. Trevor-Roper, *Archbishop Laud 1573–1654*, London, Macmillan, 1940, pp. 277–84.
15. Maurice Cranston, *John Locke: A Biography*, Oxford, Oxford University Press, 1985, p. 18.
16. Toomer, *Eastern Wisedome*, p. 267.
17. Chew, *Crescent and Rose*, pp. 515–17.
18. Ibid., p. 516; Sykes, *Persia*, vol. 2, p. 174.
19. Twells, *Pocock*, p. 38; *DNB*, 'Edward Pococke'.
20. Edward Pococke, *Lamiato 'l Ajam: Carmen Tograi, Poetae Arabis Doctissimi . . .* , Oxford, Richard Davis/Henry Hall, 1661, sig. Q8v.
21. Simon Ockley, *The History of the Saracens*, London, R. Knaplock/ Bernard Lintot, 1718, vol. 2: *Sentences of Ali*, p. 9, nos 74 and 79.
22. Twells, *Pocock*, p. 43; Trevor-Roper, *Laud*, p. 283; *DNB*, 'Pococke'.
23. Twells, *Pocock*, pp. 45–7.
24. Ibid., p. 77; Toomer, *Eastern Wisedome*, p. 146.
25. Hugo Grotius, *De Veritate Religionis Christianae*, London, John Nourse, 1755 edn, p. 240.

26. Hugh Trevor-Roper, 'The Great Tew Circle' in id. *Catholics, Anglicans and Puritans*, London, Secker and Warburg, 1987, p. 194.

27. Abraham Cowley, 'Sonnet to Reason', in A.R. Waller (ed.), *Works*, Cambridge, Cambridge University Press, 1905, p. 46; also pp. 190–1; John Aubrey, *Brief Lives*, ed. Oliver Lawson Dick, Harmondsworth, Penguin Books, 1962, p. 153.

28. Lucius Cary, Lord Falkland, *A Discourse of Infallibility*, London, 1660, p. 240.

29. Twells, *Pocock*, p. 82.

30. Ibid., p. 86.

31. Ibid., pp. 94–5.

32. Toomer, *Eastern Wisedome*, p. 157.

33. Twells, *Pocock*, p. 95.

34. Ibid., p. 96.

35. [Anthony à Wood], *Athenae Oxonienses*, London, Thomas Bennet, vol. 2, 1692, col. 107.

36. Twells, *Pocock*, p. 98.

37. Toomer, *Eastern Wisedome*, p. 157.

38. Ibid., p. 158.

39. Twells, *Pocock*, pp. 134–5.

40. Ibid., p. 136–7; Toomer, *Eastern Wisedome*, p. 158.

41. Edward Pococke, *Specimen Historiae Arabum*, Oxford, Henry Hall, 1648/50; *DNB*, 'Edward Pococke'.

42. Twells, *Pocock*, pp. 146–7.

43. Holt, *Studies*, p. 11.

44. Pococke, *Specimen Hist.*, p. 339.

45. Ibid., p. 166; Twells, *Pocock*, p. 176.

46. Pococke, *Specimen Hist.*, pp. 267–9; also Abu Jaafar Ebn Tophail, *The Improvement of Human Reason . . .*, tr. Simon Ockley, London, Edmund Powell, 1708, p. 4n. [henceforward Ockley, *Improvement*]; *DNB*, 'Edward Pococke'; Toomer, *Eastern Wisedome*, p. 162.

47. Ockley, *Improvement*, pp. 4n.–5n.

48. Twells, *Pocock*, pp. 174–5.

49. Ibid., pp. 284–6; Edward Pococke, *Philosophus Autodidactus sive epistola . . . de Hai ebn Yokdhan. In quâ ostenditur quomodo ex Inferiorum contemplatione ad Superiorum notitiam Ratio humana ascendere possit*, Oxford, Henry Hall, 1671.

50. Ockley, *Improvement*, sig. [*]4v.

51. Ibid., p. 33.

52. Ibid., p. 30.

53. Ibid., p. 37.

54. Ibid., pp. 37–8.

55. Ibid., p. 38.

56. Ibid., p. 39.

57. Ibid., pp. 39–40.

58. Ibid., p. 42.

59. Ibid., p. 43.

60. Ibid., p. 49.

61. Ibid., p. 53.

62. Ibid., p. 54.

63. Ibid., p. 57.

64. Ibid., p. 58.

65. Ibid., p. 62.

66. Ibid., p. 69.

67. Ibid., p. 77.

68. Ibid., p. 84.

69. Ibid., p. 85.

70. Ibid., p. 91.

71. Ibid., p. 100.

72. Ibid., pp. 94, 95.

73. Ibid., p. 101.

74. Ibid., p. 109.

75. Ibid., p. 112.

76. Ibid., p. 114.

77. Ibid., p. 116.

78. Ibid., p. 117.

79. Ibid., p. 121–3.

80. Ibid., p. 126.

81. Ibid., p. 130.

82. Ibid., p. 139.

83. Ibid., p. 144.

84. Ibid., p. 148.

85. Ibid., pp. 153–4.

86. Ibid., p. 156.

87. Ibid., p. 159.

88. Ibid., p. 160.

89. See David M. Lang's introductions to [John Damascene], *Barlaam and Ioasaph*, Loeb edn, Cambridge, Mass., Harvard University Press, 1967, and *The Balavariani: A Buddhist Tale from the Christian East*, London, Allen and Unwin, 1966.

CHAPTER EIGHT. ISLAM AND EUROPE IN THE EIGHTEENTH CENTURY

1. Chew, *Crescent and Rose*, p. 185; Toomer, *Eastern Wisedome*, p. 166.

2. Twells, *Pocock*, pp. 242–52; *DNB*, 'Edward Pococke'.

3. Pococke, *Lamiato'l Ajam*, sig. *4v.

4. Ibid., sig. *5v.

5. Ibid., sig. *6v.

6. Ibid., sig. *7r.

7. Ibid., sig. *8v.

8. Ibid., sig. **1r.

9. Edward Said, *Orientalism*, London, Routledge, 1980, p. 65.

10. *The Philosophical Transactions of the Royal Society of London . . .* , abridged by C. Hutton, etc., vol. 1 [for 1665–72], London, C. and R. Baldwin, 1809, pp. 614–15; G.A. Russell, 'The Impact of The Philosophus Autodidactus, Pocockes, John Locke and the Society of Friends', in G.A. Russell (ed.), *The 'Arabick' Interest of the Natural Philosophers in Seventeenth-Century England*, Leiden, E.J. Brill, 1994, p. 232.

11. John Locke, *Essay concerning Human Understanding*, 1690, etc., bk 2, ch. i, §24.

12. Ibid., bk I, ch. iv, §11.

13. Ibid., §28.

14. John Locke, *Works*, London, Rivington, 1824, vol. 9, p. 302 (letter of 23 July 1703).

15. Ibid., p. 300.

16. Russell, 'The Impact of The Philosophus Autodidactus', pp. 224–65.

17. Shelly Ekhtiar, 'Hayy ibn Yaqzan: The Eighteenth-Century Reception of an Oriental Self-Taught Philosopher', *Studies on Voltaire and the Eighteenth Century*, 302 (1992), 242.

18. Crombie, *Augustine to Galileo*, vol. 1, p. 23.

19. Alexander Pope, *Essay on Man*, ep. II, 23–30 [1733].

20. Plato, *Timaeus and Critias*, tr. Desmond Lee, Harmondsworth, Penguin Books, 1977, p. 109.

21. Alexander Pope, *Works*, ed. J.W. Croker, London, John Murray, 1886, vol. 5, pp. 518–19 [*Guardian*, no. 61 (21 May 1713), p. 381]; see also Ekhtiar, 'Hayy ibn Yaqzan', 239.

22. Edward Gibbon, *Memoirs of My Life and Writings*, Everyman edn, London, J.M. Dent, [?1920], p. 25.

23. Ockley, *History of the Saracens*, vol. 2, Preface to *The Sentences of Ali*, sig. Cc6r; see also Albert Hourani, *Islam in European Thought*, Cambridge, Cambridge University Press, 1991, p. 14.

24. Henry Stubbe, *An Account of the Rise and Progress of Mahometanism*, London, Luzac, 1911, esp. p. xiii.

25. See Wilbur, *A History of Unitarianism: Socinianism*, and H. John McLachlan, *Socinianism in Seventeenth-Century England*, London, Oxford University Press, 1951.

26. Thomas Fuller, quoted in McLachlan, *Socinianism*, p. 33.

27. McLachlan, *Socinianism*, pp. 178–9; [John Bidle], *A Confession of Faith Touching the Holy Trinity*, London, 1691, sig. D4r.

28. McLachlan, *Socinianism*, p. 216.

29. *The Alcoran of Mahomet*, tr. André du Ryer and [?] Alexander Ross, London, Randal Taylor, 1688, p. 7.

30. Ibid., pp. 172–3.

31. Richard Baxter, *Cure of Church Divisions*, London, Nevil Symmons, 1670, p. 49.

32. Maurice Ashley, *England in the Seventeenth Century*, Harmondsworth, Penguin Books, 1961, p. 157.

33. Charles Leslie, *The Socinian Controversy Discuss'd*, London, 1708, pp. iii–xiii; A[lexander] G[ordon], 'The Primary Document of English Unitarianism, 1682', in *The Christian Life and Unitarian Herald*, 24 September, 1 and 29 October 1892.

34. McLachlan, *Socinianism*, pp. 318–19; Gordon, 'Primary Document', 1 October 1892, p. 477, col. 1.

35. Leslie, *Socinian Controversy*, p. v; Gordon, 'Primary Document', 24 September 1892, p. 464, col. 3.

36. Gordon, 'Primary Document', 1 October 1892, p. 476, col. 3.

37. Leslie, *Socinian Controversy*, p. vii; Gordon, 'Primary Document', 1 October 1892, p. 477, col. 2.

38. Gordon, 'Primary Document', 29 October. 1892, p. 524, col. 1; Leslie, *Socinian Controversy*, pp. xii–xiii.

39. Gordon, 'Primary Document', 29 October. 1892, p. 523, col. 3; Leslie, *Socinian Controversy*, p. x.

40. [Stephen Nye], *Letter of Resolution concerning the Doctrine of the Trinity and the Incarnation*, London, ?1691, p. 18.

41. [Arthur Bury], *The Naked Gospel*, London, 1690, p. 4.

42. John Hunt, *Religious Thought in England*, London, Strahan, 1871, vol. 2, pp. 198–9.

43. Gibbon, *The Decline and Fall*, vol. 3, p. 336.

44. G.V. Bennett, *The Tory Crisis in Church and State, 1688-1730*, Oxford, Clarendon Press, 1975, pp. 33–4; Wilbur, *History of Unitarianism in Transylvania, England* . . ., p. 226.

45. H.R. Fox Bourne, *The Life of John Locke*, London, H.S. King, 1876, vol. 2, pp. 404–6.

46. John Locke, *The Reasonableness of Christianity*, Washington, Regnery, 1997, §§238, 239 (pp. 133–5).

47. Leslie, *Socinian Controversy*, 'The Fourth Dialogue', pp. 28, 29.

48. Charles Leslie, *The Truth of Christianity Demonstrated*, Edinburgh, Fairbairn, 1819, p. 187.

49. Lord Herbert of Cherbury, *De Religione Gentilium*, Amsterdam, 1663

50. [John Toland?], *A Letter from an Arabian Physician* . . ., London, 1706, p. 8.

51. Ibid., p. 14.

52. Lord Wharncliffe (ed.), *The Letters and Works of Lady Mary Wortley Montagu*, London, 1837, vol. 2, p. 119.

53. Thomas Chubb, *Posthumous Works*, London, R. Baldwin, 1748, vol. 2, pp. 40, 35.

54. Lord Bolingbroke, *Works*, London, J. Johnson, 1809, vol. 4, p. 501, quoted in John Leland, *A View of the Deistical Writers*, London, Tegg, 1837, p. 513.

55. Humphrey Prideaux, *The True Nature of Imposture Fully Display'd In the Life of Mahomet* . . ., London, 1697, pp. xix–xx.

56. Adrian Reland, *De Religione Muhammedica*, Utrecht, 1705.

57. Robert Halsband, *The Life of Lady Mary Wortley Montagu*, New York, Oxford University Press, 1960, pp. 67–8.

58. Wharncliffe, *Letters and Works of Lady Mary*, 1837, vol. I, p. 362.

59. Ibid., p. 359.

60. Halsband, *Lady Mary*, pp. 80–1; *DNB*, 'Lady Mary Wortley Montagu'.

61. George Sale, *The Koran Translated*, ed. E. Denison Ross, London, Warne, n.d. [?1912], 'Preliminary Discourse', pp. 131, 42, 44, 75.

62. Henri de Boulainvilliers, *The Life of Mahomet*, London, Longman, 1752, pp. 163–4.

63. Ibid., p. 163.

64. Ibid.

65. Gibbon, *The Decline and Fall*, vol. 3, pp. 1199–1200.

66. Ibid., p. 1187; see also James Harris, *Works*, Oxford, Thomas Tegg, 1841, p. 480n.

67. Voltaire, *Mahomet: Tragedie*, Brussels [i.e. London], 1742; James Miller, *Mahomet the Imposter: A Tragedy*, Dublin, 1745, p. 21.

68. Theodore Besterman, *Voltaire*, London, Longman, 1969, p. 253.

69. Ibid., p. 251.

70. Lord Chesterfield (Philip Dormer Stanhope), *Miscellaneous Works of*

the Late . . . , London, 1779, vol. 3, p. 46.

71. Harris, *Philological Inquiries*, chs vi–viii, pp. 478–96.

72. Gibbon, *The Decline and Fall*, vol. 3, p. 230 [ch. 50].

73. Ibid.

74. Ibid., pp. 231, 232.

75. Ibid., pp. 177–8.

76. Ibid., p. 230.

77. Ibid., p. 213.

78. Ibid., p. 189.

79. Ibid.

80. On Sir William Jones, see Arberry, *Oriental Essays*; also *DNB*. Edward Said's view of Jones, expressed in *Orientalism*, pp. 77–9 etc., is puzzling and perverse.

81. Quoted in Arberry, *Oriental Essays*, pp. 77–8; on Goethe, see *Legacy of Islam*, 1st edn, p. 204; ibid., 2nd edn, p. 347.

82. [Sir William Jones], *Poems Consisting Chiefly of Translations from the Asiatick Languages*, Oxford, Clarendon Press, 1772, p. 5.

83. Baron de Tott, *Memoirs . . . on the Turks and the Tartars*, 2 vols, London, J. Jarvis, 1785.

CHAPTER NINE. OTTOMAN FORTUNES: MILITARY DEBACLE, DIPLOMATIC RESCUE

1. Creasy, *Ottoman Turks*, pp. 280–3; Lord Eversley and Valentine Chirol, *The Turkish Empire from 1288 to 1914*, London, Fisher Unwin, 1924, p. 173.

2. Eversley and Chirol, *Turkish Empire*, pp. 174–5; von Hammer-Purgstall, *Histoire de l'empire ottoman*, vol. 9, p. 378.

3. J.A.R. Marriott, *The Eastern Question: An Historical Study in European Diplomacy*, Oxford, Clarendon Press, 3rd edn, 1930, p. 118.

4. Creasy, *Ottoman Turks*, pp. 290–4.

5. Eversley and Chirol, *Turkish Empire*, p. 181.

6. Ibid., pp. 189–90; Creasy, *Ottoman Turks*, pp. 319–21.

7. Creasy, *Ottoman Turks*, pp. 331–4; Eversley and Chirol, *Turkish Empire*, pp. 193–4.

8. Creasy, *Ottoman Turks*, p. 339; Eversley and Chirol, *Turkish Empire*, pp. 199–200.

9. Creasy, *Ottoman Turks*, pp. 345–6; Eversley and Chirol, *Turkish Empire*, pp. 201–2.

10. See Jonas Hanway, *The Revolutions of Persia*, London, T. Osborne etc., 1762, vol. 2, pp. 160–2; Creasy, *Ottoman Turks*, p. 347; Eversley and Chirol, *Turkish Empire*, pp. 203–4.

11. Creasy, *Ottoman Turks*, pp. 358–75; von Hammer-Purgstall, *Histoire de l'empire ottoman*, vol. 4, p. 365; Eversley and Chirol, *Turkish Empire*, pp. 207–10.

12. *DNB*, 'Elphinston'; Eversley and Chirol, *Turkish Empire*, pp. 215–16.

13. M.S. Anderson, *The Eastern Question*, London, Macmillan, 1966, p. 143.

14. Marriott, *Eastern Question*, pp. 151–3.

15. Henri Troyat, *Catherine the Great,*
tr. E. Read, Nuffield, Aidan Ellis,
1979, pp. 268–74.

16. Eversley and Chirol, *Turkish
Empire,* pp. 226–9; Creasy, *Ottoman
Turks,* p. 430; William Coxe,
History of the House of Austria,
London, Bell, 1873, vol. 3, p. 518.

17. J. Holland Rose, *William Pitt and
National Revival,* London, George
Bell, 1911, p. 490.

18. Eversley and Chirol, *Turkish
Empire,* p. 231.

19. *The Parliamentary History of
England . . .* , vol. 29 (22 March
1791–13 December 1792), col. 54
(29 March 1791).

20. Ibid., col. 55.

21. Ibid., cols 62–3.

22. Ibid., col. 78.

23. Ibid., col. 996 (29 February
1792).

24. Ibid., cols 180–1 (12 April
1791).

25. Marriott, *Eastern Question,* p. 163.

26. J. Christopher Herold, *Napoleon in
Egypt,* London, Hamish Hamilton,
1963, pp. 136–63.

27. *Déscription de l'Egypte,* Paris,
Imprimerie Impériale, 1809.

28. Christopher J. Walker, *Armenia:
The Survival of a Nation,* London,
Croom Helm, 1980, p. 55.

29. Marriott, *Eastern Question,* pp. 250,
311.

30. Peter Mansfield, *The Arabs,*
London, Allen Lane, 1976,
pp. 123–4, 155–6.

31. Quoted in ibid., p. 144 .

32. See for example H.C. Armstrong,
Lord of Arabia, Harmondsworth,
Penguin Books, 1940, pp. 13—19.
Compare T.E. Lawrence's
'The Semite hovered between lust
and self-denial' *(Seven Pillars of
Wisdom,* Harmondsworth, Penguin
Books, 1964, p. 40): an example of
Freudian transference, since
the author could more truthfully
have written, 'T.E. Lawrence
hovered between lust and self-
denial.'

33. On the Greek War of
Independence, see C.M.
Woodhouse, *The Story of Modern
Greece,* London, Faber, 1968,
pp. 125–57.

34. Lord Byron, *Don Juan,* Canto 8,
91 ff., esp. 141, and Canto 12, 27 ff.

35. Duke of Wellington, *Maxims and
Opinions* ed. G.H. Francis,
London, Henry Colburn, 1845,
p. 138 [House of Lords,
29 January 1828].

36. Mansfield, *The Arabs,* pp. 121-5;
Anderson, *Eastern Question,* p. 56.

37. Anderson, *Eastern Question,* p. 39.

38. Ibid., pp. 39–40.

39. Ibid., pp. 84–5.

40. Quoted in V.J. Puryear,
*International Economics and
Diplomacy in the Near East,* Stanford,
Stanford University Press, 1935,
p. 150; see also Eversley and
Chirol,*Turkish Empire,* pp. 284–5.

41. Eversley and Chirol, *Turkish Empire*
p. 290; *DNB,* 'B.W. Walker'; *Burke's
Peerage and Baronetage,* London,

1923, 'Sir Francis Elliot Walker', a hereditary Pasha of the Ottoman Empire.

42. G.H. Bolsover, 'David Urquhart and the Eastern Question, 1833–37', *Journal of Modern History*, 8/4 (December 1936), 445–6.

43. Charles Webster, 'Urquhart, Ponsonby, and Palmerston', *English Historical Review*, 62/264 (July 1947), 327–34.

44. Bolsover, 'David Urquhart', 465; Gertrude Robinson, *David Urquhart*, Oxford, Blackwell, 1920, pp. 52–3.

45. On the *Vixen* incident, see *British and Foreign State Papers, 1837–38*, vol. 26, pp. 2–60; Puryear, *International Economics,* pp. 49–53.

46. [David Urquhart], *Speeches Delivered at a Dinner Given by the Commercial Community of Glasgow to David Urquhart Esq., on the 23rd of May 1838*, London, 1838, p. 33.

47. Sir John MacNeill, *Progress and Present Position of Russia in the East*, Madras, 1838, pp. 110–11.

48. Richard Cobden, 'Russia, by a Manchester Manufacturer', in *Political Writings*, New York, 1867, pp. 165, 169.

49. Charles Greville, *Memoirs*, ed. Henry Reeve, London, Longman, 1888, vol. 7, p. 140 (entry for 20 February 1854).

50. Asa Briggs, *Victorian People*, Harmondsworth, Penguin Books, 1975, p. 224.

51. Charles Kingsley, *True Words for Brave Men*, London, Kegan Paul, 1878, p. 204.

52. Edwin Pears, *Life of Abdul Hamid*, New York, Arno, 1973, pp. 167–72.

53. D.C. Blaisdell, *European Financial Control in the Ottoman Empire*, New York, Columbia University Press, 1929, pp. 55 ff.

54. Anderson, *Eastern Question*, pp. 173–4; Nevil Forbes, *et al.*, *The Balkans: A History*, Oxford, Clarendon Press, 1915, pp. 113–16.

55. Anderson, *Eastern Question*, pp. 178 ff.; Edwin Pears, *Forty Years in Constantinople*, London, Herbert Jenkins, 1916, pp. 14 ff.; Eversley and Chirol, *Turkish Empire*, pp. 318–23.

56. Pears, *Forty Years*, p. 57; Anderson, *Eastern Question*, pp. 190–1.

57. W.F. Monypenny and G.E. Buckle, *Life of Disraeli*, vol. 6, London, John Murray, 1920, p. 130 (letter of 21 March 1877).

58. The despatches of Sir Henry Elliott and Sir Henry Layard are quoted in Walker, *Armenia*, p. 105.

59. Robert Blake, *Disraeli*, London, Methuen, 1969, pp. 633–4.

60. Christopher J. Walker, 'Kars in the Russo-Turkish Wars of the 19th Century', UCLA Armenian History and Culture Series, Costa Mesa, California (forthcoming).

61. J.E. McCoan, *Our New Protectorate: Turkey-in-Asia*, London, Chapman and Hall, 1879.

62. On al-Afghani and Abduh, see Albert Hourani, *Arabic Thought in the Liberal Age, 1798–1939*, London, Oxford University Press, 1967, pp. 103–60; Mansfield, *The Arabs*, pp. 163–8.

63. Ibid., p. 145.

64. On James Senua, see Jacob Landau, *Middle Eastern Themes*, London, Frank Cass, 1973, ch. 8, 'Abu Naddara: an Egyptian Jewish Nationalist'; Messrs Sotheby's, 'The Travel Sale', London, 17 October 2001, lot 518.

65. Peter Mansfield, *The British in Egypt*, London, Weidenfeld and Nicolson, 1971, pp. 167–70.

66. Walker, *Armenia*, p. 125.

67. Ibid.

68. On 1894–6, see Walker, *Armenia*, pp. 121–73.

69. Arminius Vambery, *The Story of my Struggles*, London, T. Fisher Unwin, 1904, vol. 2, p. 389.

70. See Christopher J. Walker, *Visions of Ararat*, London, I.B. Tauris, 1997 (repr. 2005), pp. 62–70.

71. Allan Cunningham, 'The Wrong Horse? A Study of Anglo-Turkish Relations before the First World War', in A. Hourani (ed.), *Middle East Affairs 4*, St Antony's Papers 17, London, 1965, 63.

72. Anon, *The Greco-Turkish War of 1897*, tr. Frederica Bolton, London, Swan Sonnenschein, 1898; Anderson, *Eastern Question*, pp. 262–3.

73. Pears, *Forty Years*, pp. 218 ff.; Marriott, *Eastern Question*, pp. 433–7.

74. *British Documents on the Origin of the War*, ed. G.P. Gooch and Harold Temperley, London, HMSO, 1926, vol. 5, p. 263, Grey to Lowther, 31 July 1908.

75. Walker, *Armenia*, pp. 192–3.

76. Aubrey Herbert, 'The Second Revolution in Turkey', *The Spectator*, 17 April 1909, p. 601.

77. Bernard Lewis, *The Emergence of Modern Turkey*, London, Oxford University Press, 1968, pp. 217–19.

78. W.E.D. Allen and Paul Muratoff, *Caucasian Battlefields*, Cambridge, Cambridge University Press, 1953, pp. 228–9.

79. *EI* 1, 'Mecca'; Pococke, *Specimen Hist.*, p. 136.

Bibliography

Abbot, G. *A Briefe Description of the Whole World*, London, 1599

Agathias, *The Histories*, tr. J.A. Frendo, Berlin, Walter de Gruyter, 1975

Allen, W.E.D. *Problems of Turkish Power in the Sixteenth Century*, London, Centre for Central Asian Research, 1963

Allen, W.E.D, and Muratoff, P. *Caucasian Battlefields*, Cambridge, Cambridge University Press, 1953

Anderson, M.S. *The Eastern Question*, London, Macmillan, 1966

Arnold, T.W. *The Preaching of Islam*, London, Darf, 1986 [1935]

Asin Palacios, M. *Islam and the Divine Comedy*, tr. H. Sunderland, London, John Murray, 1926 [1919]

Atiya, A.S. *The Crusade in the Later Middle Ages*, London, Methuen, 1938

——. *The Crusade of Nicopolis*, London, 1934

Bainton, R.H. *Hunted Heretic: The Life and Death of Michael Servetus*, Boston, Beacon Press, 1953

——. *The Travail of Religious Liberty*, London, Lutterworth Press, 1953

Barker, E. *The Crusades*, London, Oxford University Press, 1939

Barraclough, G. 'Deus le Volt?', *New York Review of Books*, 21 May 1970

Bell, R. *The Origin of Islam in its Christian Environment*, London, Macmillan, 1926

Bellaguet, M.L. (ed.). *Chronique du religieux de Saint-Denys*, Paris, 1840

Bent, J.T. *Early Voyages and Travels in the Levant*, London, Hakluyt Society, 1893

——. 'The English in the Levant', *English Historical Review*, 5 (October 1890), 654–64

[Bernard]. *The Itinerary of Bernard the Wise*, tr. J.H. Bernard, London, PPTS, 1893

Blaisdell, D.C. *European Financial Control in the Ottoman Empire*, New York, Columbia University Press, 1929

Bodin, J. *Colloquium of the Seven about the Secrets of the Sublime*, tr. M.L.D. Kuntz, London, Princeton University Press, 1975

Bolsover, G.H. 'David Urquhart and the Eastern Question, 1833–37', *Journal of Modern History*, 8/4 (December 1936), 444–67

Boulainvilliers, H. de. *The Life of Mahomet*, London, Longman, 1752 [1731]

Briggs, A. *Victorian People*, Harmondsworth, Penguin Books, 1975

Brown, P. *The Rise of Western Christendom*, Oxford, Blackwell, 1996

——. *Society and the Holy in Late Antiquity*, London, Faber and Faber, 1982

Browne, E.G. *Arabian Medicine*, Cambridge, Cambridge University Press, 1921

Bullard, R. *Britain and the Middle East*, London, Hutchinson, 1952

Burnett, C. *The Introduction of Arabic Learning into England*, London, The British Library, 1997

[Bury, A.]. *The Naked Gospel*, London, 1690

Busbequius, A.G. *The Four Epistles*, tr. N. Tate [?], London, J. Taylor, 1694

Campbell, D. *Arabian Medicine and its Influence on the Middle Ages*, 2 vols, London, Kegan Paul, 1926

Castellio, S. *Concerning Heretics*, ed. and tr. R.H. Bainton, New York, Columbia University Press, 1935

Chew, S.C., *The Crescent and the Rose*, New York, Oxford University Press, 1937

Cochrane, L. *Adelard of Bath*, London, 1994

Conder, C.R. *The City of Jerusalem*, London, John Murray, 1909

Comnen, Anna. *The Alexiad*, tr. E.R.A. Sewter, Harmondsworth, Penguin Books, 1969

Copleston, F., SJ. *A History of Philosophy*, vol. 2, London, Burns and Oates, 1959

Creasy, E.S. *History of the Ottoman Turks*, London, Richard Bentley, 1877

Crombie, A.C. *Augustine to Galileo*, 2 vols, Harmondsworth, Penguin Books, 1969 [1952]

Crowson, P.S. *Tudor Foreign Policy*, London, A. and C. Black, 1973

Cunningham, A. 'The Wrong Horse? A Study of Anglo-Turkish Relations before the First World War', in A. Hourani (ed.), *Middle East Affairs 4*, St Antony's Papers 17, London, 1965

de Beer, E.S. 'The Dictionary of National Biography', sections on 'Barton', 'Harborne', *Bulletin of the Institute of Historical Research*, 19/57, (1942–3), 158–62

Ekhtiar, S. 'Hayy ibn Yaqzan: The Eighteenth-Century Reception of an Oriental Self-Taught Philosopher', *Studies on Voltaire and the Eighteenth Century*, 302 (1992), 217–45

Eliot, C. ['Odysseus']. *Turkey in Europe*, London, Frank Cass, 1965 [1900]

Epstein, M. *The Early History of the Levant Company*, London, Routledge, 1908

Eversley, Lord, and Chirol, V. *The Turkish Empire from 1288 to 1914*, London, Fisher Unwin, 1924

Fakhry, M. *A History of Islamic Thought*, New York, Columbia University Press, 1970

Fletcher, R. *The Cross and the Crescent*, London, Allen Lane, 2003

Fox Bourne, H.R. *The Life of John Locke*, London, H.S. King, 1876

Gibb, H.A.R. *Arabic Literature: An Introduction*, Oxford, Clarendon Press, 1963 [1926]

Gordon, A. 'The Primary Document of English Unitarianism, 1682', 3 articles, *Christian Life and Unitarian Herald*, 24 September, 1 and 29 October 1892

Guizot, [F.P.G.], *Collection des mémoires relatifs à l'histoire de France*, vol. 20: Albert d'Aix, I, Paris, 1824; vol. 23: Raoul de Caen, Paris, 1825

Hales, J. *Tract concerning Schism and Schismaticks*, ?London, 1716 [1642]

Hamilton, A. *William Bedwell the Arabist 1563–1632*, Leiden, E.J. Brill, 1985

Hanway, J. *The Revolutions of Persia*, London, T. Osborne etc., 1762

Harris, J. *Philological Inquiries*, [1781], in *The Works of James Harris Esq.*, Oxford, 1841

Haskins, C.H. 'Arabic Science in Western Europe', *Isis*, 7 (1925), 478–85

——. 'England and Sicily in the Twelfth Century', *English Historical Review*, 26 (1911), 433–43, 641–65

——. *The Renaissance of the Twelfth Century*, Cambridge, Mass., Harvard University Press, 1927

——. *Studies in the History of Medieval Science*, Cambridge, Mass., Harvard University Press, 1927 [1924]

Herold, J. C. *Napoleon in Egypt*, London, Hamish Hamilton, 1963

——. *History of the Arabs*, London, Macmillan, 1968 [1939]

——. *Makers of Arab History*, London, Macmillan, 1969

Hitti, P.K. *Syria: A Short History*. London, Macmillan, 1959

Holm, F. *My Nestorian Adventure in China*, London, Hutchinson, 1924

Holt, P.M. *Studies in the History of the Near East*, London, Frank Cass, 1973

Hourani, A. *Arabic Thought in the Liberal Age, 1798–1939*, London, Oxford University Press, 1967

——. *Europe and the Middle East*, London, Macmillan, 1980

Hyman, A. and Walsh, J.J. *Philosophy in the Middle Ages*, Indianapolis, Hackett, 1977

Ibn al-Qalanisi. *The Damascus Chronicle of the Crusades*, tr. H.A.R. Gibb, London, 1932

Ibn Tufayl, *see under* Ockley, S.

Jenkins, H.D. *Ibrahim Pasha: Grand Vizir of Suleiman the Magnificent*, New York, AMS Press, 1970 [1911]

John of Damascus. *Writings*, tr. F.H. Chase Jr, New York, 1958

[Jones, W.]. *Poems Consisting Chiefly of Translations from the Asiatick Languages*, Oxford, Clarendon Press, 1772

Kantorowicz, E.H. *Frederick the Second 1194–1250*, London, Constable, 1931

Knolles, R. *The Generall Historie of the Turkes*, London, Adam Islip, 1610 [1603]

Kristeller, P.O. *Eight Philosophers of the Italian Renaissance*, London, Chatto and Windus, 1965

Kritzeck, J. *Peter the Venerable and Islam*, Princeton, Princeton University Press, 1964

Landau, J. *Middle Eastern Themes*, London, Frank Cass, 1973

Lane, E.W. *Arabian Society in the Middle Ages*, London, Chatto and Windus, 1883

Leff, G. *Medieval Thought*, Harmondsworth, Penguin Books, 1958

——. *Paris and Oxford Universities in the 13th and 14th Centuries*, 2 vols, New York, John Wiley, 1968

The Legacy of Islam, ed. T.W. Arnold and A. Guillaume, 1st edn, Oxford, Clarendon Press, 1931

The Legacy of Islam, ed. J. Schacht and C.E. Bosworth, 2nd edn, Oxford, Clarendon Press, 1974

The Legacy of Israel, ed. E.R. Bevan and C. Singer, Oxford, Clarendon Press, 1928.

The Legacy of Persia, ed. A.J. Arberry, Oxford, Clarendon Press, 1968

Le Strange, G. *Palestine under the Moslems*, London, A.P. Watt, 1890

Lewis, B. and Holt, P.M. (eds). *Historians of the Middle East*, London, Oxford University Press, 1962

McLachlan, H.J. *Socinianism in Seventeenth-Century England*, London, Oxford University Press, 1951

Mansfield, P. *The Arabs*, London, Allen Lane, 1976

——. *The British in Egypt*, London, Weidenfeld and Nicolson, 1971

Marriott, J.A.R. *The Eastern Question: An Historical Study in European Diplomacy*, Oxford, Clarendon Press, 1930 [1918]

Mills, C. *The History of the Crusades*, 2 vols, London, Longman, 1822

Minorsky, V. 'The Middle East in Western Politics in the 13th, 15th and 17th Centuries', *Journal of the Royal Central Asian Society*, 27/4 (October 1940), 427–61

Mosheim, J.L. *An Ecclesiastical History*, London, T. Cadell, 1768

Morison, R. *An Exhortation to styrre all Englyshe men to the defence of their countreye*, London, 1539

[Napoléon le Grand]. *Déscription de l'Égypte*, Paris, Imprimerie impériale, 1809

Neale, J.M. *A History of the Holy Eastern Church*, vol. 2, 'The Patriarchate of Alexandria', London, Joseph Masters, 1847

Nicholson, R.A. *A Literary History of the Arabs*, Cambridge, Cambridge University Press, 1907

[Nye, S.]. *Letter of Resolution concerning the Doctrine of the Trinity and the Incarnation*, London, ?1691

Ockley, S. *The History of the Saracens*, London, R. Knaplock/Bernard Lintot, 2 vols, 1718

——. tr. *The Improvement of Human Reason*, London, Knaplock, 1708

Palmer, A. (ed. and tr.). *The Seventh Century in the West-Syrian Chronicles*, Liverpool, Liverpool University Press, 1993

Pears, E. *The Destruction of the Greek Empire*, London, Longman, 1903

——. *Forty Years in Constantinople*, London, Herbert Jenkins, 1916

——. 'The Spanish Armada and the Ottoman Porte', *English Historical Review*, 8/21 (July 1893), 439–66

Pococke, E. *Lamiato 'l Ajam: Carmen Tograi, Poetae Arabis Doctissimi . . .*, Oxford, Richard Davis/Henry Hall, 1661

——. *Specimen Historiae Arabum*, Oxford, Henry Hall, 1648/1650

Prideaux, H. *The True Nature of Imposture Fully Display'd In the Life of Mahomet . . .*, London, 1697

Purchas, S. *Hakluytus Posthumus or Purchas his Pilgrimes*, 20 vols, Glasgow, MacLehose, 1905–7

Puryear, V.J., *International Economics and Diplomacy in the Near East*, Stanford, Stanford University Press, 1935

Rawlinson, G. *The Seventh Great Oriental Monarchy*, London, Longman, 1876

Rawlinson, H.G. 'The Embassy of William Harborne to Constantinople', *Transactions of the Royal Historical Society*, 4th series, vol. v (1922), 1–27

Read, C. *Mr Secretary Walsingham and the Policy of Queen Elizabeth*, 3 vols, Oxford, Clarendon Press, 1978 [1925]

Rodinson, M. *Mohammed*, Harmondsworth, Penguin Books, 1971

Rose, J.H. *William Pitt and National Revival*, London, George Bell, 1911

Ross, E.D. (ed.). *Sir Anthony Sherley and his Persian Adventure*, London, Routledge, 1933

Runciman, S. 'Charlemagne and Palestine', *English Historical Review*, 50 (1935), 606 ff.

——. *A History of the Crusades*, 3 vols, Harmondsworth, Penguin Books, 1965

Russell, G.A. (ed.). *The 'Arabick' Interest of the Natural Philosophers in Seventeenth-Century England*, Leiden, E.J. Brill, 1994

Scott, M. *Medieval Europe*, London, Longman, 1964

Servetus, M. *De Trinitatis Erroribus* [Hagenau], 1531, tr. E.M. Wilbur, *The Two Treatises of Servetus on the Trinity*, Cambridge, Mass., Harvard University Press, 1932

Sherley, A. *Sir Antony Sherley His Relation of his Travels Into Persia*, London, N. Butter etc., 1613

Sherley, T. *Discours of the Turkes . . .* , ed. E.D. Ross, London, Camden Miscellany vol. XVI, 1936 [original Ms, 1607]

Shirley, E.P. *The Sherley Brothers*, Chiswick, Roxburghe Club, 1848

Singer, C. and D. 'The Jewish Factor in Medieval Thought', in *The Legacy of Israel*, Oxford, Clarendon Press, 1928

Skilliter, S.A. *William Harborne and the Trade with Turkey 1578–1582*, Oxford, Oxford University Press (for the British Academy), 1977

Socinus, F. *Opera*, Bibliotheca Fratrum Polonorum, vols 1–2; Irenopolis [i.e. Amsterdam], 'Irenaeus Philalethius', post 1656

Southern, R.W. *Western Views of Islam in the Middle Ages*, Cambridge, Mass., Harvard University Press, 1962

Stenton, D.M. *English Society in the Early Middle Ages*, Harmondsworth, Penguin Books, 1951

Strachan, M. *Sir Thomas Roe, 1581–1644: A Life*, Wilton, Michael Russell, 1989

Stubbe, H. *An Account of the Rise and Progress of Mahometanism*, London, Luzac, 1911

Sykes, P. *A History of Persia*, 2 vols, London, Macmillan, 1958 [1915]

Theophanes. *The Chronicle of Theophanes Confessor, 284–813* [*Chronographia*], tr. C. Mango and R. Scott, Oxford, Clarendon Press, 1997

Thomson, R.W. (tr.), Howard-Johnston, J. and Greenwood, T. (eds.). *The Armenian History attributed to Sebeos*, Liverpool, Liverpool University Press, 1999

Thorndike, L. *A History of Magic and Experimental Science*, 2 vols, London, Macmillan, 1923

——. *Michael Scot*, London, Nelson, 1965

[Toland, John?]. *A Letter from an Arabian Physician . . .*, London, 1706

Toomer, G.J. *Eastern Wisedome and Learning*, Oxford, Clarendon Press, 1996

Trevor-Roper, H. *Archbishop Laud, 1573–1645*, London, Macmillan, 1940

——. 'The Church of England and the Greek Church at the Time of Charles I', in id., *From Counter-Revolution to Glorious Revolution*, London, Pimlico, 1993

——. 'The Great Tew Circle,' in id., *Catholics, Anglicans and Puritans*, London, Secker and Warburg, 1987

Tronzo, W. *Cultures of his Kingdom: Roger II and Cappella Palatina in Palermo*, Oxford, Princeton University Press, 1997

Twells, L. *The Lives of Dr. Edward Pocock . . .* [etc.], 2 vols, London, Rivington, 1816

Tyerman, C. *England and the Crusades*, London and Chicago, University of Chicago Press, 1988

Vasiliev, A.A. *History of the Byzantine Empire*, Madison, University of Wisconsin Press, 1984 [1952]

Vaughan, D.M. *Europe and the Turk: A Pattern of Alliances, 1350–1800*, Liverpool, Liverpool University Press, 1954

Vitry, J. de. *The History of Jerusalem, AD 1180*, tr. A. Stewart, London, PPTS, 1896

Voltaire. *Mahomet: Tragedie*, Brussels [i.e. London], 1742

Warton, T. *The History of English Poetry*, 3 vols, London, Thomas Tegg, 1840

Watt, W.M. *The Influence of Islam on Medieval Europe*, Edinburgh, Edinburgh University Press, 1972

Webster, C. 'Urquhart, Ponsonby, and Palmerston', *English Historical Review*, 62/264 (July 1947), 327–51

Wilbur, E.M. *A History of Unitarianism: Socinianism and its Antecedents*, Cambridge, Mass., Harvard University Press, 1945

——. *A History of Unitarianism in Transylvania, England and America*, Boston, Beacon Press, 1952

William of Malmesbury. *Chronicle*, tr. J.A. Giles, London, Bohn, 1847

Williams, G.H. *The Radical Reformation*, London, Weidenfeld and Nicolson, 1962

Wittek, P. 'The Turkish Documents in Hakluyt's "Voyages"', *Bulletin of* the *Institute of Historical Research*, 19 (1942–3), 57, 121–39

Wood, A. C. *A History of the Levant Company*, London, Oxford University Press, 1935

Index